# STRACHAN
## MY LIFE IN FOOTBALL

# STRACHAN
## MY LIFE IN FOOTBALL

## GORDON STRACHAN
### with JASON TOMAS

TIME WARNER
BOOKS

First published in Great Britain in 2006 by Time Warner Books

A CIP catalogue record for this book
is available from the British Library.

ISBN-13: 978-0-316-73082-2
ISBN-10: 0-316-73082-3

Endpapers image © Offside

Typeset in Sabon by M Rules
Printed and bound in Great Britain by
Clays Ltd, St Ives plc

Time Warner Books
An imprint of
Little, Brown Book Group
Brettenham House
Lancaster Place
London WC2E 7EN

A member of the Hachette Livre Group of Companies

www.littlebrown.co.uk

# CONTENTS

Acknowledgements      vii

1   The Pressure Game      1

2   Running Into Trouble      23

3   The North Star      50

4   The Hairdryer      72

5   The Big Ron Show      100

6   Howard's Way      118

7   The Life of Bryan      142

8   Whelan and Dealing      160

9   Snakes and Ladders      181

10   Off With My Head      211

11   Take the Lowe Road      230

12   Revival      246

13   Hoop Dreams      274

Index      301

# ACKNOWLEDGEMENTS

I have a lot of people to thank for this book, not least my collaborator Jason Tomas, and our editor Tom Bromley and his Time Warner team. Their hard work and patience were invaluable.

In addition to David Luxton, who played a big part in putting the project together, I am grateful, too, for the help of Ron Scott, the chief football correspondent of the *Sunday Post*; Alastair Macdonald, the former football chief correspondent of the *Aberdeen Press and Journal*; Don Warters, Leeds United's press officer; Jim Brown, Coventry's City's historian; and Jeremy Wilson, the Southampton-based freelance journalist for their factual checks.

# CHAPTER ONE

# THE PRESSURE GAME

I have always had a fear of heights and of the sea. In these instances (if not one or two others), I have to put my hand up and admit I am a coward. Yet there aren't many non-footballing experiences I have enjoyed more in recent years than that of my wife Lesley and I being propelled some one hundred feet above the Atlantic Ocean. It took place during a short holiday in Tenerife in September 2001, just after I had been sacked as Coventry City manager, when we tried our hand at parasailing. To say it was an uncharacteristic thing for me to do would be an understatement. But Lesley wanted to try it; and, in deciding whether to allow myself to be persuaded to join her, I was also influenced by the need not to give the group of English lads immediately behind us a good reason to poke fun at me.

As we were being lifted into the sky, I just stared straight ahead. Lesley, appreciating what an ordeal this was for me, was squeezing my hand – though not as hard as I was squeezing hers – and smiling at me. I was panicking.

It would have been just my luck to find two Coventry fans parasailing past us, giving me dog's abuse. Instead, something equally amazing happened. Suddenly, when we had reached the top of our ascent and I looked at the beautiful blue sky, I thought: 'This is nice.' My anxiety just drifted away and was replaced by an overwhelming sense of contentment. I was so relaxed, I really did not want to come down. I said to Lesley: 'If I throw a credit card down, do you think they will let us stay where we are for another hour or two?'

In fact, the way I felt at that stage in my career – when Coventry's slide from the Premiership to the bottom of the First Division had stamped me as a failure, and the fans screaming for my blood had made me feel almost as if I was a criminal – I did not want to come down, ever.

I have come a long way since then, at Southampton and now Celtic. Although it has hardly been a smooth ride – certainly, it was as bumpy as it could get when Artmedia beat Celtic 5-0 – I know that I am a better manager now.

Despite the success I have had, and the success I feel I am capable of achieving in the future, I also know that I will have no problems in walking away from the job.

Even now, the sarcastic gentleman who stood up at a Coventry fans' forum I once attended and asked, 'Mr Strachan, have you ever thought about becoming a gardener?' might like to know that his question was not as outrageous as he intended it to be.

I am hard-pressed to think of any job in which there is greater stress than that of football manager. Football, it is often said, is a simple game. It is – unless you are a manager and are having to deal not just with players' football problems but those of a more general nature relating to their conduct off the field and financial, domestic and family matters. In my ten years as a manager I reckon I have seen and heard it all. I have even had the bizarre experience of one player being accused of sexual harassment by his next-door neighbour – she claimed that when she was in her garden, he deliberately walked around his stark naked.

Nobody is more negative about the manager's job than Alan Hansen. He himself could easily have become a manager when his outstanding playing career at Liverpool came to an end, but he chose to give it a wide berth. 'I was never interested in that role,' he has said. 'As a player, I was generally able to push aside my problems or worries when I stepped through the front door of my home, but I think that becomes more difficult when you're a manager. If you are still same after ten or twenty years in the job, then you have done well. So many things can go wrong – so many things that are out of your control. Basically, I have kept away from this side of football because I wanted to keep my hair relatively black. Managers tend to be as competitive as they were as players, and the buzz they get from competing is like an addictive drug. It is a dangerous buzz because, unlike players, their influence on performances and results is limited. These men are obsessed with football and management in a way that I could never be.'

I am not obsessed with it, which is one of my biggest strengths.

It has never been the easiest of jobs but I have no doubts that, as a result of the game's amazing financial growth, it has been more difficult than ever in the ten years I have spent in it. Football has become big business, with clubs turning themselves into multi-faceted commercial empires and the men at the helm – the chairmen and owners – adopting very much a hands-on approach in their running.

That is probably how it should be. The financial side is now much too high-powered and complicated for managers to handle. I can see where the club chairmen and owners are coming from. Though some managers might baulk at some of their traditional responsibilities being curtailed in areas such as the buying and selling of players and the terms of their contracts, I really do not have any problems with it. Nobody wants to see clubs fall into the financial trouble that Leeds United did; and I cannot say that I enjoy being closely involved with the financial aspects of football anyway.

I am sure most managers will confirm that the aspect of the job that gives them the greatest pleasure is just working with the players – the training and coaching, combined with the dressing room banter. In some ways, it gives us the chance to become players again ourselves. It is what we know best and, by and large, what we feel the most comfortable with.

I feel less comfortable with the financial side. As in most walks of life, the amount of money washing around in football has inevitably generated greed and dishonesty. There is no shortage of people striving for a piece of the cake, and I can get quite sensitive sometimes over the ease with which some allow any sense of integrity they might have to fly straight out of the window. At Coventry, where my lack of experience as a manager meant that my skin was probably thinner than it is today, it could really get to me.

The point has been brought into particularly sharp focus with the conduct of some players' agents. They are not all bad, obviously, but the truth is that, even if one of my best friends became an agent tomorrow, I would find it difficult to have the same trust in him.

That football has become a cut-throat business, in more ways than one, is also reflected by the conduct of one or two club chairmen. Take my negotiations over a player I wanted to sign for Coventry. It was during the close season, and after we had reached agreement on the deal in principle, I was asked to hold fire on completing it for another week or two.

Not to put too fine a point on it, the chairman just strung us along. He continued to lead me to believe that the player would be coming to us – until it reached the stage, just before the start of the season, where I could not afford to wait any longer.

At that point, the chairman did a U-turn. 'He is not available,' he said.

'So you lied to us,' I said.

'Yes, that's right,' he replied, matter-of-factly. 'It's business. You should learn from it.'

'No thanks,' I told him.

So, the basic principle of managers being free to concentrate on what they are best at – purely football matters – is one that I relish.

It could be argued that managers have been restricted too much. The view that they are no longer as much in control of their own destiny as they were has been underlined particularly forcibly by reports of some chairmen advising or telling them who they should sign and even who they should select for their teams. Obviously, some modern-day managers wield greater power and influence than others but the impression of us having been sort of cut down to size and marginalised to the point where we are little more than coaches and trainers – as has long been the case with many of our counterparts on the Continent – does have a basis of truth.

Of course, while the position of managers has appeared to become weaker, that of the players has become stronger. Their high basic salaries, which have tended to represent a much bigger percentage of their overall football earnings than was the case for most of the time that I was a player, and their contractual freedom following the Bosman ruling, have made it more difficult for managers to exert the same measure of control and authority over them. You can no longer do it by leaving them out of the first team, or, if they have stepped out of line, imposing club fines on them. If either had happened to me at Dundee and Aberdeen (where I had to play in order to earn a half-decent living) I would have cried my eyes out.

Adding to the problems for managers in motivating their teams has been the presence of so many stars from different countries and cultures. They have raised the skill level of English football, and, in a lot of cases, the level of professionalism in terms of lifestyle habits. But, with such a cosmopolitan mix, it is perhaps only to be expected that their integration, in a league so different from those in other parts of the world, can be quite erratic. I would suggest that managers, in striving to get their players on to the same wavelength, and keep them there, now need to give them a bit more individual attention.

On top of all this, football has attracted greater public interest, and media coverage, than ever before. The appetite for information is insatiable. Almost everybody has an opinion on the game and, with the growth of fans' internet websites and those radio phone-in programmes, there is no shortage of outlets through which even the most outrageous views and comments (and there are plenty of them) can be voiced.

But some things never change. No matter how much he has to operate with his hands tied behind his back, it is the manager who still carries the greatest responsibility for a team's performances and results; and it is the manager who takes all the flak when the often unreasonable expectations of these are not fulfilled. This is when you are really on your own. We are living in an age when people do not just criticise you; they abuse and ridicule you. You only have to look at the list of managerial sackings to appreciate the attitude to all this of the men who employ you.

This, indeed, is a job which can easily change a person, and not for the better. I must admit that during my own time in it there have been periods when I have not liked myself; when I have retreated into a small world of my own, and Lesley and our three children, Gavin, Craig and Gemma, have not been able to communicate with me properly. At times like this, I hear them, but whether they always have enough of my attention for me to listen to what they are saying is another matter. During my fifteen-month sabbatical from football, following my departure from Southampton in the 2003/04 season, it was a standing joke in our household that the children could at last directly ask me anything they wanted, without using Lesley to deliver the message when she felt the time was right. In Lesley's case, not for nothing is there a sign in the kitchen of our house in Southampton which states: 'We interrupt this marriage to bring you the football season.'

Still, while recognising that I am not entirely the husband and father that I want or possibly need to be, I probably get higher marks than a lot of other managers. I would hate to think that I will ever have cause to feel as guilty about my commitment to football as Sir Alex Ferguson has done. I was given a poignant insight into his regrets over this when we were together at Manchester United in the 1980s, and his wife Cathy, who had been experiencing a number of health problems, was rushed into hospital. It was a very traumatic time for Fergie, and because of our long association with him, from our Aberdeen days, Lesley was more than willing to help him out by doing some of his ironing and shopping and looking after his sons, Mark, Jason and Darren. That was the closest I have ever got to Fergie, and my most vivid memory of our relationship then is of him sitting in our front room and pouring his heart out over his perception of the way he had treated his family.

Cathy's illness provoked Fergie to show a side of him that I had never seen before. While talking about not having given her and his children enough attention, he became so emotional that he burst into tears, the very last thing you would have expected of someone with his image. That memory, in fact, has helped shape my own attitude and approach to the job and, indeed, it was one of the factors in my decision to take a long break from football, instead of signing a new contract with Southampton.

All managers have to work hard, but I sometimes think that a few of them feel a need always to be seen to be doing so, to justify themselves to their chairmen, and take it to the extreme. For one thing, I have never seen the point of spending more time at a club than is truly necessary – when whatever I need to do can easily be done at home. At Coventry and Southampton, I was not entirely joking when I used to say to members of the office or coaching staff that I wanted to be back home by 4 p.m. to watch *Countdown* on TV. I found that it was a programme which helped me unwind, and I reckon I saw it enough times to be classed almost as an expert on it. Nor do I see much point in travelling hundreds of miles each week to watch games personally. During the week, some managers are out watching matches almost every night. How they can do that, and still be fresh for training in the morning, is difficult for me to get my head around. Coaching is one of my strengths and, as someone who needs his sleep, I doubt whether I would be much good to anybody in that department if I started work tired and grumpy.

Fortunately for me, Lesley likes football, which means that whenever I do go to watch a match, I can take her with me. She has accompanied me to so many games that people must think she, rather than Garry Pendrey, has been my assistant manager at Coventry, Southampton and Celtic. Quite apart from the fact that I enjoy having Lesley with me, I look upon these trips together as a good way for her to 'reach' me. With comparatively few distractions for me when it is just her and me in a car, we are able to have a laugh and joke and discuss all the 1001 little domestic and family matters that normal married couples talk about.

I am proud to say that, despite that private world I inhabit as a manager, we still have an exceptionally strong, happy marriage. I think it is unusual in this day and age for a couple to remain as close as we have. Generally, I am always at my happiest when I am with Lesley. There is no way that I would ever allow football seriously to threaten our relationship.

There are other reasons why I think I have a lot to be thankful for as a manager. Unlike others, I do not have any heart problems – the only minus point relating to my health and fitness is a dodgy hip – and I have not become a heavy drinker. I know that one or two managers have done so to the point where, when you are alongside them in the technical area during matches, you can detect their presence just by the smell of alcohol on their breath.

So, whatever one might think of the records and performances of my teams, I reckon I have been a managerial success in other, equally important ways.

Managers talk a lot about their mental strength (even those who immediately contradict their rousing speeches on the subject through their various superstitious habits). When that pressure is at its most intense, we all put a brave face on it publicly and insist that we are not allowing it to get to us. We have to do that, to set the right example to our teams. But nobody should be kidded by it. It's a charade. I do not care who he is – if any manager claims that he does not feel the pressure, then in my opinion he is not telling the truth.

One of Southampton's best performances when I was there was a 2-1 win at Liverpool in December 2003, which caused Liverpool to drop from fifth to ninth in the table. Although it was a big blow for then Liverpool manager Gérard Houllier, you would have thought that if anybody had learned not to take such setbacks too seriously, it was him. After all, only two seasons earlier Gérard had collapsed at a match and undergone major heart surgery. Yet his reaction to that defeat by Southampton prompted the feeling that his wake up call – and they do not come any bigger than being close to losing one's life – had not had the effect that one might have expected.

After the match he was the last person to come into the Anfield Boot Room where, as is the Liverpool tradition, the backroom coaching staffs of the two clubs gathered for a drink and a chat. Upon closing the door, he just stood there leaning against it, with a blank look on his face. He gave the impression of being totally shell-shocked, as if he had been involved in a car crash. Someone made a remark to him, but it did not register. He was so distant that nobody knew what to say to him to snap him out of it.

If someone like Houllier can get himself into that state, just imagine what it is like for the managers of clubs whose main aim is just to survive – the majority of clubs in the Premiership and Scottish Premier League, in fact – and whose ratio of satisfactory results and performances is considerably smaller.

A look at managers during matches, when they are in the dugout or touchline technical area, tells its own story. Andy Kilner, the former Stockport manager, has told me that he was screaming so much at one of his players that his blood pressure escalated to the point where he suffered a temporary loss of sight. He was in the technical area at the time, and had to shout at his assistant in the dugout to come over and lead him back to his seat. On the subject of managers letting their emotions get the better of them, one figure I find as amusing as anyone is Bolton's Sam Allardyce. Big Sam, a former centre-half in the traditional British tackle-first-ask-questions-later mould, cuts an impressive sartorial figure at the start of a match. But by the end of it, you can be fairly certain that he will be sweating profusely and that his tie, if not other items of his clothing, will be all over the place. He is so dishevelled that he looks like one of those fathers, brothers or uncles who have got into a fight at a boozy family wedding.

As one might expect of a fiery little ginger-haired Scot, I have been known to get het up a few times myself.

I cannot imagine any manager losing control of himself more than I did after one goalless draw at home to Bolton in my second season at Southampton. In those days Bolton were one of the teams I most wanted to beat, mainly because of their League Cup win over us shortly after my appointment in 2001 and, more specifically, their manager Sam Allardyce making a big thing – publicly – of the fact that it was achieved by virtually their second team. As daft as it sounds, I'd taken the huff with big Sam over that, so although Bolton have long been noted as one of the most difficult teams to play against, that 0-0 score line – not to mention our performance – really got to me.

Everybody could see that I was very angry; so much so that when I got into the dressing room, I found almost every conceivable member of the backroom training, coaching and medical staff gathering there – like vultures – to see what was going to happen next. It reminded me of the morbid curiosity people show in road accidents. Outside the team, there must have been ten members of the backroom staff in there.

But an audience was the last thing that I or the players needed. I hit a Lucozade bottle against the wall and shouted: 'You lot can eff off.' They all went into the massage area of the adjoining physiotherapists' room, except for Chris Connolly, the sports psychologist who had been brought into the club by the chairman Rupert Lowe. Rupert felt it important that Chris and I worked together in the dressing room, which I had no problem with usually. I liked Chris and got on well with him. On this occasion, though, I told Chris to join the others. 'What I am going to say to the players has nothing to do with psychology,' I explained. 'It is going to be all about old-fashioned honesty and home truths.' It was certainly that. I went berserk. I was told later that, as the banished group were listening to my rant, Chris – unwittingly – had them in tears of laughter through attempting to explain to them in psychological jargon what I was feeling.

The only outsider in a position to see what was going on was the club doctor, who had gone to the dressing room toilet before my tirade had started, without being aware that I had banned outsiders. He looked a bit like a startled rabbit when he came out, and his reaction to the verbal bullets I was firing was to nip back in until I had finished.

That took some time, because, just as I was running out of steam, I noticed that the dressing room television was on. 'Who put on that telly?' I asked. Nobody replied – there was total silence – which wound me up even more. 'Switching on the telly after a performance like this just goes to show how much the game means to you,' I said. I then got angry with myself because I booted the kit bag at the screen, forgetting that I was wearing an expensive new pair of lightweight shoes. I was in a world of my own – muttering to myself things like 'Only bought these shoes a couple of days ago. Cost me a fortune. You b\*\*\*\*\*\*s.' It was a wonder the players were able to keep straight faces. I went out of the room at that point, but within a minute I was back asking the same question. 'Who put that telly on?' Again, nobody said a word. 'So nobody has the guts to tell me,' I said. 'It sums up what you were like against Bolton. You are f\*\*\*\*\*g cowards.'

The subject of that switched-on television was a standing joke in our dressing room for months. It eventually transpired that the person responsible was a young virtually unknown Argentinian player whom the chairman had brought over for a trial, and who was not even in our first-team squad that night.

I do try to be Mr Super Cool. During a game, you look across at the other manager, and think: 'Daft bugger.' Then you realise you are behaving the same way. One minute, you are saying to yourself: 'You need to calm yourself down.' The next minute, you are going off your head again. I can find it quite embarrassing when I watch myself on TV, although I do believe it is important for a manager or coach to show their emotions, if only to get it across to their team that they are in the same boat. Needless to say, knowing where to draw the line in this – and preventing one's blood pressure being raised further through clashes with match officials, members of the opposing managerial staff and players on both sides – is a different matter entirely. With emotions running so high, what is happening in and around the dugout is sometimes more entertaining than the football itself. I have even witnessed a bust-up between a club's manager and assistant manager – in this instance, my old Scottish friends Walter Smith and Archie Knox when they were working together at Everton. In one match against Coventry, a dreadful 0-0 draw, they started arguing over the decision to bring on substitute Danny Cadamarteri. As the change was being made, I caught sight of Archie shaking his head, with Walter looking at him. Then, with Cadamarteri struggling to impose himself, Archie started shaking his head again.

'What the f*** are you shaking your head for?' Walter asked.

'I told you not to play him,' Archie said.

'What are you talking about?' Walter retorted. 'You are the one who said I should put him on, '

The two men, who have been very close for years and are among the most knowledgeable and likeable pros you could come across, were now heading for a full-scale row. I put my oar in by taking on the guise of peacemaker. 'Now calm down you two,' I said.

'It's him,' Archie protested. 'He is trying to blame me for it.'

'No, it was his idea,' Walter said to me.

I started laughing, 'What a pair you are,' I said. Then they saw the funny side of it and started laughing as well.

The stress managers experience can be detected in a number of different ways. You can see it in Fergie, not just through his explosive outbursts, but in his nervous cough. I became particularly aware of it when he was manager of the 1986 Scotland World Cup squad in Mexico and I occupied the bedroom next to his at our team hotel. It turned out to be quite a problem for me because the walls were very thin and his cough was so persistent throughout the night that I hardly got any sleep.

More disturbing is the effect of that stress on a lot of managers' health. Outside the occasional spells of finding it difficult to catch my breath – as happened at the start of my managerial career – my biggest scare was when I collapsed at the Coventry training ground on the day of a club fancy dress Christmas party. I was suffering from a virus, but I did not know that at the time. Initially, I just thought I was overtired. When I was finally brought me to my knees – literally – I feared that I'd had a stroke and was on the way out.

I had got to the ground at about 8.30 a.m., and as I was expecting to have to stand in for one of our injured players in training that morning, as opposed to just supervising the session, the first thing I did was to take a tablet to relieve soreness in my back and hips, a common problem for me towards the end of my playing career and to this day. Whether there was something wrong with the tablet, I don't know. But, as I was about to get changed, I suddenly felt prickly heat all over my body. Then, when I took off my clothes, I was even more alarmed to see that the colour of my skin had changed to bright red. I was burning. It was almost as if I was on fire. I felt as if I was going to be sick, so I wrapped a towel around my waist and headed for the toilet. That's when my legs and arms stopped working and I found myself in a heap on the corridor floor. I could hardly speak, although as I hit the deck, I did manage to shout for help loudly enough to attract the attention of Garry Pendrey and our physio, Andy Harvey. I think Andy was the first to reach me – my vision was somewhat blurred – and I remember him telling me: 'Okay, we will need to keep you warm.' In my befuddled state, I was also aware of the fact that I still had no clothes on and big Andy, a veritable giant of a man, was holding me in the spoon position.

In some of my quiet, reflective moments – and especially when I am attending a funeral – I sometimes think about death and how I am going to die. Needless to say, being on the floor stark naked, with somebody like Andy Harvey attached to my back, would be the very last way in which I would wish my life to end. The other surreal aspect of that experience was that, as I was on the floor, I could hear the players coming in, laughing and joking over the costumes they had brought with them for the Christmas party. Some had parts of their fancy dress on already – Noel Whelan, for example, came through the door in high heels. They could not see me, and had no idea I was so sick. But as I said to them when I had recovered: 'I am going to fine you lot. Laughing when I'm dying is not on.'

For all my jokes, nobody needs to remind me about the managers whose lives really have been threatened. It is impossible not to empathise with these figures and their families. Quite apart from the serious heart problems of men like Houllier, Joe Kinnear and Barry Fry, the general awareness of the health hazards of the job has been increased more than ever in the last couple of years through the publicity afforded to the 'Fit to Manage' scheme initiated by the League Managers' Association. The head of the scheme, Dr Dorian Dugmore, likened the health problems of managers to those of chief executives of major companies. But he made the point that the ones facing managers were exacerbated by their having 'every move examined under the spotlight'. Referring to the lifestyles of managers – their eating and drinking habits, the amount of exercise and proper rest they get – and the considerable increase in their heart rates and blood pressure during matches, he was quoted as saying: 'Add all that together and it's a recipe for potential disaster.' Dr Dugmore, one of the world's leading heart specialists, was apparently prompted to investigate the dangers facing football managers as a result of Jock Stein's fatal heart attack at sixty-two at the end of the vital Scotland World Cup qualifying tie against Wales at Ninian Park, Cardiff, in September 1985. Of course, as a member of the Scotland team that night, the memory of how the big man's passion for football finally rebounded on him is particularly poignant for me.

With Scotland needing a draw to clinch a place in the 1986 finals in Mexico, the pressure on Stein was possibly greater than at any time in his long and illustrious career. It was no secret that he had not been in the best of health. Doubts about whether he could cope with the strain of football management at the top level had first arisen ten years earlier, when he almost lost his life in car crash; and when he took on the Scotland job, it was common knowledge that he had heart problems. Before the Wales match, at the Scotland party's training base in Bristol, you could not help noticing that he was feeling the strain. The closer we got to the game, the more uncomfortable he seemed. When I was sitting with him at lunchtime on the day of the game, he looked grey and was sweating.

I do not think any of the players were unduly worried about this. Stein had remarkable managerial presence and charisma; he seemed indestructible. He might not have been as fit as he once was – he was certainly carrying a bit of weight – but for us, and no doubt for everyone else close to him then, the signs of dis-comfort that might have suggested otherwise to outsiders were only to be expected on occasions like this. Okay, he was feeling the pressure – but we all were. If anyone had the experience to cope with it, it was surely Jock Stein. The possibility that the whole situation was too much for him never crossed my mind.

I shudder to think of the anguish Stein must have been going through during the game, with Scotland falling behind but finally getting the draw they needed thanks to a late, slightly fortuitous penalty.

In a way, I was probably one of the players who exacerbated his stress in the first half. Stein had decided to play me on the left flank in place of Davie Cooper, in the belief that the Welsh, having recalled their veteran right back Joey Jones, were vulnerable on that side. I think he envisaged me wearing Jones down and then, if necessary, Davie being brought on to push him and Wales over the top. After taking my place, it was Davie, of course, who scored the Scotland penalty, but I could not take any of the credit for that result because, for some reason, I'd found it difficult to get into the game. At half-time Stein clearly cross with me, left me in no doubt that he would haul me off if the situation did not quickly improve. He just said: 'You've got ten minutes [of the second half].' I thought he was rather brusque, which did rankle with me. It was not as if I had not been trying. I knew he could be very cutting. I remember him substituting me in a match against France – about ten minutes later I had remarked to one of the other players: 'What a poor game this is', to which Stein retorted: 'Aye, but it has got a lot better since you came off.' That, though, was a wind-up, or at least I interpreted it as such. His irritation with me against Wales was different. You get used to that treatment from your club manager. It's different with national team managers – as they are effectively only borrowing you, and are thus more reliant on your goodwill, they tend to be more diplomatic.

Stein's attitude to me did not put me in the best of moods, as

Alex Ferguson – then Scotland's assistant manager – was quick to appreciate. When Stein walked away and I was sitting there muttering to myself, Fergie came up to me and said: 'The big man is not at his best. Just ignore it and go out and do your best.' I was not the only player to annoy Stein that night. At half-time, he was even more uptight about Aberdeen goalkeeper Jim Leighton having to be replaced because he had lost one of his contact lenses. As has been well documented, Stein was particularly upset that Jim had kept his need for the lenses a secret; not even Fergie, his club manager, was aware that he wore them.

At the final whistle, when Stein collapsed on the touchline and it was clear that his life was ebbing away, the obvious question was why he had subjected himself to all that responsibility and pressure in the first place. To football professionals, the answer was simple. Indeed, Stein himself provided it in a newspaper interview just a week or two earlier. Asked whether he had contemplated retirement, he replied that he could not imagine what he would do without the excitement of football. 'For me there is no life at all after football,' he said. 'No life at all.'

There are a lot of managers like that. There are also some managers who put themselves under the extra strain of setting long-term career targets for themselves, and who will do anything to reach them. They can be dangerous, not just to themselves but the people around them. Luckily, I am not one of them. I just focus on being the best manager I can be from one week to another. Even then, though I love football, I know for a fact that I can easily detach myself from it; that I do not need to be involved in it so closely in order to be happy and fulfilled. This was confirmed to me during my fifteen-months out of the game. It was the first proper break of my entire career – a career in which, with due modesty, I had nearly always been subjected to the physical and mental strain of operating at the highest of expectation levels – and it proved one of the best moves I have made. It made me realise what a vegetable I had become.

It was not initially my intention to be out of the game for as long as I was. But while waiting for the chance to step back into management, most importantly in a job which would present the stimulation of a different challenge from the ones I had experienced in management previously, and give me the scope to develop my ability, I was far from unhappy. To me, the difference between being a manager and being out of the job was like the difference between night and day. It worried me that I might reach the stage where I never wanted to return; that I would be too worried about what I would be like when I did, and crack up after just two months.

I got a lot of enjoyment out of my BBC TV *Match of the Day* and media work, not to mention the time I was able to spend with Lesley and our family. It was great for Lesley and myself to be able to indulge ourselves, in terms of travel and new experiences, and for me to wake up each morning without feeling any tension. I was so happy I found it almost disconcerting. Obviously, the money we had behind us, which we needed in order to maintain the same standard of living that we'd had before, was not going to last forever. But over those fifteen months it became clear to me that I could do other things and that we would hardly have to survive on bread and water as a consequence.

It was particularly comforting to know that when my Celtic career got off to such a bad start. In those early days at Celtic, my experience at Coventry came in handy as well.

I did not think I had done a bad job at Coventry. Yet when they lost their Premiership place in 2001, the fact that for many years their survival at the top level had been achieved very much against the odds and that I had played a part in that success in the previous six seasons, did not matter a jot to a number of their fans. They had been second from bottom when I took over; it was not as if they had been at the top and I had dragged them down.

As a player and manager, you get used to abuse from followers of opposing teams. You expect it – you even relish it because it usually means you are doing well. It's less easy to accept when it is coming from your own team's supporters, especially when their criticism escalates into the sort of mass hate campaign that was directed at me. People who pay their hard-earned money to watch their teams are entitled to criticise you. Yet when teams are not doing well, a lot of them just do not appreciate what you are going through and that you are feeling as badly about it as they are, perhaps even more so. If they did, some 80 per cent of them would probably back off. However, there is not a lot that anybody can do about the other 20 per cent – the people who I feel represent the pronounced yob culture in our society.

At one time, the people who came into that category were generally packed into specific areas of stadiums, usually the terracing. Today, there can be pockets of them all over the place. The abuse you take is quadraphonic, and the people it hurts the most are the members of your family. As a player, my mental state was quite good 95 per cent of the time. It has been different since I became a manager, which has made it considerably more difficult for Lesley to enjoy watching my matches. When things are not going well, I am very conscious of her worrying about me, and, as a consequence, I worry a great deal about her.

In my struggle to keep Coventry in the Premiership, it was not unusual for the problems to keep me awake at night and for me to try and forget about them through watching old John Wayne cowboy films until three or four in the morning. The 'Duke' has always been one of my favourite film stars, which explains why there is a seven foot statue of him – a Christmas gift from Lesley – on display at our house in Southampton. In some

Coventry matches, I reckon I could have done with the real John Wayne alongside me.

In view of all this, it does seem perverse that I now am at a club like Celtic. If the pressure of management is intense at places like Coventry and Southampton, it is nothing compared to what it is like at Parkhead.

However, one thing that everybody in professional football has in common is that we are extremely competitive people, and we love challenges. Thus, having resurrected my managerial career at Southampton, and proved that I was not deluding myself in thinking that I had something to offer on this side of the game, it was only natural that I should want to see if I could push myself further. The other factor was the knowledge that, if I was ever unfortunate enough to attract the same fire that I did at Coventry, it would be unlikely to get to me as much.

In professional football, we all talk a lot about strength through adversity; we all hold the view that it does not matter how many setbacks you encounter, it's how you react to them that really matters. The best way I can sum it up is to relate a conversation I had with Tim Booth, the rock star and song-writer who was formerly the lead singer in the critically acclaimed UK band James.

Tim, a quiet-spoken, highly intelligent man whose manner is nothing like what one would normally expect from a pop per-former, is a good friend of mine. We first got to know each other after I joined Leeds from Manchester United. He comes from Leeds, and, being a soccer fan, he wrote to me pointing out what he felt were similarities between us. Like me at Leeds, he was considerably older than the other members of his band; and like me, he loved performing but not the celebrity circus attached to what he did.

He was one of the first people to telephone me after my sacking by Coventry. He actually called before it had been announced publicly and when I told him what had happened he said that he was also feeling low because Radio One was no longer playing his music and he and his band had just decided to split up, after some fifteen years together. He then told me about a dream he'd had: 'I was a warrior and I went into a battle knowing that I was going to die,' he explained. 'Sure enough, I did get killed. But then I was reborn as a warrior again, and I felt great about it because I knew I was stronger this time. I should imagine that football managers feel that way.'

If there is one thing that all managers can be certain about, it is that one day they are going to get the sack; that they are going to 'die'. I more or less knew it was going to happen to me at Coventry some time before it did. But I still carried on because, as Tim suggested, managers have the mentality of warriors (even though I and one or two others hardly look the part).

I am happy to carry on as a warrior – as long as I know when to put the sword down.

# CHAPTER TWO

# RUNNING INTO TROUBLE

During my playing career, the only manager I can think of who could erupt as spectacularly as Alex Ferguson was Jim McLean. In fact, those associated with McLean would probably claim that Fergie was positively docile in comparison.

McLean was Dundee's first-team coach when I signed for the club as a schoolboy, and then as an apprentice professional at fifteen in 1972. But I never had the chance to work with him as he left a few months later, to take over at Dundee United. According to those who know him best, he has very fixed opinions; once he gets something into his head about a player, he never lets go of it. I have had personal experience of that. For one thing, McLean always felt I drank too much. He was right at one time – I did get into a drinking habit at Dundee. It started when I was only about fifteen and, apart from what Jim might have heard on the grapevine, one incident through which his attention was bound to be drawn to it, was the ban imposed on me at eighteen by the manager of the Scotland youth team, Peter Rice, for going out on the town after a match in Denmark.

Among the players who were with me – and who were also banned – was Dundee United's John Holt.

When I became a first-team player at Dundee, Lesley and I bumped into McLean and his wife, Doris, at a Tony Christie cabaret in a city hotel, and as I did not have a car he gave us a lift home. I'd only had a few beers, but I could tell that it bothered him. The truth is that I did not have a serious drinking problem. I was not in the same drinking league as other players, although I can appreciate why this might not always have been very apparent because, unlike them, I did not hold my drink very well. Having said that, I wasn't an aggressive 'drunk' – if anything I was a happy one! In any case, the habit was quickly curbed when I was with Fergie at Aberdeen from the age of twenty-two. From then on, I would have a social drink if Lesley and I were out on a Wednesday night, or after a match on a Saturday, and that was that. Even so, for the rest of my career in Scotland, Jim seemed to have a bee in his bonnet about it. People have told me that whenever my name cropped up in conversation with him he would say: 'Oh, he drinks a lot.'

According to my 'spies' in the Dundee United camp, another McLean fixation about me concerned my defensive work. He said I could not defend, which was news to me. Though someone of my height and build was never going to win many tackles, I felt I was as good as any attacking player on tracking back and not giving an opponent the opportunity to make runs off me.

He made me laugh sometimes, often unwittingly. Following one Scotland match at Hampden Park, I travelled back to Dundee with him and his Dundee United international players, David Narey, Eamonn Bannon and Paul Sturrock. I had filled my usual role on the right side of midfield but as Jim was discussing the match with David, Eamonn and Paul, he suddenly remarked: 'Jock [Stein] had a problem tonight – right midfield. He was so concerned about the lack of midfield quality that he was thinking of playing you there, Paul.' Paul, a striker, of course, just looked at me and smiled. I thought that McLean was either trying to wind me up – after all, I was an Aberdeen player then and there was tremendous rivalry between us and Dundee United – or that he had forgotten I was present. Either way, I could not help smiling about his comment as well.

I liked McLean. His eccentricity appealed to me. Suffice it to say that when I talk to various people in the game about him, and mention that Dundee's senior players were in awe of him when he was at Dens Park, their reaction is: 'Aye, that was before he was barking mad as opposed to slightly mad.'

He was unquestionably a brilliant coach, and when he left Dundee it proved to be very much their loss and Dundee United's gain. Traditionally, United are the smaller of the two clubs, but under McLean's management – which spanned twenty-two years – nobody would have guessed it. While Dundee declined, United went from strength to strength. In addition to McLean's move to Dundee, the reverse in fortunes for the two clubs could also be traced to the first season of the Premier League (or Premier Division, as it was then), when Dundee, Dundee United and Aberdeen finished level on points at the bottom of the table, but Dundee were relegated on goal difference. Since then, United and Aberdeen have been the only teams outside the 'Old Firm' to have won the Championship – hence the description of them as the 'New Firm'. I have the impression that McLean, considerably more dour and introverted than Fergie, never allowed himself really to enjoy his ability and that of his teams as much as he should have done. The picture I have of him is one of a born pessimist, who was as hard on himself as he was on his players. They must have felt like strangling him at times. But so many of them – and notably those who started working with him from an early age – will not hear a bad word said against him by outsiders. They recognise that they would not have progressed as far as they did without the football knowledge and, equally impor-tant, the discipline that he imbued in them.

This is where McLean is pertinent to the story of my own career because, despite his exaggerated view of my problems as a youngster, I do think I could have done without him imposing that discipline on me at Dundee.

When I joined the club, I moved from a boy's world into a man's one, a very tricky step for any footballer. I have lost count of the number of times I have told youngsters: 'You might have had a brilliant schoolboy career, but that will count for absolutely nothing now.' So many of them lose their way, and, to a degree, that is what happened to me at Dundee.

Not even Jim McLean can have disputed that I was on the right track beforehand. I was born and raised in Muirhouse, close to the banks of the Firth of Forth on the north side of Edinburgh, and I am sure that even a lot of people from outside the city and even Scotland will know that this has been one of the most deprived areas in Britain. The novelist Irvine Welsh was brought up in Muirhouse and, of course, his 1993 novel *Trainspotting* – about a group of disaffected Scottish youths turning to heroin to escape the harsh reality of their lives – was focused on the area.

Like most families in Muirhouse, my own did not have much money. We were not destitute but both my parents had to go out to work – my father Jim was a scaffolder and my mother Catherine had a job in a whisky bond – and even then, it was a struggle for them to buy enough food to last us the entire week comfortably. Up to leaving home at fifteen, I felt as if I was an only child, because, although I have a sister, Laura, she is eight years younger than me. That, combined with the amount of time I spent on my own while my parents were working, made me quite independent. I often joke that I was a latchkey kid.

For all this, my general conduct and behaviour was good.

Though I was inclined to be cheeky and always wanted to get in the last word (a bit like I am today), I was never allowed to progress beyond that. My clearest memory of the parental discipline I experienced was the reaction of my parents one day when I came out with the word 'arse'. They went berserk. In fact, my father even reprimanded me for using the word when I was 21. The other reason why I was never in danger of going off the rails in any way was my devotion to football. It was not my only sporting interest. From the age of eight or nine, I played a lot of golf. However, as with countless other lads in urban inner-city areas, it was football that truly dominated my life.

Like my father, I was a Hibernian supporter – I was only five when I first watched them – and my favourite players were Pat Stanton and Peter Cormack. I must have spent hours fantasising about being in their boots, during the huge amount of football I played, especially the impromptu small-sided games with my mates.

One of the biggest changes in the game at schoolboy level is that it has become much more organised. There is no shortage of structured football – that is competitive league or cup matches involving full teams on full-sized pitches – but for all manner of reasons you have to look long and hard nowadays to find lads having kickabouts in the street or on wasteland. I loved that form of football because there was no manager or coach telling me what positions I should be in – restricting me to whatever role he felt I was best suited to – and when I should pass, shoot or dribble.

I played by instinct and had all the scope in the world to express myself. Kids organised into proper teams cannot do that. From an early age, they are told where they should play and, more often than not, that is where they stay. All youngsters like to create or score goals but depending on where they are pigeon-holed, and the coaching advice or instruction they are given by the people in charge of their teams, some never get anywhere near a goal.

Most of the great footballers of my generation, not to mention their predecessors, learned to play the game in the same way as me, and the other important part of that learning process was the number of hours they spent practising their ball skills on their own. It was comparatively easy for us to do this because our choice of leisure or sporting activities was much more limited than it is for lads today. Outside football, there was precious little else for us to do in our spare time.

Much of my own spare time was spent working on my basic skills on a grassy area close to my home. It was an ideal place to play football because it was partly enclosed by a big wall, which kept the wind off, and you never lost the ball. You felt as if you were playing in your own small stadium. The wall was an invaluable aid in helping me develop my ability to bring the ball under control quickly – the key to creating time and space for yourself in a match – and my passing. I devoted hours and hours to hitting a ball against that wall. I doubt that there was one method of control or passing that I did not practise. I had so many touches, I was almost dizzy.

If anything, I worked even harder on my fitness. This really was an obsession with me and it always has been. That's why I was able to play at the top level for as long as I did.

There are a lot of ways in which you can prolong your career. Every little bit helps as far as I am concerned, not least when you get into your thirties – the professional footballer's old-age zone. I was nothing if not open-minded when I was in that zone, as was reflected by my much-publicised intake of porridge and bananas, seaweed tablets and my interest in bio-kinetics, the acupuncture-type art of using fingertip pressure on certain points of the body to maintain its proper energy balance and flow. All this – which I know caused me to come across as somewhat quirky – attracted a lot of publicity when I was at Leeds. Indeed, because of my success in playing at the top level until I was forty, people still mention these aspects of my old fitness regime to me today.

However, there was a lot more to my long playing record than met the eye. The real key to it was the training I did long before the start of my professional career. I still get a lot of satisfaction from the memories of my willingness to drag myself off my backside and train flat out – on my own. I cannot stress enough what it did for me and how it has influenced my outlook on the game.

Any form of training without the ball is possibly the least enjoyable aspect of football. A lot of players, believing that their technical ability is more or less all that matters, will cut as many corners as they can with their physical preparation, but I was different. I realised from a very early age that all players – even the most gifted – need a high degree of fitness and physical strength in order to use their skills and that those factors are also crucial in helping them maintain concentration and avoid mistakes.

In my experience, nothing can give a player a greater psychological boost than the knowledge that he is fitter and stronger than the man marking him and that, sooner or later, he is bound to run his opponent into the ground.

Of course, nobody should really need to be reminded of that point today. The physical side of football has become increasingly pronounced since I started playing – throughout my career in the game, this is the part of it which has progressed the most. It is often said that today's top players are more like athletes than footballers. Their height and upper-body strength and their running power are awesome. There are men like that all over the field, but the physical capabilities of the modern-day star are best encapsulated in the influential midfield figures like Frank Lampard and Steven Gerrard.

Some players cannot hope to match such midfielders, no matter how hard they try. It is just the way they are made. One vivid example can be found in my own family. Gavin, who was on the playing staff at Coventry when I was manager, and was selected for the Scotland Under-21 team, has excellent basic technical ability. Yet Gavin, who is now with Hartlepool, struggled to establish a Premiership career for the simple reason that he does not have the engine to enable him to bomb up and down the park like so many of the other midfielders at that level. It is different with his brother, Craig, who has the added advantage over Gavin of being able to score more goals. The sad irony about this, though, is that Craig has suffered more injury problems and operations than any footballer I have known and, indeed, has had to retire because of it. I was comparatively lucky in that department and, in comparison with Gavin, another big plus for me is that I have an extremely slow heartbeat. Still, I have to stress again that my heart got plenty of exercise when I was a boy.

I seemed to be running all the time and, in repeatedly pushing myself to new endurance levels, I was almost like some kind of masochist. I jogged or ran virtually non-stop during a daily milk round, from 6 to 8 a.m. – in my ordinary shoes – and this would also be the case for the two and a half mile journeys to and from my school, when I would usually test myself against the clock. In the summer, I ran at least five miles a day – not including the series of shuttle sprints I did on the Firth of Forth beach. I was absolutely shattered sometimes; once or twice, I was even physically sick. But I always picked myself up and forced myself to keep going. I was afraid to give in for fear that, if I did that once, it might become a habit and that it could happen in a game.

Running was an integral part of my life, and it has remained so. It has been difficult for me to switch off from it, even when

I have been away on holiday. One of the reasons why I remember the holidays Lesley and I took at the La Manga golf complex, at the tail-end of my career, was the wind-ups from Kenny Dalglish – who had a villa there – over my nightly six mile run around the course. Kenny would often be relaxing on his patio, having a pre-dinner drink with his family and friends, as I whizzed past and, needless to say, I got all manner of stick from him. I am sure that most people who saw me thought I was a nutcase. Running has also formed the main part of my fitness regime as a manager, although I have had to curb this more than I would have wanted to in the last year or two because of hip and back problems.

I take the view that the way I improved my fitness levels as a boy was not just great physical training: it was also great character training. I still believe that. Indeed, without wishing to come across as an old fuddy-duddy, I still prefer my approach – of pushing yourself (or being pushed) beyond the point at which you feel you are ready to drop – to some of the more sophisticated methods of improving the fitness of players these days.

In recent years, the scientific methods of the highly-specialised fitness coaches who have come into the game have been reflected by the common sight of players training with heart monitors strapped to their chests. This trend, prevalent in a lot of physically demanding sports, is based on the premise that, as the maximum heart rates of players are not all the same, they should work in different aerobic 'zones'. Though I can see the benefits of this, I have yet to be convinced that the concept is always applied properly. I cannot help thinking that, in some cases, it is taken to the point where it is little more than a gimmick, and does not equate properly with the nature and demands of the game.

One of my misgivings concerns the question of how many players, in their initial tests to ascertain their maximum heart rate (and thus what zone they should adhere to in training), will have pushed themselves enough to give a true reading. When it comes to hard physical work, players are generally notorious for looking for the easy way out. That leads me to my biggest concern about this training method – the fact that it gives players the scope to ease up and take a breather if and when their monitors show their heart rates to be too high.

This is a very negative habit for any footballer to get into as far as I am concerned. No team can afford to have players who, having made one lung-bursting twenty- to forty-yard run, will allow any feelings of tiredness, disappointment or frustration to stop them doing it again immediately. It is for this reason that all the teams I have managed have trained – at least partly – in the way that I did as a lad. The run-until-you-drop approach has not gone down very well. At Coventry and Southampton, most of the players initially hated me for it, but as they got used to it, and could see the improvement in their fitness and performances, they changed their tune completely. In fact, on the occasions that I decided to give them a bit of a rest, some of them tended to be quite neurotic about it.

When I became Celtic manager, I did not have to work very hard to get all this across to the players at Parkhead following the signing of Paul Telfer. In showing them the advantages of my methods, Paul, having worked with me at both Coventry and Southampton, was the perfect advertisement. In the pre-season fitness tests the players were given, Paul, at thirty-four, was by far the most impressive.

To some extent, my determination to work on this aspect of my game as a boy stemmed from my slight build, and the fact that I tended to play for and against teams in a considerably higher age group than the ones for which I was qualified. Most of the other players were giants compared to me (which was the case even during my professional career) but this did not create as many problems as one might have thought. In fact, being the youngest and smallest member of my teams worked to my advantage in that the other members of those sides felt an extra responsibility for looking after me. They were my friends as well as my team-mates, which often came in handy when I was in danger of being battered off the field as well as on it.

Among the most prominent teams I played for were those of the amateur club Edinburgh Thistle. I started in their Under-16 side at thirteen and, in addition to winning everything in our area, we also reached two Scottish Juvenile Under-16 Cup Finals. This led to my first representative appearance – for Edinburgh against Glasgow at fourteen – and then selection for the Scotland Under-15 team. By this time there had been no shortage of English and Scottish League clubs offering me the chance to sign for them. The first to come into the picture were Coventry, Manchester City, Nottingham Forest and Celtic; but, not surprisingly, the excitement I felt about their interest in me was nothing compared to my feelings when Hibernian came in for me. Given the number of times I had watched Hibs and imagined myself playing for them, their invitation for me to join them, initially made through a scout by the name of John Dalziel, was the realisation of an ultimate dream for me. Not even Real Madrid could have tempted me to say no to him.

However, my enthusiasm then had to be tempered as a dispute arose between the club and my father over the agreement Hibs had put forward for me to sign. There had been major changes at the club following Dalziel's approach, with Tom Hart gaining control and becoming chairman and installing Eddie Turnbull as manager. I think Turnbull, a somewhat brusque, intimidating figure, felt that Hibs had been too generous on the expense allowance they had provisionally agreed to pay me; and not being the type of person to mince words, he and my father ended up having a row over it. So, as far as my hopes of playing for Hibs were concerned, it was end of story.

The next club on the scene was Dundee – as Hibs, also in the old Scottish First Division – and because of their proximity to my home, and the high number of good players they had produced, I looked upon them as my best alternative. A lot of people were surprised that I did not set my sights on joining a big club in England. A number of Scottish boys were moving south in that period, but I was influenced more by the percentage of those who had struggled to settle there and quickly returned home. The greatest temptation to ignore this was provided just a day or two after I had verbally accepted Dundee's offer, and was waiting for the relevant contract to sign. That was when I was approached by Manchester United. In addition to telling me that they wanted me to join them – which in itself would have been a pretty good reason for any lad immediately to pack his bags and hot-foot it down to Old Trafford – I was told that when I signed on the dotted line George Best would be there to give me a personal welcome. However, apart from my concern that this could be too big a step for me, I was conscious of the fact that I had given Dundee my word that I would be going there. I think it says much about the values with which I was brought up that I could not bring myself to break it. So I signed the Dundee schoolboy forms and upon leaving school at fifteen – at Easter 1972 – I joined the Dens Park ground staff as an apprentice.

I am still quite proud of that decision not to let Dundee down; and I have no regrets at all about it, even though I don't think the professional standards during my five years at the club were always particularly high. I certainly could not have any complaints about not being given early opportunities to show what I could do. I was only sixteen when I made my first team debut; eighteen when I made my league debut; and by nineteen, in addition to having established myself in the first team (albeit in the First Division) I was even appointed captain.

Two of my most vivid memories as a Dundee teenager concerned my rivalry with a player by the name of Tom Hendrie, another lad from Edinburgh who was about eighteen months older than me, and my performance in a friendly match against Arsenal. I probably have a lot to thank Tom for. He, too, was a right-side attacking player and the fact that I was twice voted Dundee's Young Player of the Year when I was in their reserves stemmed partly from the way in which he kept me on my toes. I was always worried about whether I would be considered good enough for a place in the reserves or first-team, at his expense, and I think he felt the same about me. I must admit that I was a bit jealous of him as well because, quite apart from being a good player, he was also considerably bigger and stronger than me; brainier (he later became a maths teacher); and, worse of all as far as I was concerned, he was good-looking. We were always on opposite sides in the small-sided training games and in one of them, when we started arguing about something, I ended up allowing my envy of him to get the better of me by throwing punches at him. It must have looked hilarious because Tom was about six foot. As I said to him later: 'Your knees took a right tonking.' Fortunately for me, Tom struggled to maintain his development. He only made a couple of first-team appearances before leaving Dundee in 1976, and then became a part-time player in the lower divisions. He has also been manager of Berwick Rangers, St Mirren and, most recently, Alloa.

As for that match against Arsenal, when I was eighteen, the game was arranged to mark the laying of a new Dens Park pitch, and I did so well in direct opposition to Alan Ball that when I was substituted near the end – to a standing ovation – Ball himself gave me the ultimate compliment of applauding me. The following day, the headline to the report of the match in the *Sunday Post* read: 'Strachan roasts Alan Ball. Dundee find a new Billy Bremner.'

All very flattering, but the other side of the story was that I was not doing myself any favours with my conduct off the field. I was not a bad lad – there was no way I was ever going to land myself in what I would call serious trouble. But like many teenagers when they are undergoing the transition from boys to men, I tended to be easily led into daftness.

This was probably inevitable for me once I started living away from home and coming into closer contact with senior professionals whose own standards of discipline did not always present the best examples for me to follow. The managers I had at Dundee, Davie White and Tommy Gemmell, both recognised that I had a wayward streak and was not looking after my body as well as I should have done, and did try to knock some sense into me. But neither man was in the mould of an Alex Ferguson or Jim McLean; and on the premise that it is the approach and attitude of the leading players at a club that can often influence youngsters the most, there was nobody remotely like a Roy Keane in our dressing room either.

I rubbed shoulders with some tremendous players at Dundee, like Jocky Scott and Gordon Wallace, who formed one of the best scoring partnerships in the post-war history of Scottish football, and John Duncan, who later moved to Tottenham. It is difficult to think of any strikers who have worked better together than Jocky and Gordon. A lot of my early knowledge about creating space for yourself was picked up from those two, which might well have been something of a sore point with Jocky, given that I eventually took his No. 10 first-team shirt off him at Dundee and then did it again at Aberdeen. I was like a black cloud hanging over him.

From a technical viewpoint, I like to think that most of the players at Dundee helped me. However, in a setup which could best be described as being too relaxed, it would have been just as helpful to me to have players who could also help shape my mentality.

Before I started living in Dundee I was one of a number of players who commuted to Dens Park from Edinburgh each day, but it became more tiring for me than it did for them, for the simple reason that I could not return home after training at midday; as the only apprentice in the group, I had to stay behind and carry out various general duties throughout the afternoon. Having left home at 6.15 a.m. to catch a bus to Waverley Station and then a train over the Forth and Tay Bridges to Dundee, I rarely got home before 7.15 p.m. By the end of the week, I was knackered. The other problem for me was that one of my morning travelling companions was centre half George Stewart – a great one for card games, who had no compunction about persuading me to become a regular member of his school and relieving me of as much of my £13-a-week Dundee wages as he could. I am not sure that this is a good way for a relationship between a senior professional and a wet-behind-the-ears apprentice to be conducted, but I did like George.

The Dundee youngsters to whom I formed the closest attachment were George Mackie and Alec Caldwell, two of the lads I shared digs with. They have remained among my best friends to this day. Since our time together at Dundee – where Alec made more than a hundred league appearances, compared to just half a dozen by George – our lives have mostly taken us in totally different directions. Alec was a defender and after he left Dundee he played for St Johnstone and Forfar, and filled management positions at Inverness Caledonian and Elgin City. George, a right back or midfielder, went on to play for Partick Thistle, Albion Rovers and Brechin and then tried his hand on the management side at Meadowbank and Arbroath.

For some years, George and his former Meadowbank and Arbroath managerial sidekick, Donald Park, were also partners in a hotel and bar business in Edinburgh. I loved that bar on a Saturday night. It was very Gaelic-orientated and, with people playing Irish songs on fiddles and guitars and almost everybody singing, the atmosphere was electric.

One of my best decisions as Coventry manager was to appoint George to oversee our youth setup with Richard Money. Though he'd established an excellent reputation as a youth-team coach at Dundee United and with the Scotland Under-16 and Under-17 squads, it did bother me that my choice of George for the job would be construed merely as an old pal's act. Both Andy Roxburgh and Craig Brown, effectively his Scottish Football Association coaching bosses, had no hesitation in putting George's name forward when I asked them who they felt I should pick. My reaction was: 'Oh no – he's my mate.' However, as they said: 'You must not allow that to stop you hiring him if he has the right qualifications for the post.' I am glad I didn't because he and Money steered us to two FA Youth Cup Finals and a semi final, which is not bad going for a club like Coventry.

Alec Caldwell, who spent a week with me at Coventry to study our training methods when he was preparing for his Uefa coaching badge, is a good coach as well but both he and George have recently spent some time out of the game. That, sadly, can easily happen in our profession. George has been working for the logistics department of a supermarket chain, while Alec, who was operations manager for a national courier company, has started a new life in Spain.

However, in one way, the link between the three of us can never be broken. One example of the depth of our friendship was when George and I played against each other in an Aberdeen–Partick match, in my first season at Pittodrie. We were both among the substitutes and, as we were chatting in the dugout, George, appreciating that my Aberdeen career had not got off to the best of starts, said: 'If we both get on, I will try to help get the crowd behind you. When you get the ball, and I am in a position to tackle you, you feint to take it left and then go right and I will go the other way. You will beat me, no bother.' A good idea in theory, but it was a different matter in practice because when I did get the opportunity to take him to the cleaners I got his instructions the wrong way around and we ended up bumping into each other.

Still, at least nothing like that happened when George was the best man at my wedding (Alec was also pushed into the picture as an usher) and I filled the same role at his.

For our twenty-fifth anniversary in the summer of 2002, following my first season at Southampton, Lesley and I invited my two old pals and their partners, together with Lesley's bridesmaid and her other half, to help us celebrate with a week's holiday on a yacht on the French Riviera. The lease of the yacht – which had a crew of seven and virtually every mod con you could think of – cost me an arm and a leg. To do it again I think I would need to be manager of Real Madrid or Juventus (or, looking at Sven-Göran Eriksson's salary, England). But it was worth every penny. Being with George and Alec again helped make it one of the most enjoyable holidays I have ever had. I still laugh at the thought of what the locals, not to mention the glamorous looking, well-heeled people on the other boats, will have made of us when we were moored at St Tropez. The three of us are red-headed, and with our Scottish accents and pasty faces and bodies, we must have represented quite a culture shock for them. They probably thought we were members of the kitchen staff on a day off. It was very much like going back in time for me because the rapport between us was no different from what it had been when we lived together as teenagers. It was the same when George, Alec and me joined up in Portugal to see some of the 2004 European Championship matches together.

I have so many great memories of my association with the pair. George was seventeen or eighteen, and playing for the reserves when I joined Dundee at fifteen and it was through him that I started living away from home. Unfortunately, his initiative in bringing me into the digs in which he was living was probably not the best move he has ever made. This was even more the case with the decision of the landlady, the mother of the former Dundee defender Ronnie Selway, to agree to it. Displaying the sort of unruly accident-prone habits that should have seen me banned from every nice house in Scotland, I broke Mrs Selway's television on my first night there; and no sooner had I been forgiven for that – after all, I was only trying to improve the picture quality – I shattered one of her most valued antique ornaments.

Not surprisingly, she sent me packing and, with George electing to follow me – no doubt because of some misguided sense of responsibility to look after me – the next port of call was the lodgings which Alec shared with a centre-forward by the name of Keith Wyllie.

The four of us had to sleep in one room – a small attic room, in fact – and if there had been a TV camera there I am sure our antics would have provided more entertainment than *Big Brother* or any other reality programme ever has. Needless to say, the other three were much taller than me and when we were all in the room together there was hardly room to swing a cat. Keith was the tallest, at six foot four inches, and had to sleep in a bed that was not really big enough for him. He used to sleep with his feet dangling over the end, and a small electric fire – kept on all night – as near to them as was possible without him getting burned.

That fire was the only source of heating in the room, and as we quickly mastered the art of getting constant power without having to pay for it by sticking a match in the meter, it was on virtually all the time. Even so, the room was so cold in the peak winter months that we had to sleep with our clothes on. It was not unusual for us to nick clothes off each other, especially if they were relatively fresh. No matter who they belonged to, clean clothes were like gold dust to us. When it came to 'borrowing' my gear, it mattered little to George, Alec and Keith that they had to be almost double-jointed to get into it.

The other element of farce in the challenge of getting a good night's kip was that George was a sleep-walker. It was always on the cards that you would wake up in the middle of the night to find George hovering over you and demanding that you get out of 'his' bed.

Crazy stuff, and it got crazier still when Keith was involved. A regular visitor to the bookies, and both a drinker and smoker, Keith was a character with a capital 'C'. When I played with him in the reserves, there was one occasion when the manager wanted to bring him on as a substitute, only to discover that he was no longer on the bench. He was having a fag in the dressing room toilet. As for his ability, we teased him unmercifully by referring to him as 'the striker who cannot strike'. He did not have the best scoring record even for the reserves. I do remember one goal he scored, though – at Dunfermline – because we travelled back to Dundee by rail together, and, by the end of the journey I reckon everybody in the train must have known about it.

I do not think Keith made any first-team appearances for Dundee in competitive matches, and we lost touch with each other after Dundee gave him a free transfer. The last time I saw him was in 1996, when I bumped into him in London before the Scotland–England European Championship clash at Wembley, but as he was late for an appointment with some friends, we were not able to have a proper conversation. It was impossible not to like this guy and as I have no idea what has happened to him since he left Dundee, it would be great to see him again to find out.

One of the daft things the four of us got up to in that room, to relieve the boredom of being in such a confined space, was the occasional game of strip poker. How sad is that? It gets worse: Keith liked to sit by the window, because of his smoking – which created a problem when he was losing and had no clothes on, as the window overlooked a school. Keith – in a world of his own when he was gambling – could easily be seen by the children when they poured out of it. On one occasion it was not only the kids who were subjected to the disconcerting sight of Keith's bare backside. To her horror, our landlady, who happened to be putting out the washing at the time, also got a glimpse of it. She was not impressed, although we were by the speed with which she charged up the stairs to point out the error of our ways.

After eighteen months in those digs, Keith left Dundee and Alec and I, having started courting the girls who were to become our wives, decided to rent a flat together. The arrangement worked well, even though Alec and I did have a big falling out over my views about his partner, Carol. She is a strong character, who I felt was too forthright and opinionated – as I was when complaining to Alec about her. Still, the issue was quickly sorted out. One day, when I went too far in criticising her, Alec gave me a fully deserved punch in the mouth. It says much about my knowledge of what makes a good relationship that Alec and Carol have been happily married for more than thirty years.

The path towards my own happiness in that department started when Lesley and I, both seventeen, met at a Dundee disco. I was looking for someone shorter than me – a mission impossible, you could say – but as Lesley was so stunning, the fact that she did not meet that criterion quickly became irrelevant. At least I could look her straight in the eye – well, almost. So it was quite a shock to both of us when we realised that the height difference between us was greater than we had originally thought; we had not noticed it before because she had been dancing in her bare feet and I was wearing platforms. The result was that, although we arranged a date, neither of us showed up for it.

In my case, the other reason was that I only had about 45p in the bank. Still, as I knew where she worked (in a Dundee Co-Op Insurance office) and where she went for lunch, it was not as if I was never going to see her again. I would hate anybody to think that I was a stalker – let's just say that I kept discreet tabs on her. We met again at another disco a few months later, and this time we immediately became an item. We were engaged at eighteen and married at twenty.

I shouldn't imagine many people will have felt this was a good idea from Lesley's point of view because, during our courtship, I was not the most mature of teenagers.

All of which brings me back to that drinking habit which Jim McLean keeps going on about.

The start of it can be traced right back to the day I received my first Dundee wage packet, at fifteen. All the players got paid each Thursday afternoon, and once they had the money in their pockets it was not long before most of them headed for the pub. I saw no reason not to join them. I did not know any better. Nobody said to me: 'Gordon, you should not be doing that.' In fairness to the players at Dundee, I think it was the norm at a lot of clubs in Scotland in those days. Players seemed to take the view that as long as they did not have a drink the day before a game they were okay. They were good pros.

Of course, the other reason why I shouldn't have been involved in those Dundee pub sessions was that I was under age. You would have thought that, as I was five foot six and nine and a half stone, I would have stood out like a sore thumb in any pub. Yet, strange as it might seem, I cannot recall a single person behind the bar (let alone any of my colleagues) ever questioning my right to be on the premises. I think the reason was that I had an old face: I might have had a fifteen-year-old's body, but my face then was little different from the one I have now.

In addition to the practice of regularly going out for a drink with the lads – an easy trap to fall into, I feel, given the boredom and sense of confinement of living in the sort of digs I had – I also picked up a bad eating habit. The flat Alec and I rented was above a fish and chip shop and, if we had our windows open, the smell of that artery-clogging fried food wafting through them made it difficult to resist. We were also frequent visitors to the Chinese takeaway, or 'carry-out' as such places are called in Scotland, across the road, not to mention all manner of other fast-food establishments. The 'fuel' I put into my body was all wrong. It shows how little I knew in those days that I used to wonder why I occasionally felt lethargic.

Even when I was a so-called 'star' first-team player, being with Dundee was no picnic. It is often said that the leading young players of today are too pampered, and I can certainly relate to that view when I look back on my Dundee career. Alec Caldwell and I had to take two buses to get to Dens Park from where we lived, and to save money it was not usual for us to walk there, even for the game on a Saturday. As far as the Dundee public was concerned, you might have been someone special during a match, but outside that, the attention paid to you was underwhelming.

There was nothing remotely glamorous about Dundee FC behind the scenes, especially when they ran into serious financial difficulties following their relegation and there were fears that they might have to go part-time. It was like the football equivalent of *I'm a Celebrity, Get Me Out of Here*. The players' training kit – including our pants – was only washed once a week. After we had trained in it on Tuesday, Wednesday and Thursday, often in terrible weather, imagine what it was like on a Friday.

I could easily cope with the thought that I was not among the cleanest and sweetest-smelling footballers in Scotland. More difficult for me to come to terms with was the feeling that I had reached the end of my development with Dundee. Obviously, part of this was down to their slide into the First Division, under Davie White's managership, in 1976, after finishing midway in the table in the two previous seasons and winning the League Cup in 1974. Dundee's failure to bounce back in 1976, my first season as a first team regular, led to White getting the sack and Tommy Gemmell – Dundee's captain – replacing him.

Tommy was a popular choice for the job. He'd initially been brought to Dundee as a player by White in 1973, and through the stature he had gained in Celtic's superb teams of the 1960s under Jock Stein, and his extrovert personality, he was as charismatic as anyone I have ever worked with. I was only sixteen when he joined Dundee, and like everybody else who had been thrilled by his trademark explosive long-range shots – notably the one that helped bring Celtic their epic win over Inter Milan in the 1967 European Cup Final – I could not wait to see him produce them in our training sessions. Hardly a day went by without one of us imploring Tommy to show us one of his 'thunderbolts'. It must have driven him mad because, by that stage in his career, the necessary power in his legs had diminished. However, he still had plenty left in other areas of the game, as Celtic were to discover when he led Dundee to victory over his old club in the 1974 League Cup Final.

It was a great feather in my cap when, with Tommy out of action because of injury, Davie White chose me to take over from him as captain; and even more so when Tommy gave me the responsibility after he had become manager. In truth, I was much too young for that role. I did not have much of a grasp of what I should have been doing on the field, let alone what the players in other positions should have been doing. Even so, being appointed captain by someone like Tommy Gemmell did my self-esteem and image no harm at all.

I did have my doubts, though, that Tommy was the type of manager who could help turn me into a better footballer.

The dressing-room atmosphere had begun to change at the time of his appointment, with some players losing their focus and more or less just going through the motions. Tommy, being the somewhat laid-back character that he was, did not really get to grips with that. This side of him was also reflected in the level of organisation and intensity in our approach to matches. Training would usually consist of a bit of running and shooting, maybe a small-sided game and that was it. There was little work on the team shape and tactics and, indeed, we did not even know what the team would be until the day of the game. For a team of our standard, too much was left to chance.

You could hardly say that about the teams produced by Fergie and Jim McLean, although in fairness to Tommy I should imagine that a lot of managers in Scotland at that time struggled to match their attention to detail and drive. On the premise that great footballers do not necessarily make great managers, it is also worth pointing out that, unlike Fergie and McLean – neither of whom were great players – Tommy did not need to address himself to much in-depth technical and physical work during his long Celtic career. As one of the best attacking full backs in the world, in one of the best attacking teams, the game was comparatively easy for him. For many years in domestic football, the only times Celtic were stretched were when they played Rangers.

Tommy was only Dundee manager for a few months before I was transferred to Aberdeen in November 1977, for a fee of £50,000. It was in that short space of time that another legendary figure from Celtic's European Cup-winning team, the incomparable Jimmy Johnstone, was brought on to the Dundee playing staff. Like countless others who had watched him, I was absolutely infatuated with the wee man; whenever I think of his astonishing dribbling ability, the way he could make opponents look like fools, and that engaging personality of his, I still am. But, of course, the other side of the story with Jimmy was his wayward, self destructive streak.

He was thirty-three when he came to Dundee from Sheffield United, and it quickly became obvious that all his years of not looking after himself properly off the field, and, it should be added, the physical punishment meted out to him by opponents on it, had taken their toll. Tommy arranged for me to train with him, to help push him. Jimmy did work hard, but the sad reality was that his legs had gone. He could hardly kick the ball any distance at all and though he could still produce the occasional flashes of individual magic in matches, he would tend to get tired after just ten minutes. It is well-documented that Jimmy's life was not as successful as it should have been. Of all the players who did not make the most of their talents, Jimmy, who died tragically at the age of 61 in March 2006 following a long struggle against motor neurone disease, has long been held up as one of the most poignant examples. I once said that a video of Jimmy's life should be made compulsory viewing for every young professional footballer in Britain. When I was at Leeds, and had the responsibility of helping to guide the young players there, my own copy of the video was often shown on the team coach.

In talking to them about the dangers of drinking, it was also good for me to be able to tell them about the day that Jimmy and I got drunk together.

It happened after one of our first Dundee training sessions, when he invited me to join him at his hotel for lunch. During the meal, it did not bother me that he was ordering and consuming a fair amount of alcohol. Let's face it: when one of your heroes has invited you for lunch, you are hardly going to say: 'You should not be drinking – it's unprofessional.' As for myself, I was so engrossed in his views on the game, and his anecdotes, that I was drinking without really being conscious of it. By the end of the lunch, Jimmy and I should have called it a day and tried to get some sleep – especially me. Having accepted that I was never going to match him as a footballer, it was obvious that I was never going to be able to match him as a drinker either. But not being in a fit state of mind to make such a decision, I joined him on a bar crawl, which eventually took us to the village of Errol. We must have been in a bad way to go there because Errol was where Tommy Gemmell lived. He owned a hotel there and happened to be looking out of one of the windows as Jimmy and I staggered past. Needless to say, Tommy was not amused. He read us the riot act. It was at that point that the penny at last began to drop and I decided that I had to clean up my act.

Ironically, like Tommy Gemmell and Jimmy Johnstone, the Aberdeen manager who bought me from Dundee, in November 1977, was an equally high-profile member of that Celtic 'Lisbon Lions' 1967 European Cup-winning team – Billy McNeill, the captain and centre-half. I was fortunate, inasmuch as Dundee, who had made a good start to the season, quickly establishing themselves among the leading promotion contenders again, needed to let me go in order to keep themselves afloat financially. Tommy has said: 'The Dundee chairman [Ian Gellatly] told me on the Monday that unless we got £50,000 by the Friday, then the banks would be closing the club down.'

It was fortunate for me, too, that when Dundee were on the wrong end of an embarrassing hammering in a second-leg League Cup tie at Queen of the South – in what proved to be my last match for the club – I at least gave a good impression through my work rate and determination. I often refer to that match when talking to players about the importance of never allowing their heads to drop, and how this can provide seemingly unlikely defining moments in careers. Dundee had been beaten 3-1 by Queen of the South in the first leg at Dens Park, and for the return tie I think the thought at the back of most players' minds was that they would be better off saving their energy for the league match against Hearts – also among the table leaders – three days later. As a consequence Queen of the South beat us 6-0.

On the face of it, I could have done without that, given that Queen of the South's manager, Mike Jackson, and Billy McNeill were close friends. However, when the pair were discussing the match the following day, and Billy asked Jackson what I'd been like, he was told: 'Not great, but unlike one or two other Dundee players, the wee man worked his socks off.' I cannot help wondering if I would have ended up at Aberdeen if Jackson has said: 'He looked as if he wasn't bothered.'

## CHAPTER THREE

# THE NORTH STAR

It took me a long time before I could look Billy McNeill in the eye without being embarrassed. I have always had a great deal of respect and admiration for the big man, and it is one of the biggest regrets of my career that, because of my poor early form for Aberdeen, I did not properly repay him for the faith he showed in me. After bringing me to Pittodrie, he was only there until the end of that season before returning to Celtic to succeed Jock Stein. I am sure he was very happy to see the back of me. In the time we worked together, a lot of people felt he made a mistake in signing me. Quite apart from a number of the fans, who made their negative opinions about me plain enough during matches, I know for a fact that Billy's assistant, John Clark – yet another ex-Celtic star – did not fancy me. On one occasion, I overheard him telling Billy: 'I wouldn't have had Strachan.' The way I was playing, though, I could hardly quibble with that comment.

It was a difficult time for me outside football. I had only been married for about five months when I joined Aberdeen, and on top of the adjustment problems common to all newly-weds, Lesley and I, having some difficulty in finding a house we liked and could afford in Aberdeen, spent some time living in a hotel. On the football side, I was hampered by an ankle injury, sustained in training before my first Aberdeen match; and shortly afterwards, while I was still struggling to find top form, another injury put me out of action for four weeks.

None of this was of much consolation to me. My absence meant a slight re-organisation of the team, the most significant part of which was John McMaster being brought into the central midfield area. John was superb and the new line-up worked so well that, upon my recovery, I was kept out of the side. For the rest of the season, I could only be reasonably sure of a place in the starting line-up in the Scottish Cup, which was largely because Steve Archibald, who had been signed from Clyde, was ineligible. Even then, when Aberdeen reached the Scottish Cup Final against Rangers (which they were to lose 2-1), I was not even on the bench. There were fourteen players in the first-team squad, but only two substitutes were allowed then, and I was the one who drew the short straw and had to watch the action from the stands, despite the fact that I had been one of the subs for the semi-final and played in all the previous ties.

The team for the final was announced after our training session the day before the game and, with no part to play, I spent that night and much of the day of the game on my own. That memory was particularly strong when, as Southampton manager in 2003, I had to tell players like Paul Jones, Fabrice Fernandes and Kevin Davies that they would not be in our team for the FA Cup Final against Arsenal. It was never going to be easy, but knowing what I felt like when it happened to me made it even more agonising. One of the factors which helped stop my spirits sinking too low in that first season at Pittodrie was my contact with Teddy Scott, the club's long-serving trainer and kit man.

Many clubs have a Teddy Scott on their backroom staff. Such figures, whose job descriptions tend to incorporate all manner of dressing room duties on behalf of the players, usually know everything that is going on at their clubs and the players probably trust them more than anyone else.

At Aberdeen all the players loved to congregate in Teddy's room, a general store of a place in which this wonderful character – an inveterate hoarder – kept everything we could possibly need or want both on and off the field. Teddy had to take a lot of stick from us – I think that is par for the course for all the men in his role – but when it came to anybody else taking liberties we were all fiercely protective of him.

On an Aberdeen European trip, I remember Fergie – who was as fond of Teddy as we were, it has to be stressed – losing his rag over him having packed the wrong training kit.

'Well, why don't you sack him, then?' I said tongue in cheek.

Such was Fergie's rage that the joke was lost on him.

'Aye, I think I might,' he replied.

That ignited my temper as well. 'Well, if you are seriously thinking of doing that, you are off your head,' I said.

Teddy was a big help to Fergie, as the manager acknowledged in 1999 when he brought Manchester United to Pittodrie for Teddy's testimonial match. Teddy was a great help to me as well, especially when he was in charge of the Aberdeen reserve team I played in.

He could be brutally honest. 'How do you think you played on Saturday?' he would ask me.

'Okay, not bad,' I'd say.

'Nah, you were crap.' End of conversation. But he was also a great person to talk to when you were down; he had a knack of speaking to you in the right way, without patronising you. He was one of the figures who represented the heart and soul of the club.

That was also the case with the chairman, Dick Donald. It is the chairmen of clubs who set the standards and principles by which they are run, so I think that any explanation of why I found so much happiness and contentment at Aberdeen would have to start with the influence of Donald. After all, it was Donald who appointed Fergie to succeed Billy McNeill, despite Fergie's sacking by St Mirren. Not only this, Donald, one of the old-school football chairmen who believed in letting his managers manage, was a steadying influence on Fergie. As he once said: 'He can be very impatient and impulsive, so now and again it is just a question of saying to him: "Hang on, Alex. Let's think about this".'

Donald was clearly a stronger character than he might have seemed. To the players, this delightful man, once an Aberdeen half-back, came across like one's favourite uncle. He would always have a bag of sweets in his pocket, which he'd happily dispense to all and sundry when he came into the club, not to mention some loose change to give to any of the staff's children who happened to be at Pittodrie when he was there.

You never actually had to see him to know he was around because he was forever whistling and did a sort of soft shoe shuffle when he walked.

Outside football, he had an entertainment empire, incorporating dance and bingo halls, theatres and cinemas. He kept all manner of paraphernalia from these – stage props, seating etc – in a big warehouse, and he took me there one day to try and find a front door for the house that Lesley and I had bought. He'd heard me talking about our need for one while I was having lunch in the Pittodrie canteen and, typically, he immediately offered to help.

Unfortunately, the door he picked out, while being the right size, had the word 'Exit' on it. Strange as it might seem, he seemed a bit surprised when I told him that I did not think it was suitable. 'I thought it was perfect,' he told me. I felt like saying to him: 'Okay, I will take it – but can you also throw in a couple of usherettes to show our visitors to their seats?'

Until Fergie came along, of course, I was in danger of being shown another exit – the one at Pittodrie. Fergie has said that in one of his initial meetings with Donald to discuss the players he wanted to sign or let go, the chairman suggested that I might be in the latter category. Fortunately for me, Fergie's response was that he would not decide either way until he'd had the opportunity to assess me properly.

When players are at a low ebb, there is nothing quite like the presence of a new manager to stimulate them. Fergie's arrival was a big fillip for me. Having let Billy McNeill down, I felt as if the slate had been wiped clean and I could make a fresh start. The other good news for me was that John Clark had moved to Celtic with Billy and the man Fergie appointed as his Aberdeen assistant was Pat Stanton. In addition to being one of my favourite players as a boy, Pat was the only other member of the Aberdeen staff who was born and raised in Edinburgh. That somehow made me feel less isolated.

My clean slate began to look even better as my fortunes at Aberdeen improved. In Fergie's first season, when Aberdeen finished fourth in the Premier Division, and reached the semi-finals of the Scottish Cup and the final of the League Cup (in which we were again beaten by Rangers), I played in all but half a dozen of our forty-nine matches, mostly from the start. Outside the occasional injuries, it was the same story in my five other Aberdeen seasons. In view of what Aberdeen achieved, I can only describe the experience of being part of a team like that as a privilege.

No team has ever undermined the power of the Old Firm quite like Aberdeen did under Fergie. I am not usually into statistics, but it is difficult to ignore them when talking about Aberdeen's success under him.

In 1980 Aberdeen became the first side other than Celtic or
Rangers to win the title since Kilmarnock in 1964/5. We were
one of only fifteen teams to have broken the Old Firm hold on
the title in the entire twentieth century. That was just for
starters – during my time at Aberdeen we won the Championship again; the Scottish Cup three times; the League Cup; and
the European Cup Winners' Cup and European Super Cup. The
European Cup Winners' Cup success in 1983, when Aberdeen
overcame the likes of Bayern Munich in the quarter-final and
Real Madrid in that epic rain-soaked final in Gothenburg,
formed the major part of a trophy double with the Scottish Cup.
There was also a double for us – that of the Championship and
Scottish Cup – in 1984. No team outside the Old Firm has ever
won those two competitions in the same season. Though the
Cup Winners' Cup triumph – the only time that a Scottish team
other than Celtic or Rangers has won a European trophy – was
the achievement for which Fergie's Aberdeen are probably best
remembered, there is little doubt that the first Championship,
the first major honour of Fergie's reign, was the most significant.
It was one thing to beat Celtic or Rangers in the occasional
match; to overshadow the Glasgow giants over a season was
something else. Indeed, the Old Firm's domination of Scottish
football had created something of a psychological barrier for the
other teams and the breaking of it – at the expense of Celtic particularly – was an immense turning point for us. Having proved
to ourselves that we could do it, we became hungrier, if not
greedier, for more.

Fergie amassed a lot of good players at Aberdeen and, as I
have said, they were strong characters.

It made for an interesting life behind the scenes because some
could be quite difficult. Steve Archibald, who did a great job for
Aberdeen in that first Championship-winning season before
joining Tottenham, was certainly in that category. Off the field,

Steve was very much a loner, and would tend to detach himself from the rest of the lads. Whatever we decided to do as a group, you could bet that Steve would want to do something else. He was also very single-minded about scoring – like all the top goalscorers – and very demanding when it came to getting the service he felt he needed. Occasionally, on the premise that goalscorers have the most difficult and important jobs in the game, he could give the impression of thinking that everything should revolve around him. While I could appreciate his desire to make the most of his ability, for the good of Aberdeen as well as himself, it did not make him the easiest of people to work with.

In the 1979/80 season, he and I had a terrible row during an 8-0 Scottish Cup win over Airdrie. He started it by having a go at me for not passing to him when he was in the box. I just did not think it was my best option, but Steve felt otherwise and did not mince his words in letting me know. Our argument got very heated. It was not unlike the clash between Newcastle's Kieron Dyer and Lee Bowyer in April 2005, but without the fisticuffs. Steve was still going on about it immediately after the match, despite the score line – and despite the fact that he had scored four of the goals.

'I do not think you and I should talk to each other again until the end of the season,' he told me.

'Is that going to be a hardship for me?' I said.

Despite such dressing-room friction, we were all very much on the same wavelength when it really mattered. No set of players had greater respect for each other or worked harder for each other than Aberdeen's; and no team had greater mental strength. That, I think, was the key to our success in breaking out of the Old Firm's shadow.

In Scotland, Celtic and Rangers had become used to playing against teams inhibited by their reputations. The approach of the opposition, especially at Parkhead or Ibrox, was often based mainly on damage limitation. They would sit back against Celtic and Rangers and try to frustrate them. Fergie, referring to their efforts to take the heat out of the game, would often draw attention to the attitude of some teams when they were awarded throw-ins and corners against the Old Firm – the fact that, even in good attacking positions, they were in no hurry to get the ball back into play. Aberdeen were different. Our aim was to defend as high up the field as possible – something of a fixation with Fergie and, to use his words: 'Get at their f*****g throats.'

This was carried out to stunning effect over the last lap of the 1979/80 title race, when Aberdeen won at Celtic not just once but twice. The first victory, 2-1, through goals by Drew Jarvie and Mark McGhee, and a Bobby Clarke penalty save from Bobby Lennox, came on 5 April. By the time we revisited Parkhead on 23 April, our fifth match from the end, the two teams were level on points – thanks to a shock 5-0 Celtic defeat by Dundee the previous week – and we had a game in hand.

I know the word cauldron is a football cliché, but it is still the best word I can use to describe what Celtic Park was like that night. It was a hot evening for a start, and the crowd of 48,000 made so much noise that the number of people in the stadium seemed more like 70,000. I have been in friendlier atmospheres, but even before kickoff the Celtic fans were given an indication of our mindset when big Doug Rougvie elected to do his warm-up right in front of the notoriously hostile 'Jungle' end of the ground – totally ignoring Fergie's instructions for our warm-ups to be carried out in more shaded areas. That was typical of Doug, one of the most physically intimidating players I have ever worked with and, needless to say, a cult figure among Aberdeen supporters.

But he was not the only Aberdeen player with the bottle to pay a visit to the 'Jungle'. Steve Archibald did it as well, going over to that part of the ground and shaking his fist at the stunned spectators after giving Aberdeen the lead. It went a bit pear-shaped for us when Celtic equalised with a George McCluskey penalty, and I then had a penalty saved by Peter Latchford. But if anything, these setbacks made us even more belligerent, and things certainly turned out well for me. I was involved in the move which saw Mark McGhee put us back in front with a header and early in the second half I pounced on a mistake by Latchford to make it 3-1.

Celtic were a point ahead of us after the next two matches, in which they beat Partick and Dundee and we overcame St Mirren but drew with Dundee United. But, because of our superior goal difference, it was all over on 3 May, when we beat Hibernian 5-0 in our penultimate game and Celtic's last fixture against St Mirren ended 0-0. We finally increased our lead over Celtic to one point with a 1-1 draw at Partick in our last match.

That season, in which I played in all but three of the thirty-six league matches and was Aberdeen's third highest scorer, was the making of me as well as of the club. I was voted Footballer of the Year by the Scottish football writers – the first part of what was to become a unique double when I picked up the English version of that award in 1992. In the close season, my personal profile was raised again when I was brought into the Scotland team for the first time for the (now defunct) British Championship matches against Northern Ireland, Wales and England, and the 1982 World Cup qualifying ties against Poland and Hungary.

If any player deserved to be singled out for applause, though, it was our underrated midfielder Andy Watson. Teams need a blend of many different qualities and attributes to achieve success, and quite often the most important players are those who, because of the nature of their roles, get the least public recognition. Andy – the Aberdeen player then who probably took the most stick from the fans – was a perfect example. He did not have the ball skills of someone like John McMaster, who could hit forty-yard passes to your feet with no bother at all, but through his amazing work rate and drive he was important to the team in other ways.

Andy came into the team midway through the season, when Alex McLeish, who had been playing in central midfield, was moved back to his 'natural' position of centre-half. It was no coincidence that, with Andy in the side, we were unbeaten in our last fifteen league matches, all but three of which we won. Epitomising Fergie's desire to have an abundance of physical power in his central midfield department, Andy, a tremendous tackler who could also get in the box and score, brought extra dynamism to the team. At the time, that was what we most needed.

I have my doubts that Aberdeen would have won the title without him, but even after that season, the fans were not totally sold on him. That was quite irritating to his team-mates – the people who truly understood what he brought to the side. Nobody thought more highly of him than Alex McLeish, whose managerial career at Motherwell, Hibernian and Rangers was forged with Andy working alongside him as his assistant.

Everybody is entitled to his or her opinion, but not – surely – when criticism becomes personal. If there is one aspect of football that is always liable to raise my blood pressure it is that of supporters belittling players on those radio phone-in programmes – I keep asking people if they know one of these idiots, but I've yet to find one who has. The first time I can recall reacting to this was when I heard one fan having a rant about Andy on the radio following a 1-0 win over Albania's Dinamo Tirana in our European Cup Winners' Cup-winning season.

'The guy [Watson] looks as if he is dead,' the caller said. 'He should be put back in the grave.' I could handle that – just – but what made it worse as far as I was concerned was that the presenter seemed to think it was a bit of a laugh. He was not laughing when he then had someone else on the line – me. 'You are a disgrace to encourage comments like that,' I told him. 'It is just unedited rubbish.'

As one of the so-called 'flair' players at Aberdeen, I generally had an excellent relationship with the fans – as, indeed, was the case at all the clubs I played for. I always knew that people love to see players beating opponents and creating and taking scoring chances, but even I was taken aback by the reaction of one supporter after my extra-time goal in the 4-1 win over Rangers in the 1982 Scottish Cup Final. The goal itself was a simple tap-in. This, though, was followed by a celebratory somersault which the fan – watching on TV at his home – was moved to try and copy. Sadly for him, he collided with his stone fireplace and broke a leg. When I heard about it, I immediately arranged to visit him. I thought it was the least I could do!

However, while I was among the Aberdeen crowd favourites, and was probably the player who attracted the most media plaudits, I have always been extremely conscious of how much I benefited from the ability of the other players and the way Fergie set up his teams tactically.

It is often said that the best way to judge a team is through the standard of the men down the middle, or 'spine', of it. Nobody could say that the most famous of Fergie's Aberdeen line-ups, with Jim Leighton in goal, Alex McLeish and Willie Miller at the heart of the defence, Neil Simpson and Neale Cooper in the central midfield area, and Mark McGhee and Eric Black in the striking roles, was not exceptionally strong in those positions.

Today, it is easy to forget Jim Leighton's stature at Aberdeen, given his subsequent problems at Manchester United under Fergie and, as a keeper who was never a good kicker of the ball, his problems in adjusting to the change in the back-pass rule. At Aberdeen, though, where he succeeded Bobby Clarke, we looked upon him as the best keeper in the world. I certainly think he was the bravest.

Jim took a lot of pressure off his defence, particularly through the number of times he came for crosses. It was the same with Steve Ogrizovic when I worked with him at Coventry, but the big difference between Steve and Jim was that Steve was stronger physically. Jim took some horrendous knocks, even in training. Indeed, there were quite a few times that, as one of the few players with a car, I had to take him to hospital. We used to say to him: 'Look, if you carry on like this, you are going to find yourself in a coffin. You do not have to come for everything.' But it did not make any difference.

The central defensive partnership involving Alex, a tremendous attacker of the ball in the air, who was deceptively quick and skilful for a man of his build, and Willie, a supreme reader of the game and as hard as nails, was as solid as any you could name. Willie's middle name should be 'Immaculate' – that's what he was not only in his performances but also in his everyday life. You could tell that he was the captain just through his clothes and his house and the way he conducted himself. The rest of us could come across as a rabble. We always seemed to be laughing and joking. But Willie wanted to be seen as a man apart in that respect.

Willie was one of those players who showed that one cannot always accurately access a footballer on what he does in training. As a manager, you demand 100 per cent from everybody. But Kenny Dalglish was not a good trainer – he looked as if he had lead in his boots – and it was the same with Willie. We used to joke that, outside matches, he was in almost permanent hibernation. He spent most of his time resting at home, and having to come in for training was a chore to him.

Willie was never a good athlete, but because of his great football brain he did not need to be. He, and Alex, were also helped by the high-octane style of play of the men immediately in front of them, Neil Simpson and Neale Cooper.

It is fair to say that Simpson and Cooper, two of the leading young graduates from the excellent schoolboy and youth system that Fergie developed at Pittodrie, were very much the essence of Aberdeen's approach. It was important to Fergie that Aberdeen performed at a high tempo, and did not allow opponents to settle on the ball, and these two, with their boundless energy and enthusiasm, provided the perfect lead. Their power and determination could intimidate opponents, and in the big matches Fergie was always liable to exploit this by winding up the pair to the hilt. In one match against Celtic, for example, Neale Cooper was booked after about three seconds. From the kickoff, the ball was knocked to Charlie Nicholas, and as he laid it back to a midfield player, Neale, in his eagerness to show Celtic the sort of pressure we intended to put them under, sent Charlie flying. Charlie did not know what hit him.

One drawback to all this for me personally was that, instead of teams seeking retribution against Neale or his equally combative partner, they would take it out on me. I was an easy target, and the sight of me taking physical punishment for the misdeeds of others would cause all hell to break loose. I did not mind it so much myself. Throughout my career, I could usually see a foul coming and get out of the way, and even when I didn't, being kicked did not bother me as much as one might think. As a player noted for his skill on the ball, I looked upon it merely as an occupational hazard. To me, if someone was not trying to kick me I was not doing my job properly. Still, against Celtic and Rangers it was more than a little comforting to know that we had Doug Rougvie – everybody's arch-protector – in the line-up.

It has been argued that the physical intensity required of Neale Cooper and Neil Simpson eventually rebounded on them. Fergie himself, referring to his determination not to overplay Ryan Giggs in his first few seasons as a full-time professional at Manchester United, has gone on record as saying that he regrets not adopting that approach with his young midfield dynamos at Aberdeen.

No player likes to be out of a team, especially if it has a significant effect on their earnings – which was very much the case during the early part of my career. When you are young and doing well, you feel almost invincible. A rest is the last thing you think you need, so part of a manager's job when he is dealing with youngsters is to protect them from themselves. Both Cooper and Simpson were finished as top-level players well before the age of thirty, although in view of what they achieved at Aberdeen I am pretty sure that if they had the chance to wind back the clock, they would be happy to take on the same physical and mental pressures again.

The tempo and intensity of Aberdeen's play was also mirrored by the individuals up front. The movement and work rate of Eric Black and Mark McGhee – not to mention other strikers I played with there, such as Archibald and John Hewitt – were fantastic. The one thing defenders could be sure about when they faced these strikers was that there would be no rest for them. Mark and Eric ran defenders all over the place. I had a special affinity with Mark. He was Fergie's first signing for Aberdeen, from Newcastle in March 1979, and Lesley and I invited him and his wife around to the guesthouse we were staying in for a weekend drink. The place was a huge, exquisitely furnished granite house right in the centre of Aberdeen, and as Lesley and I were the only people in when the McGhees called – the owners had gone away for a wedding and we had agreed to look after it – Mark thought that the house belonged to us. Catching sight of him and his wife whispering to each other about it, as I poured them a drink in the massive sitting room, I asked: 'Do you like it?'

'Oh, yes,' Mark replied. 'It's amazing. How much do you think it would cost us to buy a house like this?'

When I told him, his face was a picture. He turned to his wife and said: 'I have made one of the biggest mistakes of my life. The terms I agreed with Fergie were much too low.' Imagine his relief when he learned the truth.

As a centre-forward, Mark led the line brilliantly. He was exceptionally strong, which No. 9s had to be in those days because of the number of times defenders could get away with kicking strikers from behind. Mark took such a battering, it was a wonder that he played so many matches. He was an unpredictable player – the type who might give the ball away one minute, and then beat three or four players the next. But generally, because of his ability to help us push our play up the field – into the last third – he was possibly our most important attacking player.

For any player in possession in the build-up, there is nothing better than people up front repeatedly giving you good passing options. Mark has said that I was the player at Aberdeen who set up the vast majority of his goals. But because of his movement, he made it easy for me. He could read me perfectly, inasmuch as there were very few times that he came short when I wanted to play the ball long, or vice versa. Surprising as it might seem, not all strikers can be relied upon to do that.

In an ideal world I like to think I would have played in central midfield. I believe I had the technical ability to play there, even though there was a slight difference of opinion between Fergie and myself on that one. Fergie has said that when he put me there for one or two of his early matches at Aberdeen, he felt I played too many short balls and did not open up the play enough. He might have been right, but from my point of view it was important that the opposition were drawn towards us before I could think about playing any killer balls. As Aberdeen started to push up on teams, thus bringing me into more advanced attacking positions, his point about my passing possibly became less pertinent anyway.

As it happened, Fergie was the only manager who voiced misgivings about my passing range. In contrast, Andy Roxburgh, one of my Scotland managers, described me as one of the best players in the country at switching the play from one side of the field to the other, and Ron Atkinson raved about my performances when I filled a central midfield role for him at Manchester United. However, I had to agree with Fergie when he also cast doubts on me as a central midfielder on the grounds of my build. Working in such a congested area was always going to be difficult for me, especially on poor playing surfaces and against teams more interested in smashing people about than concentrating on football.

So operating just outside that fiercely contested central zone, wide on the right (and occasionally the left), was perfect for me at Aberdeen. The only thing that bugged me about my role was that people were inclined to describe me as a winger. I hated that. Though I could go forward with the ball, and get in crosses, I did not really have the pace and strength to take people on over a long distance. In order to get from the edge of our box to a crossing position, I needed to play off somebody. My game, which revolved around a lot of one- or two-touch play, was more like that of an inside-forward (to use the old-fashioned term) than a winger. If anybody played like a winger on my side of the field, it was our right back, Stuart Kennedy.

That is precisely why I have no hesitation in saying that Stuart was the person who helped me the most at Aberdeen – by a million miles. His overlaps were magnificent. I think we must have set some kind of record for the number of times I came off the touchline and he bombed down it, taking the attention of opponents away from me. Throughout my career I was always at my best when I had full backs who could do that. Other examples were Mike Duxbury, John Gidman and John Siveback at Manchester United and Mel Sterland at Leeds. If I did not have someone in that mould supporting me, I struggled.

I often say that people such as Stuart put five or ten years on to my career, whereas I probably knocked five or ten years off theirs!

Stuart was a wonderful character as well as a great footballer. His biggest idol was Burt Lancaster and I remember how delighted he was when he managed to meet the American film star and get his autograph. It happened after Aberdeen's 1982 Scottish Cup triumph, when our visit to the Gleneagles Hotel for our celebration bash that night coincided with Lancaster taking a short holiday there. Lancaster, who had been on location in Scotland for the film *Local Hero*, was astonished by Stuart's knowledge about him. Stuart was even able to recite some of his best lines back to him.

Sadly, Stuart's good fortune as exemplified in meeting Lancaster was conspicuous by its absence at important stages of his soccer career.

One disappointment for him was his failure to get into Scotland's 1982 World Cup squad, after being selected for the provisional pool of forty. It did not help matters that Alex McLeish, Willie Miller and myself, who did make it, were given a £25-a-week rise by Fergie when we returned, while he only got an extra £20. It really upset him. I was sharing a room with Stuart when Aberdeen started training for the new season, and he went on and on about it. On the first day he turned to Alex and Willie and said: 'If there are any 50-50 balls to win, don't expect me to do it. As you are getting more money than me, I will leave it to you to do most of the tackling.' He was still on about it a couple of years ago, when he stayed with Lesley and me in Southampton for a few days.

But the biggest blow for Stewart was the bad knee injury he suffered in the European Cup Winners' Cup semi-final against Belgium's Waterschei. Bizarrely, it happened through Stuart's studs getting caught on a wooden hoarding attached to the boundary wall. In addition to causing him to miss the final against Real Madrid, it pretty much marked the end of his career. It said much about Fergie's admiration and respect for Stuart that he named him among the Aberdeen substitutes for the Real Madrid match. Even though Stuart was on crutches, there was no way that Fergie was going to allow him to feel that he was an outsider. It was a wonderful managerial gesture by any standards.

I often feel that managers and players can learn more from setbacks than they can from successes, so when I think of the Cup Winners' Cup wins over Bayern Munich (when we twice came from behind to beat them 3-2) and Real Madrid (when we also came from behind for a 2-1 victory), it is difficult to over-look the lessons we were handed by Liverpool in the 1980/81 European Cup. Liverpool and Brian Clough's Nottingham Forest were dominating the competition then and our ties against Liverpool provided the perfect yardstick by which to measure where we stood in relation to the game outside Scotland.

It was a chastening experience for us, to lose 5-0; and, fol-lowing our success in brushing aside the Old Firm, I think we probably needed it. We knew Liverpool were good, but we did not think they were that good – or that we were that bad. We did not have our strongest team out and after just five minutes of the first leg at Pittodrie, John McMaster had to go off with knee damage after a challenge by Ray Kennedy. John was arguably Aberdeen's most talented player. But there was no point in our making any excuses. Liverpool were much too strong for us, technically and physically.

In that first leg, Kennedy had caught John just below the knee, and it was while John was on the ground that Liverpool broke away to score the only goal of the game with a superb Terry McDermott chip over Jim Leighton from near the byline. We were doing okay in the second leg at Anfield, until seven minutes before half-time. That's when Willie Miller, attempting to clear a corner, sliced the ball into his own net. A minute later, it was 2-0. Just before we were due to go out for the second half, we were all stunned again when Drew Jarvie, who'd been playing up front with Mark McGhee, shouted: 'Come on, lads – three quick goals and we are back in it.' That has to be one of the most amusing half-time comments I have heard in any dressing room, although I am not sure that Drew was joking.

That Liverpool success stretched their unbeaten home record to seventy-seven matches. Mark, after watching a video of the game some years later, likened it to a *Spitting Image* sketch. 'Compared to us, people like Alan Hansen, Graeme Souness and Kenny Dalglish looked like giants from a different planet,' he said. I could not help remembering that when I met Liverpool's chief executive, Rick Parry, during my sabbatical from the game after leaving Southampton, to discuss the possibility of me being considered for the Anfield manager's job in place of Gérard Houllier. 'What would you do to make Anfield an intimidating place for visiting teams again?' I was asked. 'There is only one thing that can do that.' I said. 'The quality of your players.'

In those Aberdeen matches against Liverpool, I seemed as out of my depth as anyone. I made no impact on the games whatsoever, which many people attributed to the Liverpool manager Bob Paisley's 'mind games' in praising me in his media interviews during the build-up to the ties. The wily Paisley, a master at using the press to gain a psychological edge over opponents – I daresay he could have taught even the likes of Fergie, José Mourinho and Arsène Wenger a thing or two about that – was widely quoted as saying that I was the best player in Britain, and was worth as much as £2 million. That was some compliment, given that this figure was almost double the British record transfer fee at that time, and in the light of my performances, it was tempting for people to suggest that I'd allowed Paisley's remarks to go to my head.

It was very strange in that it did not work in the way they might have expected.

I was an instinctive player and going into different areas and using my imagination on the ball was a big part of my game. However, far from Paisley's comments prompting me to fall into the trap of taking this to the extreme, of running about all over the place, trying to nutmeg people, I went totally the other way. In the Liverpool setup, no player did much in possession – it was all about simple passes and not giving the ball away, and for some reason that is how I tried to play. I cannot recall ever moving away from the right flank and virtually every time I got the ball the next step was a safe square pass. Instead of playing like Gordon Strachan, I tried to play like Sammy Lee.

If anybody at Anfield could take the credit for leading me into that, it might well have been Graeme Souness.

When Graeme and I started playing together in the Scotland team, I know that he had mixed feelings about whether I was a top-class player by English or European standards. There is more than one way to play the game but Graeme – quite understandably in view of the ascendancy of his Liverpool teams – felt that the highly disciplined, machine-like way they approached the game was the be all and end all. He and I got on well, but as I was not what he would have described as a typical Liverpool player, it took time for him to appreciate the value of what I had to offer.

I did not go into those games against Liverpool thinking: 'I am going to prove you wrong about me.' However, it could be that his opinion of me, combined with Paisley's comments, had a subconscious effect.

The Liverpool matches left Aberdeen and me with a lot to prove, not least to people in England. The following season, we were given the perfect chance to do that when we were drawn against Ipswich, the Uefa Cup holders, in the first round of the competition. Under manager Bobby Robson, Ipswich, who were the Championship leaders at the time and were to finish runner-up for the second year in succession, had some wonderful players. That Ipswich side, including Mick Mills, George Burley, Frans Thijssen, Arnold Muhren, John Wark and Paul Mariner, probably oozed more class than any small-town team I have ever seen. But we held them to a 1-1 draw at Portman Road, and thanks to a brilliant second half performance by Peter Weir, beat them 3-0 at Pittodrie.

We were knocked out of the competition in the third round, by Hamburg. However, what we had learned in Europe was enough to bring us the greatest prize in Aberdeen's history the following season.

It has been said that Aberdeen's achievement in Gothenburg was a little misleading, in that the stature of Real Madrid as a club was probably not matched by the team they had then, and that Aberdeen's best performance was arguably our quarter-final win over Bayern Munich. Given Real's majestic European Cup background, it has also been suggested that the Cup Winners' Cup did not mean as much to them as it did to us. They had never won the Cup Winners' Cup and the final in Gothenburg – their third in this competition – only attracted a crowd of 17,800, of which some 15,000 were Aberdeen followers.

However, Real are the team that all professional footballers dream of playing against and objectivity does not come into it if you can also tell your grandchildren that you got the better of them. I doubt that the Aberdeen team against Real, and the extra-time goal by substitute John Hewitt which clinched the win, will ever be forgotten. As we were up against the biggest and most glamorous club in the world, that is how it should be.

Real, of course, are also the club that all players dream of playing *for*, so in terms of helping me keep my feet on the ground, I suppose it was no bad thing that although they made an enquiry about me to Aberdeen, I did not learn about their approach until the latter stages of my career. But by that time I was far too content with what I had achieved to be interested in trying to find out more about it.

# CHAPTER FOUR

# THE HAIRDRYER

One common characteristic of short people is their tendency to be 'gobby'. I daresay a number of the people I have worked with would suggest that I am a good example of such a person. When I was picked on by bigger lads as a kid, I found I could invariably talk my way out of trouble. I often did it by making them laugh, which is something I seem to be quite good at to this day and which has become an integral part of my public image. I can usually see the funny side of most things. This does have its disadvantages; it occasionally bothers me that it might cause people not to take me seriously as a coach or manager. Still, I often say that it's not growing old that worries me, it's losing my sense of humour. When that happens, that will be the time for me to go six feet under – a place where some of the people I have crossed swords with over the years would love to have put me.

When you are built like me, your mouth can become your most effective weapon. As a player, there was no way I could make opponents wary of me through hard tackles or fouls. If they nailed me, the only way I could get back at them – other than with my ability – was with my tongue. For example, when an opponent kicked me, my first reaction would be to get to my feet as quickly as I could, force a smile – which because of the pain could be more like a grimace – and ask: 'Is that the best you can do?' Leaving aside the odd occasions when I discovered it wasn't, I have always been generally acknowledged to be quite good at the verbal cut and thrust that goes on in professional football.

Mick Hennigan, a wonderful character who was assistant manager to Howard Wilkinson at Leeds when I was there, used to refer to me as 'King Tongue'. He said: 'Your tongue can kill a man at ten paces.' This has not always something that I've been able to take any pride in, but as a self-defence mechanism it did come in handy for me when I played for Fergie.

As he has been the most successful manager in the history of British football, most people assume that my experience of working with him for nine years – at Aberdeen from August 1978 to August 1984, and at Manchester United from November 1986 to March 1989 – was the making of me. They are right up to a point. Until his arrival at Aberdeen, my career was going nowhere. In the early days, he was the manager who gave me the strongest platform for my ability, with the standard of the team he built at Aberdeen and his discipline and organisation. His confrontational methods helped me to develop my mental strength. If I could handle Fergie, then as a player or manager I felt I could handle almost anything.

However, I would only single him out as having had the greatest influence on me in relation to one aspect of my career. As for the other parts – notably those when I was more experienced and thus more receptive to what I would call a less controlling and dictatorial form of management – I think I owe just as much (if not more) to men like Ron Atkinson and Howard Wilkinson.

As much as I admire Fergie for what he has achieved, I have to admit that this is offset by the memories of the deterioration in our relationship. I think it was similar to the renowned split in the relationship between Fergie and David Beckham. When David and I talked about this upon meeting for the first time at the Real Madrid–Bayern Munich European Champions League match in Madrid in the 2004/05 season, one of the points on which we were in agreement was that towards the end of our association with Fergie we did not get much enjoyment from it.

As indicated by his comments about our time together in his 1999 autobiography *Managing My Life*, it would seem that Fergie is not too enamoured with me either.

Those comments, which related mainly to my desire to leave Aberdeen and Manchester United, and included Fergie stating that I 'could not be trusted an inch', both surprised and disappointed me. I know I made one or two mistakes in my dealings with him, as one might expect in any volatile player-manager relationship like this, but I feel there were mitigating circumstances. In any event, I would have thought that the service I gave him at Aberdeen – when I was looked upon as one of his key players – and the numerous great moments we shared would have counted for more in his eyes than what he said about me in his book seemed to suggest.

Since becoming a manager, not all my relationships with players have been harmonious – far from it. Football is a highly emotional game, and the occasional bust-ups with colleagues are an unavoidable part of the job, especially for somebody like me. I do not think some of my players have treated me properly (and I daresay some have an equally good reason for believing the reverse). In that respect, the player with whom I have had arguably the most difficult relationship was Carlton Palmer at Coventry. However, as with the others, the anger I felt towards him when I believed he let me down has long since disappeared. Indeed, I still have a lot of time for Carlton. I can understand where he was coming from and certainly, I have no urge what-soever to write about him, or abnybody else, in the way that Fergie wrote about me.

Since then, Fergie and I have hardly spoken to each other. On the occasions our paths have crossed, we have tended to com-municate no more than has been necessary. Many will have found it more surprising that, despite the publicity given to Fergie's views about me, I have always kept a discreet public silence on them. I have preferred to take the option of trying to retain a sense of dignity and not give the media any scope to turn the matter into a full-blown controversy.

Nevertheless, I have always felt deep down that it would be good for me one day to give my side of the story. In doing so now, I have no wish to score any points off Fergie. I just want to put the record straight from my point of view.

Perhaps the best place to start is with our temperaments and per-sonalities – how they brought us together and then pushed us apart.

By now, I do not think anybody needs to be reminded about Fergie's autocratic, abrasive style of management. In the light of the ways in which he likes to control his players and, of course, the ferocity of those renowned 'hairdryer' verbal tirades against those who have displeased him, many might find it strange that the response from his teams has been so stunning.

But Fergie came to the fore in an era when players were in a weaker position – both financially and contractually – than they are now and managers could virtually hold them to ransom. Since then, Fergie has also been helped by the remarkable stature he has achieved through winning so many trophies. His record and reputation make him the British manager with possibly the greatest charisma and presence. He has become so powerful and influential that, if you fall out with him, you wonder if you'll ever work again.

Thus, though he might have modified his approach – he himself has said that he has become mellower – he has not had to do so by very much.

While his explosive public persona might occasionally suggest otherwise, nobody should doubt that Fergie is an exceptionally astute manager. In recent years, more and more clubs have called in sports psychologists to help them get the best out of their players; I have worked with some of them myself. Yet I often say that, for all their specialist training and knowledge, I cannot believe they can do a better job of motivating professional footballers than Fergie. He is the game's motivational master as far as I am concerned.

It is no secret that Fergie is a great believer in creating or developing what he calls a 'common cause' in his teams and that his favourite method of doing so is to instil in them a siege mentality. He often used to say that players can be at their best when they are angry or resentful. That's why, in his team talks at both Aberdeen and Manchester United, you could always rely on him to make comments that would cause the players to feel as if everybody – notably referees, the media and the general public – was against them.

Because of Fergie's confrontational manner in his dealings with his players, it was not unusual for that collective dressing room anger or resentment to be directed at him. I am not sure to what extent, if any, this situation might have been engineered by him, but one thing I am pretty certain about is that at Aberdeen the atmosphere at any party attended by Fergie and his first-team squad would not have been very relaxed. At least half of the players would not have wanted to talk to him; and I daresay, some would have been itching to rip his head off. As a manager, you would have to be a very tough cookie indeed to function in that sort of atmosphere.

In my experience of him, Fergie is not really one for dealing with players in ways best suited to their individual temperaments and personalities. He has a very fixed idea of the sort of characters he is looking for. In a sense, he looks for carbon copies of himself. So all his players get the same treatment, and if an individual cannot handle it, so be it; he is quickly discarded. There have been a number of casualties of his management style – I often think that it might have been a different story had Fergie shown a bit more sensitivity with some of them. However, it is difficult to be critical of him over this when you look at the standard and ascendancy of most of his teams.

Fergie is a man who thrives on conflict, and it is no coincidence that the vast majority of the players who established themselves under his management at Aberdeen were strong enough characters to stand up to him when the need arose. I think it is significant that a number of those players have since become managers. Fergie himself has often used Steve Archibald, his former Aberdeen centre-forward, as an example. It is well documented that the two men had a number of clashes and that, perverse though it might seem, this was one of the reasons why Fergie had so much admiration for him.

Among the others in that mould was Aberdeen's captain, Willie Miller. Willie might have seemed a quiet, unobtrusive figure, but this was very misleading. He had no compunction about going into battle against Fergie, not just for himself but on behalf of his team-mates. As captain, he was our leader – and he took that responsibility very seriously.

On one occasion, a half-time row between Willie and Fergie, over the manager's comments about some of the other players, led to Willie taking off his jersey and telling him: 'You can stick this up your backside.' As Willie stormed off into the bath area, we made a joke of it with comments like: 'Hey, Willie, do you want some shampoo?' and 'Hang on a minute Willie we'll be joining you soon.' Fergie had to leave him out for the second half.

This element of abrasiveness was very much a part of my own personality and temperament.

I feel I was considerably self-motivated as a player, partly because I did not go into any match thinking that I was a better player than the man I was facing. I was confident that I could get the better of him, but only if I performed to my potential on the day. There was always that wee bit of insecurity in me – no matter who I was playing against, I took nothing for granted. At the same time, I recognise that I am the sort of person who usually benefits – in the competitive football sense – from being in a bad or angry mood. Some people lose it when they are like that, but, as I have said, I don't. As a player, anger always seemed to make it easier for me to be properly focused. This has been the case even when I have been playing golf. If I get upset over a bad shot, my game does not go to pieces as a result.

So, at the outset, you could argue that Fergie was the perfect manager for me, even though being regarded as one of his most influential players seemed to bring me more stick from him than most of the others received. To an extent, picking on me was his way of emphasising to all the other players that reputations did not matter to him. I am sure he took the view that if the other players saw him giving me a rollicking, then nobody could feel as if he was safe from them.

Those trademark Fergie 'hairdryer' tirades – with the person on the receiving end looking as if he is standing in a wind tunnel – have long been a favourite topic of conversation among those who have worked for him. In retrospect, most of his outbursts are quite funny. I reckon I could keep an audience entertained for hours with my own recollections of them.

Among my personal favourites was his post-match rant at the former England winger Peter Barnes at Manchester United – or rather the lengths that Peter went to in order to get out of Fergie's firing line. Peter, anticipating that Fergie was going to have a go at him – he had not played well and had been substituted near the end – headed straight for the dressing room after being taken off and hid himself.

The first question Fergie asked when he came into the dressing room was: 'Where's that Barnes?'

'He must be in the bath, boss,' someone replied.

Fergie looked from the entrance to the bath area and could not see him. 'Not there, the b*****d,' he said. This clearly upset Fergie even more and for the next quarter of an hour or so he got it out of his system by letting rip at other players. Finally, he went out of the room and, as the players were discussing his conduct – 'He's a bloody maniac' etc – Peter suddenly appeared with towels around his waist and head, water dripping down his face. He had been in the bath, but the reason Fergie could not see him was that he had been hiding from him under the water. 'I am freezing – has he gone?' Peter asked.

I cannot think of any player I have worked with under his management who completely escaped his wrath. You could possibly understand it at times, such as Aberdeen's 5-0 aggregate defeat by Liverpool in the 1980/81 European Cup, when he actually banned the players from laughing on the team coach on our journey back home. 'Anyone who laughs will be fined £10,' he said. He even kept turning around to try and catch someone out.

He could adop a similar attitude in victory. Take Aberdeen's 1-0 Scottish Cup Final victory over Rangers in 1983. Although it was not the best of Aberdeen performances, there were some good reasons for it. Just ten days earlier we had beaten Real Madrid after extra time in the European Cup Winners' Cup Final in Gothenburg, still one of the greatest achievements by a British club. In a season in which we also finished Championship runner-up – just one point behind Dundee United – the key players had appeared in more than sixty matches each. In other words, we were mentally and physically knackered.

I am sure this would not have gone unrecognised by Fergie, but it meant a lot to him for Aberdeen to show the ability that had brought us that remarkable result against Real and to end the season on home soil with a flourish. When it did not happen, his frustration got the better of him.

Unlike most managers whose teams have just won a Cup Final, he lambasted us. He initially got stuck into us in his post-match TV interview on the field and was still so uptight when he came into the dressing room that I got a verbal volley from him just for suggesting that we open the bottles of champagne that had been made available to us. The only players he exonerated from any blame for the performance were Alex McLeish and Willie Miller, much to the pair's embarrassment. Fergie was so critical of the others, and especially the more creative players such as me, that Alex and Willie both felt it necessary to make the point that it had been relatively easy for them to battle through their staleness and do good jobs. 'It is okay for us,' Willie remarked. 'As central defenders, we have the play coming to us, whereas the midfielders and strikers have to make the play.'

But it did not make any difference – his black mood just went on and on.

For Aberdeen's post-match reception at St Andrews that night, Fergie cancelled the arrangement for the players' wives and girlfriends to travel there with us on the team coach, and throughout the two and a half hour journey he continued to ban us from drinking. It was all gloom and doom, although I do remember the laugh we had at the expense of midfielder John McMaster after nominating him for the unenviable job of approaching Fergie at the front of the bus to ask him to change his mind. It was typical of John not to appreciate fully what he was letting himself in for. As we anticipated, Fergie gave him an earful.

By the time of the reception, at which the atmosphere was subdued to say the least, I'd had enough of him. I just said to Lesley: 'Come on, we are leaving', and we spent the rest of the evening at a friend's pub. My walkout was wrong – I knew it – and I had no complaints about the £250 club fine that Fergie imposed on me as a result of my action. I deserved it – as I acknowledged by making a public apology to the club. In fairness to Fergie, he also apologised – albeit in private – to the players for not putting that performance against Rangers into its proper perspective.

It was very rare for Fergie to say sorry. During those nine years of working with him, there were countless Fergie bullets aimed at me; I can recall only one occasion that he put his hand up and admitted he had gone over the top. That was after a Manchester United–Aston Villa match, in which he lambasted me for giving the ball away on the halfway line, a mistake which led to Villa scoring. The following Monday he asked to have a 'quiet word' with me, and said: 'Sorry about that on Saturday – I went over the top.' Generally, however, his favourite line was: 'The day I stop reacting like that is the day you need to worry. It is for your own good.'

I was the player involved in arguably the most famous of all his dressing-room explosions – in the second leg of Aberdeen's second round Uefa Cup tie against Arges Pitesti in Romania in the 1981/82 season.

Aberdeen had won the first leg 3-0 and for the return Fergie elected to switch from our usual 4-4-2 or 4-3-3 system to a 4-5-1 shape, with Mark McGhee as the lone striker. The earlier result meant that Arges Pitesti had to attack strongly – they needed to get as many men forward as possible, and Fergie felt that his 4-5-1 system would give us the best chance of stopping them getting behind us and hitting them on the break. Because of the change, our wide attacking players – Peter Weir on the left and myself on the right – were called upon to operate close to the touchlines, partly to stop the Arges full backs bursting through. This was more of a problem for me than it was for Peter. He was essentially a winger – used to hugging the touch-line whereas I was a wide midfielder who liked to be in more central areas. I had never played in a 4-5-1 system before, and, having only discovered that we were going to play that way the day before the game, I really did not have a clue what I should be doing.

The first half was a nightmare for me, as it was for Aberdeen, who fell 2-0 behind. In the opening forty-five minutes, I was playing on the side of the pitch where the dugouts were situated and Fergie spent most of his time trying to talk me through the game – or should I say scream me through it? It was a bit like a schoolteacher or parent haranguing a kid. I could appreciate that I was causing him a great deal of frustration, but his inces-sant nagging and cajoling started to get on my nerves and, before long, we were at each other's throats.

'You don't know what you're f*****g doing,' he shouted.

I cracked. 'Shut up – you don't know what you are doing either,' I fired back.

It got even nastier in the dressing room at half-time. He tore into me, as only Fergie could; and my response was, typically, to hit back at him with quips. Needless to say, this quickly brought him to boiling point. In his rage, he took a swipe at a big tea urn, but he had not appreciated how heavy it was, and hurt his hand.

His reaction to the pain was to sweep some of the cups of tea on the table in my direction. None of the cups hit me, or anybody else. But, unluckily for Alex McLeish and Willie Miller, who were sitting close to me, most of the tea went over them.

As if to emphasise my point about the advantages of anger as a motivational conduit, I did better in the second half (I could hardly have done worse). What made it particularly pleasing for me was that I converted the penalty to increase our aggregate lead to 4-2 and it ended up as 5-2. Of all the spot kicks I took, this was probably the one that carried the greatest pressure for me. In view of the earlier friction between us, it was difficult to avoid thinking of Fergie's reaction if I missed. Indeed, as crazy as it might seem, I almost felt that Fergie half wanted me to miss, thus giving himself a further excuse verbally to rip my head off.

Hence the fact that when I despatched the ball into the net – a beauty, right into the top left hand corner – my first reaction was to stick two fingers up at him. It was just as well that I was camouflaged by half a dozen other Aberdeen players and Fergie did not see the gesture.

As a person who abhors the yob culture in our society, I am quite embarrassed by that memory. But that's the state that Fergie could get players into. The players at Aberdeen were extremely close knit, and it was typical of the us against him attitude he could create that they seemed to relish the moment as much as I did. As I was gesturing to Fergie, they were shouting: 'Well done, wee man.' They were so delighted about that converted penalty, you would have thought I had just dribbled past half a dozen players and hit the ball in from twenty-five yards.

From my point of view, one of the problems in my relationship with him was that the longer we worked together, the more I needed him to adopt a different attitude and approach with me. I needed him to treat me as an adult, not a kid; to have some respect for the fact that I was an experienced professional to

whom abuse from the manager had become more of a motivational turn-off than a stimulus. I needed him to appreciate that
my penchant for having a laugh and a joke, which he might
have interpreted as a sign that I did not take my career seriously
enough, was misleading.

Not long after he joined me at Manchester United, and took
up from where he had left off with me at Aberdeen, I remember
telling him: 'Listen, you spoke to me like that nine years ago. It
might have worked well then, but it is not going to work now.'
But the screaming and shouting did not cease – it just got worse
and more personal. The reason it did so at Aberdeen concerned
my decision to leave when my last contract there expired at the
end of the 1983/84 season.

This was not the first time that I had wanted to go elsewhere.
The previous time was before my sixth Aberdeen season, when I
returned from playing for Scotland in the 1982 World Cup Finals
in Spain. It was the first time I had ever been on a stage as big as
that and it was inevitable that it should make me think of trying
to develop my career on a bigger club platform. Though I like to
think it was not reflected in my performances, the somewhat
claustrophobic nature of Scottish football, with Premier League
teams facing each other at least four times a season, and the
ease with which Aberdeen were able to get the better of most of
those teams, had begun to affect my enthusiasm for the game.

Alex McLeish, another member of Scotland's 1982 World
Cup team, also wanted to leave and, in fact, we arranged to go
to see Fergie about it at the same time. I was the first to go into
his office, and when I told Fergie I wanted to ask for a transfer
his reply was nothing if not short and to the point. Reminding
me that I still had two years left on my Aberdeen contract, he
just said: 'Stop wasting my time – eff off.' I was not going to
argue, 'Okay,' I said, and off I went, my tail between my legs.

'What did he say?' Alex asked.

'He just told me to eff off,' I said. 'Are you going to ask him?'

'Er, no,' Alex said. 'I think I will leave it for another week or two.' Wise man.

From then on, while I was happy to see out my contract at Aberdeen it was increasingly clear to everyone concerned that I would not be signing a new agreement. That is one of the reasons why, in the 1983 close season, Fergie bought Billy Stark from St Mirren. It seemed obvious that Billy, who was also a right-side attacking player – albeit one with a different style of play from mine – was viewed as an eventual replacement for me. The following season, it was public knowledge that it was going to be my last at Pittodrie.

I thought it was the right time for me to go for many reasons. Quite apart from the lack of any real challenges left for me in Scottish football, and the familiarity-breeds-contempt problems of working with the same manager for so long, I also felt I was justified in seeking a move for financial reasons. Money has never been the be-all and end-all for me. At the same time, as I was a married man with a family – the first of my three children, Gavin and Craig, were born in 1978 and 1982 respectively – I do not think anybody could call me greedy for wanting to exploit my earning potential a bit more.

Though the move from Dundee to Aberdeen in 1977 had been a good step up the ladder for me, I still struggled to save. My basic wage at Aberdeen was only a third more than it had been at Dundee, and though the transfer brought me a signing-on fee of £3000, I remember how quickly the elation of that disappeared when Lesley and I were looking for a house in the Granite City. Having agreed the sale of our Dundee home for £9000, we discovered that an equivalent property in Aberdeen would cost at least £14,000. It was some time before we could afford central heating, and my first car, bought just before Gavin was born, a Fiat 127.

My gross annual income in my best years at Pittodrie was £30,000–£35,000. Not bad for Scotland, but far below what the leading players were earning in England, without having to make much of an impact. In that respect, the Aberdeen figure I have quoted included my signing-on fees (spread over the duration of my contracts) and all the bonuses for my first-team appearances and, of course, the trophies we won. It even included my payments for Scotland matches. Just how important it was for me to play in the vast majority of Aberdeen's games and for the club to keep achieving major honours is underlined by the fact that my basic salary was only around £12,000. Contrast this with the offers I received from the two clubs who wanted to sign me from Aberdeen. Cologne were willing to pay a basic starting salary of £64,000, whereas in Manchester United's case it was £70,000.

Thus, it was only when I left Pittodrie, at twenty-seven, that I started to feel some measure of financial security and that Lesley and I were able significantly to improve our lifestyle.

In those days, the trend of Scottish footballers moving to England tended to be a sore point with Fergie. He appeared to interpret it as those players having somehow sold out – it seemed to offend his socialist principles. He could get particularly touchy about it when noting the trappings of wealth and fame some of those players displayed on their visits back to Scotland to join up with the national squad. In my own case, his behaviour towards me made me think that he looked upon my decision to leave Aberdeen as a personal slight.

As a manager myself, I have always remembered that treatment in my own dealings with players on similar issues. With the possible exception of the current stars at Real Madrid and Chelsea, all leading players can present a reasonable case – professionally, financially or both – to go elsewhere. For obvious reasons, I had to deal with a lot of that at Coventry and

Southampton, but generally, if the players concerned had done a good job for me, and gone about their desire to move in the right manner, I saw no reason why I should not help them achieve their goals. When I signed a player for Coventry or Southampton, I would tell him: 'If you want to leave for a bigger stage at the end of your contract, I will not have a problem with it because if you do get the chance, it will be because you have done well here and you have helped me.'

I wish I'd had more confidence in Fergie taking this stance with me.

It was an unsettling time for me – as such situations are for all players – and with so much media speculation about my future I can understand Fergie being concerned about the effect all this might have on my performances and those of the team. If this was the case, his fears did not materialise – Aberdeen won the Championship–Scottish Cup double in my last season; and though Fergie has gone on record as saying that I was a shadow of my true self, I nevertheless played in almost every game and was Aberdeen's second highest scorer behind Mark McGhee.

If I really was a shadow of my true self, that was as much down to Fergie as it was to me, as far as I am concerned.

In common with a lot of players in those days, I did not have an agent or personal management company looking after my interests – I relied on Fergie to do that. Certainly, as clubs could command transfer fees for any out-of-contract players then, the onus was on him – for the benefit of Aberdeen at least – to find prospective new employers for me. It was the same for all managers in this situation. Under the transfer fee rules for out-of-contract players, Aberdeen needed to sell me to an English club in order to get the most money for me. But to this day I have precious little knowledge of what went on behind the scenes, outside Fergie's claims in his book that Manchester United (who were eventually to pay £500,000 for me) baulked at Aberdeen's initial £800,000 asking price and that Arsenal lost interest because of worries about some pelvic trouble I had been experiencing.

Fergie seemed to me to be making life as difficult as he could for me. It was agonising enough that he kept me in the dark about the situation. On top of that, I also had to deal with his negative attitude towards me at team meetings. It was not unusual for him to make disparaging remarks about my ability, and tell me that I would be struggling to find any decent club willing to take me off Aberdeen's hands. 'Where do you think you are going?' he would say. 'Who would want a c**p player like you?'

The thought that all this might just have been Fergie's way of trying to keep me on my toes and help give me that aggressive edge he was so fond of seeing was of little consolation to me. The truth is that I was in absolute turmoil.

During this period, when the atmosphere between us was tense, to say the least, I was very fortunate to get as much support as I did from the other players. The one I was the closest to was Mark McGhee – at Aberdeen the one player who could leave even Fergie speechless. Mark is as intelligent and articulate a person as one could meet in professional football, and would tend to score points off Fergie through words and explanations that went above the manager's head. During one argument with Mark, Fergie just turned to Archie Knox and said: 'Archie, Mark is in his Scrabble mood. Get the board out for him.'

Mark was a wonderful dressing room ally for me. For example, Fergie occasionally felt that when Mark went on one of his trademark mazy runs with the ball, I did not move into the middle to support him quickly enough. Mark was an extremely individualistic striker, as I pointed out one day when Fergie had a go at me over leaving him too isolated. 'Mark is not the easiest of players to read,' I explained. 'There are times when I don't have a clue what he is going to do.'

How's this for looking cool and composed? Pat Stanton, captain of the Hibernian team I supported as a boy. (COLORSPORT)

The late inimitable Jimmy Johnstone, when he was at the height of his Celtic career in 1968. One of my all-time favourite players and people, his lack of inches was misleading – he was a soccer giant. (OFFSIDE)

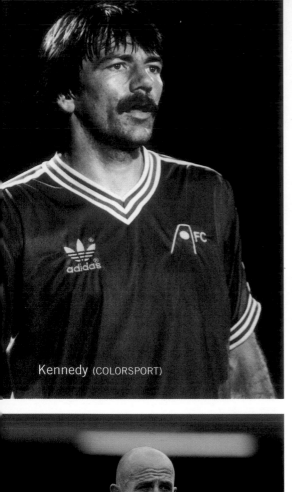

Kennedy (COLORSPORT)

Robson (OFFSIDE)

McAllister (COLORSPORT)

Three of the players who helped shape my career. Stuart Kennedy (Aberdeen), Bryan Robson (Manchester United) and Gary McAllister (Leeds and Coventry).

My high-octane matches for Aberdeen against Celtic. Roy Aitken, Celtic's captain is not telling me how much he loves me. (COLORSPORT)

Nor is the Celtic fan who has come onto the pitch to confront me. (EMPICS)

Fergie winds himself up for the Hairdryer treatment. (COLORSPORT)

We celebrate his and our greatest Aberdeen achievement – the winning of the European Cup-Winners' Cup in 1983. (COLORSPORT)

Celebration times in England – Manchester United win the FA Cup in 1985, and Leeds capture the Championship in 1992. (COLORSPORT)

Trying not to look out of place (some hope) against the best team I ever played
against – Brazil – in the 1982 World Cup Finals. (COLORSPORT)

Another side of South American football – battered by Uruguay in the 1986 Finals.
Jose Bastia was sent off for a foul on me after 55 seconds. (COLORSPORT)

My major managerial influences. Howard Wilkinson (with his assistant Mick Hennigan), at Leeds. Big Ron Atkinson and myself at Coventry. (OFFSIDE)

Did I really achieve this? My greatest personal football honour. I follow
legendary figures like Bob Paisley and Sir Stanley Matthews in getting the
PFA merit award in 1995. (EMPICS)

'Gordon's got a point, gaffer,' Mark added. 'I do not know what I'm going to do either.'

Fergie shook his head. 'I might have known that you bloody two would stick up for each other,' he muttered.

Mark left Aberdeen at the same time as me, as did Doug Rougvie, who went to Chelsea, and in that last season he was perhaps the only person at Aberdeen I felt I could really confide in. The Aberdeen contracts of Mark and Doug were also due to expire in the summer, although one difference between us was that their decision to leave was made some time after mine. I know Mark had been thinking about it since the start of the season, but it was not until a couple of months before the end of it that he finally made up his mind to leave. I am sure that a number of the other players, who were on longer contracts, would have liked to have been in our shoes. But, as far as my own situation was concerned, I know that they were all behind me. In a way, they looked upon me as something of a trail-blazer for them.

I owed a lot to them. While Fergie would seemingly attempt to knock me down in the dressing room, they would build me up. As we were going out on to the field, they would say: 'Don't let it bother you, wee man. You are the man for us, the one who can do the most to make us play, so go and show it.' They probably showed more belief in me than I had in myself.

Even so, the closer we got to the end of the season, without me having any knowledge about where or how I might end up, the more stressed out I became. I started getting a number of unsolicited calls at home from people purporting to represent various continental clubs. It became very confusing – if not disturbing. One club who approached me was Verona of Italy. I was not sure that I could adjust to living and working in a southern European country, and we left it that they would be the first club I would talk to if I decided to try. This was followed by a call – late at night, when I was in bed – from a guy who said he was acting on behalf of another Italian club, Genoa. He claimed that Fergie and the agent Dennis Roach had lined up a transfer for me to Genoa, and, when I explained the situation concerning Verona, he started threatening me.

It was against this background, when I was feeling totally lost and even a bit scared, that I panicked and elected to take matters into my own hands by signing a provisional agreement to join Cologne just before the end of the season. The pre-contract agreement, which was instigated and brokered by the German agent Bernt Killat, and which I was honestly under the impression would not be binding if I eventually decided not to work in Germany, was signed in the Aberdeen team hotel before our European Cup Winners' Cup semi-final first leg against Porto in Portugal in April 1984. 'Look, there is only six weeks to go before the end of your [Aberdeen] contract,' Bernt reminded me. 'What happens if you do not sign [for Cologne] and between now and the end of the season, you break a leg? You have to do something.'

He did not have to twist my arm; I knew I had to do something myself, if only to avoid going completely off my head.

I really was desperate. Most players start to decline when they are in their thirties, so in terms of financial security alone I felt that I was fast running out of time. After all, how was I to know then that I would play at the top level until the age of forty (and, of course, that I would then establish a managerial career)? As I saw it, it was better to have something in the bag – anything – than nothing. The Cologne deal would at least take a lot of the pressure off me. It meant that I could at last get some sleep at night and enjoy my football again.

In his book, Fergie wrote that he knew nothing about the deal, and that, as it coincided with the successful culmination of his transfer fee negotiations over my move to Manchester

United, he was 'stunned' when he heard about it. He said: 'Though I always felt there was a cunning streak in Strachan, I had never imagined that he could pull such a stroke on me.'

Fergie's point about being in the dark on my dealings with Cologne, through Killat, surprised me. True, I did not discuss the matter with him or anybody else in the Aberdeen hierarchy, but no manager had his ear closer to the ground than Fergie and I did wonder if Killat might have mentioned it to him. Killat, who was also involved in Mark McGhee's transfer to Hamburg at the end of that season, was well known to Aberdeen, as the organiser of some club tours to Germany, and he and Fergie seemed to have a good relationship. I'd been told that Killat had been known to stay at Fergie's house on his visits to Aberdeen and when Killat went to Mark's home to discuss the Hamburg transfer – before the Scottish Cup Final against Celtic – the agent mentioned that Fergie had driven him there. My meetings with Killat included one in an Aberdeen hotel in the weekend before the first leg against Porto, when Cologne's general manager and Lesley were also present. Fergie also came into the hotel and though I am convinced he saw us together, he did not bat an eyelid.

I must admit that, because of the importance of the matches against Porto – both of which Aberdeen lost 1-0 – this was not the time to be doing what I did. But, again, I go back to the point I made about the stress Fergie created for me. Much of it could have been alleviated if Fergie had given me the sort of help I needed and, indeed, I felt I deserved to get after six and a half successful years together. For that reason, contrary to what he wrote in his book, I did not deem it pertinent to apologise to him for the fiasco. I did, however, apologise to Aberdeen's chairman, Dick Donald, and the other Aberdeen players, and fortunately both parties appreciated my predicament. Interestingly, the players' reaction was: 'So what? We would probably have done the same.'

Basically, my feelings about Fergie's comments are simply that it works both ways. It boils down to the fact that, because of his attitude to me, I did not trust him either.

Maybe I was not alone in this. For example, it might have been significant that Eric Black, having worked with Fergie for thirteen years, ever since he was a boy, did more or less the same as I did the following season. He, too, went his own way in finding a new club for himself, and only revealed to Fergie that he would be leaving, to join Metz in France, two weeks before the Aberdeen–Hearts Scottish Cup Final. Fergie was so upset about not being in the loop that Eric was effectively booted out there and then. Fergie, of course, was spot on when he said that Manchester United were a far better club for me than Cologne – and most other clubs – could ever be. Even now, I can easily break out in a cold sweat when I think of how close I came to missing out on playing for United. My rashness created a big problem because Cologne, insisting that the agreement I had signed tied me to them no matter what the circumstances, took their case to Uefa. It was a very complicated issue and, fortunately for me, it was eventually settled – to the satisfaction of all parties – by Aberdeen giving Cologne a token compensation payment, and United arranging to play a friendly against them in Germany.

Ironically, while Fergie played a part in getting me to Old Trafford, it could be said that I might have played a part in his own arrival two and a half years later, through the praise I lavished on him during a conversation with the then United chairman Martin Edwards. Once I got to United, I took the view that all my past problems with Fergie were dead and buried – all my ill feeling towards him disappeared. So when Martin asked for my opinion about his ability, I spoke very highly of it.

For his part, I think that joining Manchester United was even more of a dream come true for Fergie than it was for me. I remember that after Aberdeen and United had reached agreement on my transfer, and I had approved the provisional personal terms, Fergie asked me if I would object to him joining Lesley and myself on our trip to Old Trafford for my contract signing. It was an unusual request – his job in relation to my move had been done – but to Fergie the opportunity to meet the leading figures at United and look around this extraordinary club was too good to miss.

Our relationship then went through a good spell. He rang me for a chat a few times during the following season, and at the end of it I was delighted to have him and his wife Cathy among my guests at Manchester United's FA Cup Final banquet, following our 1-0 Wembley win over Everton. On the morning of the match, at nine o'clock, he called me at the team's hotel to wish me luck. He was in London himself then, and I said: 'Look, we will be at the Royal Lancaster Hotel tonight, for the club reception. If you fancy a drink with me, pop along.' He and Cathy turned up at 8 p.m. and were with me and Lesley all evening. We had a great time together – nobody would have guessed that the season before we had been at each other's throats.

Indeed, Fergie, not being the instantly recognisable figure in England that he is now, was even mistaken for my father. United's goalkeeper, Gary Bailey, had come over for a chat, and upon noting Fergie sitting next to me, laughing and joking, thrust out his hand and said: 'Nice to meet you, Mr Strachan.'

The atmosphere between us was also cordial when we worked together again later that summer at the World Cup Finals in Mexico (where I was voted Scotland's best player). Fergie was caretaker manager of the Scotland squad, of course, and there was increasing speculation about how long he would remain at Aberdeen. I knew that Tottenham had wanted him to join them – he told me at that FA Cup Final banquet – and one morning over breakfast we had a chat about his situation. 'I have been very happy at Aberdeen,' he told me. 'I have had plenty of offers to go elsewhere, but the only clubs I would want to go to would be Manchester United and Barcelona.'

A few months later, in November 1986, he joined me at Old Trafford, a great move for him and Manchester United, but not, as it turned out, a great move for me. I had loved playing for Ron Atkinson at United. After being beaten with a big stick for so long at Aberdeen, it was refreshing to have a manager who truly trusted and appreciated me, and treated me as an adult. When Fergie moved to United, I had to endure the big stick again.

In some ways, I could understand that. As a newcomer to English football, Fergie needed quickly to impose his authority on the Manchester United dressing room, to show everyone what was in store for them if they stepped out of line; and what better way to achieve that than through his dealings with me? Following the criticism he attracted over his decision to select Willie Miller for the 1986 World Cup squad at the expense of Liverpool's Alan Hansen, he might also have felt the need to show that he did not have any favourites. None of this, though, was of much consolation to me. Our relationship soon deteriorated again and by the time I left United, the personal turmoil I was experiencing was as great as it had been at Aberdeen.

I did not want to leave United – who would? Being with a club of their stature was one of the most stimulating experiences of my life. My family were so happy in Manchester that, on the day we left, Lesley and the children were in tears. I was torn because, while I wanted to stay at United, I knew that I could no longer work with Fergie.

In his book, Fergie wrote that when he arrived at Old Trafford I bore little resemblance to the player he remembered at

Pittodrie. 'There was little evidence of the zest and cocky assurance that characterised his play in Scotland,' he said. 'Verbally, he was as assertive as ever, with an acid wit that was often used in criticism of his team-mates. But in matches, he appeared to be diminished by living in the shadow of [Bryan] Robson, [Norman] Whiteside and [Paul] McGrath.' This observation will surely have come as a surprise to Ron Atkinson because, even with Robson, Whiteside and McGrath in his team from the start of my United career, he still singled me out as his best player in my first season. I personally felt I was on fire, not just in that first season but, in my first eighteen months at United. I probably played the best football of my career over that period.

My United form did become more hit and miss, partly because of injury, and it is true that I was not playing well when Fergie joined United, in my third season there. It was disappointing because I had done quite well in the World Cup Finals in Mexico, although I do not think I am making excuses in pointing out that a number of the players who took part in the competition – in exceptionally difficult climatic conditions – suffered a subsequent dip in form at club level, and also that United, with Robson, Whiteside and McGrath having played in Mexico, too, were not at their best either.

With my contract due to expire at the end of the 1987/88 season, there is little doubt in my mind that I would not have been offered a new one but for two factors. Firstly, that Fergie was unable to sign Trevor Steven from Everton, and secondly, that I had a good end to the season.

As far as Steven was concerned, Fergie told me himself that he intended to buy him as a replacement for me. I had no problems with that. Fergie had left me in no doubt that he thought I had passed my sell-by date as a United player, and, deep down, I felt the same – at least insofar as working with him was concerned. In addition to the abrasive nature of our relationship, I felt that

I was also beginning to suffer through not being given enough responsibility. As one of the senior pros at United, I felt I had more to offer than just being another cog in the wheel.

Steven, six years younger than me, was a different type of player. I was more of a ball player, whereas he was a superior crosser of the ball and was physically stronger. He was quite similar to David Beckham, and he was playing so well at the time that most teams would have been pleased to have him.

I do not know how close Fergie came to persuading Everton to let him go to United at the end of the season, but the fact that he did not succeed (Steven remained where he was until 1989, when he signed for Rangers) meant that I was no longer surplus to his requirements. The other factor which prompted Fergie to think about keeping me were my performances and goals in my last few matches of the season. When asked by the media whether I was on my way out of United, he said: 'You cannot lose a player who gets goals like that.' Hence United's offer of a new one-year contract, which was followed by another major row with Fergie over my deliberations on whether to reject it and sign for the French club Lens instead.

One part of me liked to think that the relationship would get better and that it was worth giving it another go for twelve more months; the other part of me told me I was being naïve and that I would live to regret it if I did not go somewhere else. I was every bit as stressed as I was when I had signed that pre-contract agreement with Cologne.

All my United negotiations over the new agreement were with Martin Edwards. I did briefly speak to Fergie once or twice, but Martin was the United figure who was by far my closest point of contact. We have always got on well, and that was certainly reflected in the amicable nature of our dealings with each other on this particular matter. At our meeting to discuss the contract, I told Martin that I was happy with the terms and wanted to stay at Old Trafford. At the same time, I also mentioned my one area of uncertainty – the problems in my relationship with Fergie – and said that I would have another think and get back to him.

That is when Lens came into the picture, and I decided that, if I liked their setup when I went across for personal talks, a fresh start there would be my best option. Fergie accused me of breaking my word to Martin. In his book, he wrote: 'I forgave him [for the Cologne affair] and refused to let the incident affect my judgement of him as a person, preferring to put it down to immaturity and insecurity. But he was now a seasoned pro in his thirties and if he could break his word without a qualm, it was sickening.'

As far as I am concerned, I did not break any promise to Martin – which might explain why our relationship after this was as harmonious as it had been before it. When I told him about the likelihood of me going to Lens, there was no sign at all of any negative vibes in his reaction. Also, when the Lens move did not materialise – as a result of the coach who had apparently wanted me being sacked – the chance for me to stay with United was still there. Fergie was right when he said that I would not have come back to United if there had been a better offer else-where. But then he would not have wanted me back if he had signed Trevor Steven.

In that last season, although I did not make a bad start it was difficult for me to avoid the thought that I was living on bor-rowed time, especially when it became clear that the FA Cup was the only competition United had a realistic chance of winning. I knew I was not playing as well as I could and that once the Cup run was over I would be on my way out.

That's the way it turned out, with the end of my United career being marked by the 1-0 FA Cup quarter final defeat by Nottingham Forest in March. Fergie, pointing out that he had previously singled me out as 'the man who could take United to Wembley', was highly critical of my performance against Forest's left back, Stuart Pearce. He said: 'Strachan to me was like a tri-allist who had found himself completely out of his depth. He seemed to be intimidated by Pearce.'

I was certainly wary of him. Any player who came up against Pearce – or 'Psycho' as he was commonly known – had to be. But that is not why I did not have a good game. You cannot always explain why you have not played well; it just happens – and this was one such occasion. I needed to be at my technical best against Pearce because he was one of the most physically powerful full backs in the world and, for obvious reasons, there was no way I was going to be able to match him in that department. As it was, because I was not as sharp as I could have been, he was able to get close enough to me to brush me aside. Not one of my greatest matches, but whether my performance merited Fergie's description of it was another matter. The following day, Fergie was knocking on my front door to tell me that he no longer wanted me at United and that the club had agreed a deal for me with Leeds. I am not one to keep mementos of my career, but among the few still in my possession is the letter of congratulations that Fergie wrote to me after Leeds won the Second Division Championship in 1990. It was a nice gesture, and he even suggested that he might have made a mistake in allowing me to leave United when I did. Knowing Fergie as I do, I would imagine that he felt less kindly disposed to me when Leeds pipped Manchester United for the old First Division Championship in 1992. It was tempting for some people to imagine me looking upon this as the ideal way for me to get back at Fergie and gloat over the situation. In the light of what he said about me in his book, I have often wondered if he felt this as well. If that was the case, then nothing could have been further from the truth. As far as I was concerned, my transfer from Manchester United to Leeds was the best move for United as well as myself, so the thought of making Fergie pay for it never crossed my mind. It says much about the tension in our relationship, however, that even as a manager I have found it difficult to discount the possibility of Fergie taking a particular interest in putting one over on me.

The results which condemned Coventry to relegation, on the penultimate weekend of the 2000/01 season, were our defeat at Aston Villa and the surprise 1-0 win by Derby – also in dire relegation trouble – at Manchester United. Derby's success was not as difficult to explain as it might seem, because United had already retained the Premiership title and cannot have been expected to be as charged up as they would have been in normal circumstances. Indeed, Fergie did not select what was considered to be his strongest team for that match which, again, is hardly unusual for a manager in his position. Even so, given his belief that I let him down as a player, I have always viewed United's approach to the match against Derby with a degree of paranoia.

It is sad that our relationship has come to this. One day it would be great to sit down with him and have a proper chat about our clashes, to bring our relationship closer to what it was like in its most harmonious periods.

# CHAPTER FIVE

# THE BIG RON SHOW

There is more than one way to be a successful manager. Certainly, the approach to the job of the three men under whom I achieved the most success as a player at club level – Fergie, Ron Atkinson and Howard Wilkinson – differed considerably.

Ron and Howard were poles apart. Ron was more of a manager than a coach, whereas with Howard it was the other way around; and anybody who knows anything about football will not need me to point out the differences between them in their personalities, temperaments and public images. However, I feel privileged to have worked with both. They were the managers who played the biggest part in preparing me for my own managerial career. This is not meant as a slight against Fergie. It was just that Ron and Howard showed more respect for me as a senior professional, and gave greater responsibility.

It was Ron who signed me for Manchester United in 1984. I only worked with him for a couple of years there before Fergie succeeded him but when Fergie finally decided that my time was up at Old Trafford in 1989, Ron – then at Sheffield Wednesday – tried to sign me again. He did so, of course, in 1994, when he brought me to Coventry, from Leeds, as his successor-elect.

I love big Ron. He is an absolute gem of a guy. He has a fantastic personality – he is one of the funniest men I know for a start – and in many ways the experience of working with him has enriched me. This has been the case in the professional as well as social sense. I feel it is necessary to make that point because, as a result of the flamboyant image he has created with his one-liners, his love of champagne and his so-called flash appearance, I am not sure he is taken as seriously as he deserves to be. He is no Arsène Wenger, but nonetheless, Ron, with his passion and enthusiasm for the game, not to mention his knowledge of it, is very much a real football man in my view.

What a character this man is. It is well known among those who have worked with him that Ron takes a great deal of care over his appearance. It was typical of him that he had a sun bed in his office at Manchester United and, if you needed to have a chat with him there, it was not unusual for the conversation to be conducted with him lying on the bed, wearing his protective dark glasses (and little else). He can be quite obsessive about his personal grooming. When I was his assistant at Coventry, the other members of the coaching staff and myself would often tease him about the time it took him after training to have a bath and wash his hair. Occasionally, it was no laughing matter because Ron did not like anyone else present when he was going through the routine of sprucing himself up, so the first thing he did when getting back into the dressing room we used, would be to lock us out. We had to wait outside until he had finished, which was more of a hardship than you might think because, no matter how cold, wet and muddy we were, Ron believed in taking his time. When he was ready to let us in, he looked a million dollars, whereas each of us looked like something the cat had brought in.

It is also well known that Ron's approach to coaching is rather laid back. He does not have a lot of time for the basic technical work in training, the numerous drills to improve the fitness, organisation and shape of teams. He much prefers to play practice matches, especially when he can take part in them. There is an element of the Walter Mitty in all of us in these training games, but that is particularly true of Ron. The games in which he was involved tended to be a bit like the TV programme *Stars in Their Eyes*, with Ron attempting to impersonate someone like Franz Beckenbauer, Pelé or Maradona and inviting his players to guess his identity.

As all this indicates, Ron – never a top-class footballer himself – loves working with those who have reached that standard. Not only this, he has a tremendous appreciation of what is required to get the best out of such men. The better the players he works with, the more effective he becomes. That might seem an obvious statement, but getting the best out of good players can be just as much an art as doing the same with lesser players. I would say that Ron, through his feel for the right team blends and his ability to encourage players to express themselves, would have made an ideal England manager.

I must admit that his training approach occasionally led to some irritation and frustration for me. As his first-team coach at Coventry, I worked hard in planning and organising the various team drills I felt were necessary to improve our results, but there were a number of times when Ron would suddenly scrap them at the last minute.

As we were about to start, he would come out of his office and say: 'Right, kid, what are you doing?'

'We're going to work on the midfield players closing down [putting pressure on opponents in possession] and pushing across [to stop opponents catching us out when they suddenly switched the play],' I'd explain.

But Ron's reaction was: 'No, no, no. Let's have a six-a-side.'

On one occasion, as we were doing our pre-training stretching exercises, Ron – desperate to get a game started – came out of his office with a ball, and amused himself by doing fancy tricks like stepovers with it. In fact, while one of the lads was doing his warm-up, Ron dribbled the ball towards him and stuck it through his legs. 'Right, pick the sides,' he shouted at me, and off we went. It would have been another of Ron's *Stars in Their Eyes* days – except that, having had a particularly late night the previous day, he was not feeling his usual self.

'I feel a bit sluggish,' he said. 'I do not think my touch is going to be very good, so today I will be David Rennie [Coventry's centre-half].'

You had to laugh, although my smile at times like that could be rather forced. It was difficult to accept not having the scope to do all the training and coaching work I felt a team like Coventry needed. I tried to make light of it – there is no way that any assistant manager or coach should undermine his manager in front of the players – but I am not sure that I was entirely successful. I think my body language said it all. Even worse for me was that when the players arrived at the training ground and saw me setting out the cones and other equipment on the pitch, they'd say: 'What a waste of time that is.'

In all fairness to Ron, I think that my coaching methods needed to be controlled in those days; I probably took them to the extreme and tried to cram too much into the players' minds. To me, though, Ron went to the other extreme. In any event, I have seen one or two other coaches or assistant managers in the situation I was in with Ron and, for all their determination to hide their frustration, you can see that they have felt it just as much as I did. That aspect of my relationship with Ron made me realise that, if I wanted to stay in the game and fully explore my potential as a coach, it would need to be in a position from which I had full control.

Of course, Ron's attitude to the sort of work I wanted to do at Coventry made a lot more sense concerning the Manchester United team he brought me into. United in those days might not have been the most successful team I have played for, but they were certainly the most talented.

It is generally acknowledged that it is difficult for players from smaller clubs to adjust to Manchester United. However, the step was less daunting for me because of my experience of playing for Aberdeen against top European clubs, and the fact that United then were not as big and powerful as they were to become under Fergie. The other main factors in the successful start to my career at Old Trafford were the influence of Bryan Robson and Ron.

It was a privilege for me to work with Bryan. Everybody knows about his tackling and his drive and anticipation in getting into scoring positions inside the box, but I have often felt that people did not fully realise what a good passer of the ball he was. He was not just a supreme all-round footballer – I also found him a great man, which is what helped make him an outstanding captain. He was like Willie Miller in that he showed a strong sense of responsibility towards his colleagues and did a lot of work behind the scenes to help knit everybody together. He made me, indeed everybody, feel part of the family; we were all treated with respect by him, regardless of what we had achieved and our ability. Thus, despite the difference between United and Aberdeen as clubs, I found the dressing room spirit very similar.

As for Ron, he provided a massive culture shock compared to what I had experienced with Fergie. I was so relaxed, it wasn't true.

In some ways, being a manager is similar to that of being a schoolteacher. I make the point because, when I was at school, the teachers who tended to get the best response from me were those who had a sense of humour and were not too strict and intense. I was reminded of that with Ron at Manchester United and, indeed, I have tried to apply the same principle in my own approach to the job.

Ron was no pushover. He did not lose his rag often, but when he did there was no way you could take it lightly. At the same time, he never made you feel as if you might be subjected to a public flogging if you did not win.

There were considerably more team meetings at Aberdeen than at United and in his pre-match briefings Fergie gave you the clearest of pictures of the opposition's strengths and weaknesses and how you were going to approach the game tactically. Fergie was great at this – he might only have watched a team once, but his knowledge of them was so good that you felt he must have run the rule over them at least half a dozen times. In addition to this, he was very sharp and concise in the way he passed the most pertinent information on to you.

Contrast that with the nature of Ron's team talk before my Manchester United league debut against Watford at the start of the 1984/85 season.

I was sitting close to him and when I saw he had a briefcase, I thought: 'His tactical notes will be in there.' When he opened it, however, the only items in it were a can of hairspray and a bottle of aftershave. He then told us who was playing and said: 'We just have to get the ball to the wee men, Strachan and Olsen, as quickly as possible, and we'll win the game from there.' That was it – that was our tactical briefing. It was vintage Ron Atkinson. It was of little concern to him that other teams worked harder than we did on aspects of the game such as fitness, organisation and set pieces. He believed that if you had the best players, and let them do their own thing, you were bound to win.

I was given another example of this philosophy before our 5-0 win against Stoke towards the end of the season. I had been very doubtful for the game because of a swollen ankle and when we came in for training on the Friday morning, I suggested to the club physiotherapist Jimmy McGregor that I would have nothing to lose by seeing if I could run it off.

At this point, just before training was due to start at 10.30 a.m., Ron came into the treatment room and said to me: 'I want to see you, kid.'

We went into his office and just as the lads started running around the track – you could see them from his office and they could see us – a member of the canteen staff brought in a plate of bacon sandwiches and a pot of tea.

'Want a bacon sandwich?' he asked.

'No, really, I am going to have to train soon,' I replied.

'No, have a bacon sandwich,' he said.

'Listen, I want to go and train,' I told him. 'You know what I am like – I have to train – and I need to find out if I am going to be okay for tomorrow.'

But Ron was adamant. He pointed towards the players on the pitch – the likes of Paul McGrath, Bryan Robson and Norman Whiteside – and said: 'Those guys need to train, you don't. Have a bacon sandwich and a cup of tea, and then get yourself home and we will see you again tomorrow for a game of football.'

The way he said it, I went away feeling that I was a superstar and all the others were mere mortals.

Of my four full seasons at United, that first one – in which I played in almost every match and was the club's second top First Division goalscorer – was unquestionably the best for me. For all United's hunger to win the Championship again, I did not feel that finishing fourth for the second successive season was anything to be ashamed about; and, of course, the icing on the cake for me was that I completed a Scottish Cup–FA Cup winners double.

I remember how thrilled my father was when he met Bobby Charlton – by then a United director – and Charlton told him that I was one of his favourite players. To this day, that ranks as one of his proudest moments. Throughout the entire season, I felt I was buzzing, which was hardly surprising given that the United team included not only McGrath, Robson and Whiteside but also Jesper Olsen, Mark Hughes and Frank Stapleton.

Paul, Bryan and Norman were like the Three Musketeers. They were inseparable socially, and it is no secret that they all liked a drink. The three of them lived off the Hale Road in Cheshire and because of the amount of alcohol they consumed we used to joke that joining them was tantamount to taking the 'road to oblivion'.

Bryan was able to handle his drinking better than Norman and Paul. These two, on their way home after a Saturday night out on the town together, would occasionally stop off at my house – in the early hours of Sunday morning – for something to eat. If I knew this was on the cards, Lesley and I would make sure all the lights were off and the curtains drawn. But it did not make any difference. No matter how late it was, or how long Lesley and I had been in bed, Norman and Paul would still be knocking on our door. 'Oh no,' Lesley would mutter. 'It's those two again.'

In common with so many great players, Paul and Norman were not the most disciplined of people in their personal lives. But it is virtually impossible to condemn them for the simple reason that the only people they harmed were themselves. I always remember that, when I joined United, Paul and I agreed to swap cars – I gave him my big Ford Granada (because I felt it was costing me too much in petrol) and I took his smaller Ford

Escort. Everybody was laughing their heads off at the deal because the state his car was in when I got hold of it had to be seen to be believed. The interior looked as if he had been living in it and it was not too clever mechanically either. I only had it for about two weeks before it started breaking down. To me, it was a good example of the way he looked after himself as a professional footballer. However, it was a different matter in relation to his contribution to his team. You could not fault him at all in that respect, and it was the same with Bryan and Norman.

Players of their ability can sometimes be selfish. Some of them are only happy when they are the centre of attention. But Paul, Bryan and Norman were not like that at all. They were happy to blend into the picture. Essentially, they were 'givers', not 'takers' – maybe too much so at times. There is a limit to the amount of responsibility a small group of players can take on their shoulders.

Manchester United's centre-forward, Frank Stapleton, was another in that mould. Frank, one of the hardest working players I have ever known, seemed to want to do everyone else's job, as well as his own. I used to say to him: 'Frank, just be a striker, would you?'

I am surprised that Frank, a wonderful all-round striker, did not go on to become a top manager. His thirst for football knowledge was insatiable, and he was forever talking about the game. Even when it was clear that you wanted to switch off and relax, he would want to have a long discussion about whether we should play 4-4-2 or 4-3-3 and subjects like that. I remember him even wanting to talk to me about football at a club Christmas party, when he was dressed as a clown and I went as Freddie Starr-cum-Adolf Hitler. I often a joke about it. For example, on the eve of one United match away from home, when I was having difficulty getting to sleep at our hotel, I rang Jimmy McGregor in his room and said: 'Jimmy, I need a sleeping pill – but on second thoughts, can you send Frank up?' For United air trips, the players had to board the plane in alphabetical order. 'Frank,' I said to him, 'I think I am going to change my name by deed poll. It is going to be Gordon Aardvark.'

It was all taken in good spirit and, indeed, Frank could never have been in any doubt about how much I and everybody else at Old Trafford valued him. As with Steve Archibald, Mark McGhee and Eric Black at Aberdeen, he made it easy for me to bring him into the game and, once I gave him the ball, I never feared that he might not look after it and the other team would be able to hit us on the break.

This was also the case with his fellow front man Mark Hughes. He was the best shielder of a ball among all the strikers of my generation – although initially, I did find him a frustrating player to work with.

Mark was only nineteen or twenty when I started playing with him and because of his inexperience he was inclined to hold the ball too long. It could be annoying for a player making a thirty- to forty-yard run to get the ball from him only for him to ignore you or not make the pass quickly enough. It also irritated me that, even when a run in support of him had helped create the space for him to hold the ball, he would not acknowledge it. 'Mark, give me a wave from time to time, will you?' I'd say. I admit I was hard on him – but no harder than some senior professionals at Dundee had been on me when I used to make the same mistake at Dens Park. There was nothing vindictive in my attitude to Mark – I was just trying to help him, me and the team – and, indeed, Mark appeared to have no difficulty whatsoever in handling it.

Not that I can take much credit for the way he blossomed as a player. If anybody at Manchester United could do so, it was surely Frank Stapleton.

In that 1984/85 season, Frank's knowledge came in handy for us in the FA Cup Final against Everton, when he took over from Kevin Moran at centre-half, after Kevin's controversial sending off for a challenge on Peter Reid twelve minutes from the end of normal time.

United's win, thanks to Norman Whiteside's goal after twenty minutes of extra time, was no mean achievement. With men like Neville Southall, Gary Stevens, Reid, Trevor Steven, Graeme Sharp and Andy Gray, Everton had proved the best team in the country over the season by winning the Championship. Because of their tremendous teamwork and organisation, they were the most difficult of sides to play against with eleven men, let alone ten. Still, it is not unusual for teams to raise their game when they have had a man sent off, especially when they feel as hard done by over the decision as we did.

Players who have taken part in an FA Cup Final often say that, because of the excitement of the occasion – very much a unique one in terms of the interest the match attracts throughout the world – they have difficulty remembering what happened in any great detail. I can relate to that. I cannot remember much about any of the Cup Finals I played in, but that was especially the case with the match against Everton. Strange as it may seem, although I had a video of the game, it was only a couple of years ago, during my football sabbatical after leaving Southampton, that I watched it.

One thing that struck me about it was the poor quality of the play, and how combative the game was in those days. At half time, I recall saying that our players needed to be brave on the ball, to be prepared to take and hold it knowing full well that we were going to get whacked. You could certainly appreciate that point in the opening twenty minutes. Some of the tackles were horrendous – in the climate of today's game, there would have been at least six bookings. There were a lot of good players out there, but with the two teams squeezing up to compress play, and expending so much nervous energy, space – almost anywhere on that Wembley pitch – was at a premium. I was quite taken aback by the number of times both teams lost possession. Because of the stricter interpretation of the rules by referees, and the high number of foreign players in English football, I doubt that you would get that in a game between teams of a similar standing today.

In that match against Everton we did start to get more space as the early sharpness of the two teams began to wear off and the pace dropped. The longer the game progressed, the more dominant we became.

I certainly felt this about myself. I did not have the easiest of direct opponents in Pat Van Den Hauwe, an exceptionally strong, powerful full back not unlike Stuart Pearce. But it is amazing how little you tend to worry or even think about things like that when you and your team are playing well. United's attacking ascendancy meant that they could afford to have me looking for the ball in other positions, so I did not have to face Van Den Hauwe all the time anyway.

One of the most pleasant surprises for me when I watched the video of it concerned a run I made in extra time, when I picked the ball up just outside our penalty area and took it some sixty yards forward. That sort of run was rare for me – it showed me to be quicker than I had ever imagined myself to be. I also derived a lot of satisfaction from my part in Norman Whiteside's wonderful goal.

A lot of people will not have noticed it – all they will have seen was Norman receiving a ball from Mark Hughes on the right and then, instead of trying to take it behind the Everton defence, suddenly switching the ball on to his left foot and hitting a magnificent curling shot past Neville Southall from twenty-five yards. My small contribution was that, as the ball was played up to Norman, I pushed up on the outside of him, on the premise that, as he wasn't great on his right side, in order to get the ball closer to the byline he needed help. He could not see me, so as I ran towards him I shouted: 'Hold it', and when I was about two yards from him, I signalled for him to release the ball for me by shouting 'Yes'.

Fortunately for United, Norman then elected to do his own thing. However, my overlap had not been in vain – it had the effect of pulling Van Den Hauwe towards me, thus giving Norman a vital extra yard.

That goal deserved the setting of a much better match than this one, and my small contribution to it was very much my greatest personal moment of the game.

The win over Everton should have been the launching pad for even greater things for Ron Atkinson and United. It certainly looked that way the following season, when we won our opening ten league matches to establish a nine-point Championship lead. But then came a spate of injuries, the most damaging of which was the one to Bryan Robson which put him out of action for twenty matches. By the time of our sixteenth match, when we suffered our first league defeat at the hands of Sheffield Wednesday, United had used eighteen players – four more than the number Everton had called on in winning the title the previous season.

Even then, few can have visualised United slipping as far as they did. By the end of the season, it was Liverpool who were on top, with us twelve points behind them in fourth place.

There was a deterioration in my own performances that season, mainly because of the difficulty I had in getting over a dislocated shoulder. It occurred in our 5-1 win over West Bromwich Albion in our ninth league match, and although I only missed the next six matches, the knowledge that such injuries can keep recurring – as was to be seen with Bryan

Robson's dislocated shoulder problems in the 1986 World Cup Finals in Mexico – did have an adverse psychological effect. When I started playing again, my attempts to protect the shoulder meant that in some situations I was playing too much within myself. It was very much a subconscious thing. In fact, as far as I was concerned, I was doing all right. The first time I was forced to accept that this was not the case was when Gary Bailey pointed to me after a United defeat and said: 'When are you going to start playing again?'

Deep down I knew he was right, but once you get into the sort of trough I was in, it is difficult to get out of it. It did take me a while.

After doing well in the 1986 World Cup Finals, I was looking forward to the next season at Old Trafford, and another crack at the First Division title. But it wasn't long before everybody realised we would be among the also-rans again; and, even more unpalatable, that we might even end up being relegated. The difference in our results over the first ten matches, compared to the previous season, was extraordinary. We won only two of those matches, and were third from bottom. The inevitable speculation about Ron's future had not helped, and by the time he was sacked and replaced by Fergie – in November – we were second from bottom. Where did it go so wrong for him?

In his account of his early days at United, Fergie attributed the club's slide mainly to the 'drinking culture' spearheaded by Paul, Bryan and Norman. To varying degrees the trio were in decline when Fergie became manager. They were not the only ones – others who had faded included me. However, Paul, Bryan and Norman were the team's big-hitters and, in addition to their slide, some of the younger players Ron had brought into the team had difficulty raising their game to the standard expected. In other words, the decline of the Three Musketeers coincided with the supporting cast getting weaker.

It is possibly unfair to put too much emphasis on that drinking culture, bearing in mind the handicaps that Paul, Bryan and Norman suffered through their injuries. It was incredible that Bryan kept going for so long – with such a high level of physical intensity – given the number of broken bones, muscle strains and tears he had. The other two, with their serious knee problems, also deserved medals for the way they pushed themselves through it.

Even so, I have often felt they did not help themselves in the way they looked after their bodies off the field; and although I am not sure anyone could have put them on a different track, you could say that this represented the downside of Ron's managerial approach. Basically, he was only interested in what happened on the field on a Saturday; as long as the players performed for him when it mattered, anything outside that was more or less irrelevant as far as he was concerned. This was the attitude of a lot of football professionals of his generation, and his time at Old Trafford was the time it started to change.

I also believe, though, that Ron did not get as much success as he deserved at Old Trafford.

The United team I played in over my first two seasons there epitomised not just his ideas on how the game should be played but also the footballing traditions of the club. For those who appreciate inventive, all-out attacking play, no team was better to watch than we were. It was the right team to win a Championship – but not at that time.

The 1980s was generally the ugliest of footballing periods in England, with a number of teams compensating for their shortage of quality players by pushing up to squeeze the play, and getting the ball from the back to the front with just one or two passes. Some matches were more like games of head tennis than football. These teams put a great deal of thought into maximising whatever ability they had, and did not miss a tactical trick.

This, indeed, was the period when Wimbledon were able to become one of the most successful sides in the country on little more than aggression and physical power. Wimbledon brought English football to an all-time low in my view. I cannot think of any team which did more to try and intimidate you, even off the field. The one thing you could be sure about when you played Wimbledon was that the ball would be in the air a lot and you would be kicked all over the place.

I was a member of the United team when Wimbledon's John Fashanu and our Viv Anderson had their infamous a fight in the Plough Lane dressing room tunnel. I can't say who started the fight, but as I followed them I saw Fashanu fell Viv with two of the quickest punches I have ever seen. The players behind me saw it as well, and in their vain attempts to get past me – the tunnel was only about two yards wide – meant that they pushed me towards the fracas as well. Jimmy McGregor was the only member of the United party in front of me and, as he has a stutter, I still have to laugh when I think of his shouts to me to avoid blocking his route to safety. Being the devout coward that I am, I was happy to allow myself to be propelled beyond Viv and Fashanu and, with all sorts of battles going on among the big guys, to scramble into the dressing room, out of harm's way. Jimmy and I sat there by ourselves, with me keeping my foot against the door.

Viv had been on the ground when I went past him. Later, I told him: 'All I can say, Viv, is that if I trod on your fingers, I am sorry!'

As a lover of good football, playing against Wimbledon was not really my scene. Ron left me out of the team for one match against them. My initial reaction was to moan about it – no player likes to miss a match when he is fit – but in this instance it was easy for me to see where he was coming from.

Obviously, not all teams gave the ball a headache. In that

respect, if there was one consolation about the standard and
nature of English football then, it was that the Championship
was dominated by Liverpool and Everton. I honestly do not
think they had greater individual skill than we did, but one
important difference was that they were bigger teams physically.

In his book Fergie says: 'Our squad [when he took over] suffered from having too many players who were physical
lightweights.' I am certainly with him on that one. With players
like myself, Arthur Albiston, Mike Duxbury, Remi Moses and
Jesper Olsen, the team in my first two seasons at United must
have been one of the First Division's smallest. That handicap
was compounded by the overall standard of the pitches in those
days; in the peak winter months, even the one at Old Trafford
was not the best of surfaces on which to exploit our ability. The
conditions definitely made it easier for opponents to nail us,
and though all our players worked hard enough to get the ball
back, the physical shortcomings of the likes of Jesper and myself
meant that others – notably Bryan Robson – were probably
forced to stretch themselves more than they should have been.

I have often wondered whether United would have won the
FA Cup in 1985 had the Final not been at Wembley; and
whether we would have won the title the following season had
the conditions remained as they did during the early part of the
season.

Under Fergie, my United career lasted barely three seasons
and, as I have said, the nature of our relationship made it an
increasingly troubled period for me. It was a troubled period for
him, too, because United's best achievement in our time together
there was finishing runner-up to Liverpool in the 1987/88
Championship – by nine points. In the other two seasons, United
finished eleventh.

It is well documented that Fergie would probably have been
forced to follow me out of Old Trafford in the season after my

departure had United not won the FA Cup. Subsequent events proved that this would have been possibly the biggest mistake in United's history. It has also shown, of course, that my transfer to Leeds, which many might have interpreted as merely a move to a last resting place for a thirty-two-year-old apparently past his prime, was the best thing that could have happened to me.

## CHAPTER SIX

# HOWARD'S WAY

I have two confessions to make about my transfer to Leeds in March 1989. It could not have seemed the best of career moves at the time, especially as I also had the chance to link up with Ron Atkinson again – and stay in the First Division – at Sheffield Wednesday. I have to be honest and say that, while I recognised Leeds' potential, the main reason I chose to go to Elland Road was financial. Leeds, who paid a transfer fee of £300,000 for me, offered me double what I had been getting at Manchester United, an extraordinary deal for any club to present to a player in his thirties, let alone a middle-of-the-table club in the Second Division. I have always prided myself on not being particularly money-conscious, but at that stage in my career the contract Leeds offered was virtually impossible to turn down. I also have to own up to the fact that I pulled the wool over Leeds' eyes at my medical.

It's an appropriate way to put it because I am half blind in my right eye – the result of an accident as a boy, when I tripped during a kickabout in the school playground. I did not realise that I had a pen in my hand, and as I tried to protect my face as I hit the floor it went straight into the eye socket, damaging the optic nerve. The best way I can describe the effect of this is that, if I am looking at someone with my left eye closed, I can only see their bottom half. Though the injury caused me to be rather wary about the ball hitting me on that side of my face – hence my unwillingness to join defensive walls at free kicks and the temptation for me to turn my head away from the ball when I was set up for a header – it did not really have a significant effect on my performances. However, when I learned that Leeds were more thorough than other clubs with their medical examinations and that mine would include an eye test, I panicked.

The test was conducted by the Leeds physio Alan Sutton, who started it by getting me to read the letters and numbers on the board with my hand over the right eye. No problem. Then, when he asked me to change over, I just covered my bad eye with the other hand. He did not notice what I'd done so, again, no problem. I am pretty sure that, even if my sight problem had been detected by Leeds, the transfer would still have gone ahead, and I did let Alan into the secret afterwards – albeit about two years afterwards.

As far as the financial aspect of my move was concerned, I believe it made me the highest paid player in Leeds' history. But I found so much happiness and contentment at Leeds that this quickly became incidental.

My career at Elland Road, from the ages of thirty-two to thirty-eight, was transformed in a way that nobody can have predicted. It was not just my age that made my new lease of life at Leeds so surprising but also the trouble I had with an injury dating back to my last season at Aberdeen, and which still bothers me to this day.

From time to time, when I was running flat out, I would

experience a sharp cramp-like pain in my leg. It was originally diagnosed as a hamstring problem, and it was only when I got to Leeds – and the trouble became increasingly worse – that it was found to be sciatica. The build-up of calcium meant that I had to undergo three successive close-season 'clean-up' operations, the first after Leeds' Championship win in 1992. Towards the end of that season, it had got so bad that I could not train and was only barely getting by in matches.

This marked the end of my international career. Having been recalled to the Scotland team – after missing the 1990 World Cup Finals in Italy – and gained my fiftieth cap against Finland in March 1992, I had to rule myself out of the running for a place in the squad for the European Championship Finals in Sweden in the summer. That disappointment, though, was more than offset by what was happening to me at Elland Road.

The success of the team when I was there, which also included winning the Second Division Championship in 1990, was one of two big bonuses for me. The other was my close relationship with Howard Wilkinson.

That relationship played the biggest part in bringing me into football management, if only because Howard made me captain and involved me in so many of his decisions that I was virtually an assistant manager. I obviously learned a lot more about this side of the game at Leeds than I did at Manchester United, Aberdeen and Dundee. Hence the fact that Howard is often described as having been my managerial guru, and, since I started in the job, he has always been among the first people I have turned to when I've felt I needed some advice or, more pertinently, a shoulder to cry on. I feel a little guilty about it sometimes, in that I only seem to contact him when I am in trouble.

As I have said, Howard was very different from Ron Atkinson. While Ron was an idealist, Howard – outwardly dour and studious – was very much a football realist. While he appreciated skilful attacking play as much anyone, he took the view – quite rightly – that as a manager dependent on good results, you can only play in a way that suits the ability of the players at your disposal. His expertise in getting the best out of teams who do not have an abundance of top class players was instrumental in helping me to better understand the game.

This was partly why I also enjoyed working with Andy Roxburgh and Craig Brown, in the Scotland set-up. Andy and Craig, who like Howard are former schoolteachers, had outstanding organisational skills, which was just what the Scotland team needed when they took charge of it at the end of Alex Ferguson's spell as caretaker manager in 1986. In striving to compensate for the decline in the individual quality of the players available to them, these two did not miss a trick in their preparations for matches.

It is no secret that some players were not very receptive to some of their methods. Neither man had been a player or manager at a particularly high professional level and there was a feeling that their approach was similar to that of headmasters dealing with their pupils. I personally had a great deal respect for Andy and Craig, though. After all, it was under their management that I was brought back into the Scotland team, when I was at Leeds, and had five matches as captain of the side. One of those games was the 2-2 draw against Switzerland – after we had been 2-0 down – in Berne in September 1991. That was probably the best Scotland performance throughout my time in the side.

I think Scotland did benefit from their attention to detail, although I have to agree that this was taken to the extreme at times.

On one occasion, as we were walking onto the training field, Craig suddenly said: 'Stop – we can't have this.'

'What do you mean?' I asked.

'Well,' Craig explained, 'you have your socks down while Roy Aitken has his rolled up. You must all be the same.'

So we all went back into the dressing room, and found the ideal solution. We all came out again, with one of our socks down and the other up.

Basically, the thought that Andy and Craig put into their jobs helped motivate me. It was the same with Howard Wilkinson. When I watched him in training – the work he did on set-pieces and making us more effective as a unit – I thought: 'Someone is really trying to get a result here.'

I feel very strongly that Howard does not have the public recognition he deserves – nothing irritates me more than the negative way he has tended to be portrayed in the media. Some of the managers in jobs at the moment are not in the same league as Howard, in my opinion. To me, he has suffered from the fact that, unlike a lot of managers, he does not talk a good game. He does not put any spin on his knowledge and ability. He does not answer questions without giving them some thought, and he does not talk in the sound-bite language of newspaper head-lines. An exceptionally intelligent, well-read man Howard can often come across as idiosyncratic even to his players.

'Good morning,' I said to him once.

'Hmm, is it a good morning?' he replied. He then started to talk about the differences between being a player and a manager. 'It might be a good morning for you,' he said, 'but life for a man-ager is more complicated.'

'Look, gaffer,' I replied. 'I only said: "Good morning".'

He and I were chalk and cheese personality-wise, so he would laugh at me and vice versa. Some of his one-liners were so subtle that it was almost as if it was his ambition to crack a joke that nobody would get. I'd say to the other players: 'Whatever joke he cracks, even if you do not get it, just laugh.'

One or two of his team talks could be hard to follow as well. I remember one for a match against Chelsea, when Howard – who seemed particularly keen to beat them – made what amounted to a speech about the friction between the two teams in the past, Ken Bates and what he saw as differences between us in our cultures and values. He must have gone on for about twenty minutes, without anyone really knowing what point he was trying to make.

When he asked us: 'Are you with me?' we were looking at each other with blank faces.

'Sorry, gaffer,' I said. 'I think some of us were with you ten minutes ago, but now you have lost the lot of us. Can you simplify it?'

It was great to work with Howard at Leeds then, not just because of him but also the players he gathered there and the extraordinary people – like the managing director Bill Fotherby and Howard's right-hand man, Mick Hennigan – helping him behind the scenes.

Bill, who played a major part in developing Leeds' commercial income, was the man responsible for negotiating with the players Howard wanted to sign and their clubs. It was not difficult to see why he was good at it. Bill – as gregarious and verbose as Howard was introverted and quiet – epitomised that old saying about some people being able to sell snow to Eskimos.

He has never allowed me to forget the time that I went into his office to negotiate an extension to my contract. Although I was happy with the money I was getting, I felt that I should ask for something to sign a new agreement, as a token. But Bill went into a long speech about Leeds' finances and how much it had cost them to build their new stand, etc. The upshot was that I did not get a rise, but was persuaded to splash out on an executive box for the next match.

After Howard had decided he wanted to sign me, he and Bill interviewed me together. Bill – typically – did most of the talking, so by the time the pair had finished with me I felt as if my name should be Maradona and that Leeds would soon be competing on level terms with Real Madrid. It was an ego massage in stereo. 'We see you as Leeds United leader – the man to take us back into the top flight', I was told. It was great for me to hear that, following the stick Fergie had given me at Manchester United.

As for Mick Hennigan, of all the people I have come across in professional football, he is one of my favourites. The first time I met him was when he came to pick me up at a service station in Hartshill, Staffordshire, before my first Leeds match at Stoke. He was driving a battered Nissan Sunny and the way he was dressed, I thought he must be the groundsman. It came as no surprise to discover that one of his nicknames among the players was 'Steptoe'.

I thought the world of Mick – all the players did. He was a bit like Teddy Scott at Aberdeen in that there was nothing you felt you could not discuss with him and nobody worked harder than him. Such was his devotion to Leeds that when we were particularly late in arriving back at Elland Road after a midweek away match, Mick, having put all the kit away, would occasionally sleep in the laundry cupboard. Nobody was a better judge of character than he was and I might also add that nobody could give a team talk like him either.

He only gave one that I can recall at Leeds and it was bizarre, to say the least. It was before a Second Division away match, and was conducted at our hotel, in a ground-floor conference suite with big windows looking out onto the entrance and grounds. He was sitting on a chair when he started, but then he stood on it and starting telling us what he would be able to see if he were God looking down at us from Heaven. It was hilarious, especially as the curtains had not been drawn properly and people arriving for a wedding reception were looking through the windows – with puzzled expressions – to see what was going on. We were in stitches.

Mick, who had previously worked with Howard at Sheffield Wednesday, was as good an assistant manager as you could find. What I particularly liked about him was his loyalty to Howard.

After one match, in which we had been launching balls into the box from almost every area of the pitch, thus making it difficult for me to get into the game, I made the mistake of allowing my frustration to boil over and shooting my mouth off to Howard about his tactics in front of the other players. 'Our approach was rubbish,' I remarked to him. 'How are we meant to win games like that? We are so predictable.' Howard did not reply, and walked away. The following morning, however, Mick took it upon himself to give me a ticking-off about it. 'I don't think you realise how badly you let Howard down,' he said. 'He trusted you and it was just not right for you to turn around and have a go at him in front of the rest of the team.' He was right, and it was the last time I did anything like that. If ever there was a time at Leeds that I felt badly about myself, that was it.

Mick was also instrumental in one of my proudest moments when he was quoted as saying: 'Gordon is the only player I have come across who, in addition to being the highest paid at his club, is also the best trainer and the best player.'

All of which brings me back to the buzz I got out of the responsibility Howard gave me. This was probably as much of a factor in helping me to maintain my effectiveness as a player as all the fitness work I'd done and my lifestyle changes.

One example of that stimulation was that in a Leeds career spanning a total of some 244 first team matches, I played 120 games on the trot, and all but one of them for the full ninety minutes. At Aberdeen, people had told me that when I got into my thirties, I would have to think of ways to conserve my energy and change my style of play. But this did not become necessary until my late thirties, the tail-end of my Leeds career. I generally did not do as much on the ball at Leeds as I had at Aberdeen and Manchester United, but probably worked harder and was more influential.

It is surprising how much you can stretch yourself when you are the team captain and have the respect and admiration for the manager that I had for Howard.

On the days when things did not go well for us, I possibly let it get to me even more than he did. On one such day, after we were held to a 1-1 draw by Bradford near the end of our 1989/90 Second Division Championship-winning season, my reaction prompted Howard to look at me as if I had gone crazy – which I had. Bradford's last-minute equaliser stemmed from the referee allowing them to take a free kick some twenty yards closer to our goal than I felt it should have been. I simply exploded and as I was ranting and raving about it in the dressing room, our full back, Jim Beglin, actually threatened to punch me on the nose if I did not calm down. What Howard and Bill Fotherby had said to me about being the man to lead Leeds back into the First Division was particularly difficult to get out of my mind in our last two matches.

Only two teams were promoted then, and at the time of our penultimate game against Leicester – our last at home – we were level on points with Sheffield United, with Newcastle, the only other team involved in the promotion battle, two points behind. In all the stadiums I have been in, I have never experienced an atmosphere inside a ground as highly charged as it was at Elland Road that day. Nor can I ever recall expending so much mental, emotional and physical energy in a match, especially the last twenty minutes of it. By that stage of our clash with Leicester, it was 1-1, with Mel Sterland having put us ahead and Gary McAllister – at that time Leicester's star player – equalising. On a warm afternoon it was clear that if either team was going to get a winner, it would stem from a mistake borne of tiredness.

Amid unbelievable tension, that decisive error came, uncharacteristically, from Gary, in misdirecting a clearance to my feet a few minutes from the end. When I got the ball about twenty yards out I knew I was dying on my feet and that it would almost certainly be the last significant chance for me and maybe anyone else to get our winner. I knew I had to shoot with my left foot, and as I wound myself to strike the ball, I thought: 'If you don't get this right, forget it.' I caught it perfectly – it was like one of those great long golf shots, where the point of impact seems more like a ping than a full-blooded hit – and the ball flew past the keeper about two feet under the bar. My first goal for Aberdeen was scored with my left foot, as was my last for Leeds. But, of course, that one against Leicester was the most special of them all for me, so much so that I can still remember exactly what the shot felt like – when I think of it, I can still feel the sensation of my contact with the ball. Moreover, though I am not one to surround myself with reminders of my soccer successes in my personal life, a painting of me celebrating the goal is on display in the family room at my Southampton home. This, and the selection of medals kept in a discreet cabinet in the same room, is the only visible sign of my football career in the entire house. Howard Wilkinson has said that he has never seen a player look as gaunt as I did after scoring against Leicester. 'Skeletal' was the word I used to describe myself when watching the highlights of the match on TV. I must have looked even worse immediately after the match when we learned that Vinnie Jones's information that Newcastle had lost, thus enabling us to clinch promotion, was wrong. Both Newcastle and Sheffield United had won, so we had to win our last match – at Bournemouth – to be sure of going up and pipping Sheffield United for the title. On a day when Leeds fans who had travelled to Bournemouth without tickets for the match caused mayhem, we overcame Bournemouth 1-0, thanks to a header by Lee Chapman. By the final whistle, I was so stressed out I could hardly speak. In fact, on the coach journey back to Leeds, I fell asleep.

The other game I would use as an example of the effect that my position at Leeds had on me was the home game against Blackburn in April 1993. A number of Leeds fans feel this was my best game for the club. It needed to be, because we were without three key players – Tony Dorigo, Gary McAllister and David Batty – and were just four places above the First Division relegation zone.

The day before the game, without Howard's knowledge, goalkeeper Mervyn Day and I organised a team meeting to try and sort out what we felt had been going wrong. Howard had been taking a lot of flak over the situation, and I said to Mervyn: 'We cannot hide behind that. One or two of the players are not doing as much as they should be doing and as you and I have been here the longest, it is up to us to try and rectify it.'

As I was Leeds' Player of the Year, this was tantamount to me putting my head on the chopping block. I felt I had been playing well, but having criticised players for not doing so, the last thing I wanted was to give them a reason to get back at me the following day. So, as an extra motivational idea, that team talk probably worked for me just as much as it might have done for them.

We beat Blackburn 5-2 and I scored a hat-trick, including two penalties. I put Leeds ahead from a spot kick, and made it 2-0 from another after I had been brought down in the area by

Stuart Ripley. It was quite a relief to see those two go in, because I did not usually take penalties in those days; it was the job of Gary McAllister and Tony Dorigo. My third goal came following an exchange of passes with Jamie Forrester and a shot from twenty yards and I also set up a goal for Rod Wallace.

I cannot ever recall getting greater media praise for a performance than I did for that one, but the most valued compliment came from Howard. He was quoted as saying: 'Leadership was required and Gordon gave it in every respect.'

One of the most important ways in which Howard was a leader to me was that he opened my eyes to different ways of playing the game.

At Aberdeen and, especially, Manchester United I had been used to being in teams which deemed it essential to retain possession and, when necessary, were quite happy to knock the ball around and wait for gaps to appear in the opposing defence before striking at goal. Leeds, because of the players they had at the time I joined them and the pragmatic nature of the game in the Second Division, were more direct. Generally, the number of passes they used in their build-up play was considerably fewer.

With Leeds, it was mainly a question of hitting the ball from the back to the front – straight up to big Lee Chapman at centre-forward – and working from there. A lot of teams were like that then. To a great extent, it was a reflection of their managers' exploitation of the back-pass rule as it was then; the fact that, with goalkeepers allowed to handle such passes in those days, players could afford virtually to push as far up the field, as far away from their own penalty box, as they wanted. It was a good way for teams to keep the ball a safe distance from their goal, and to put maximum pressure on the opposition.

The negative side of it was that defenders and midfielders

who liked the ball to their feet and to use their imagination seemed to become almost redundant. Howard and I often talked about it in my first few months at Leeds, when I was still striving to come to terms with their style of play. For all my reservations about the trend, it was difficult to argue against him.

On one occasion, for example, he asked: 'Why is it that, when teams are 1-0 down with about fifteen minutes to go, they stop trying to play through the opposition and just keep launching balls into the box?'

'They are hoping the other team are going to make a mistake,' I said. 'They think it is the best way they can get the ball into the net.'

'So why should they not do it in the first fifteen minutes as well?' he replied.

He also reminded me of the famous comment by the former Liverpool manager Bob Paisley: 'Good football is not about short balls or long balls – it is about the best balls.'

One saving grace for me about Leeds' approach was that it was not taken to the extreme. Our first ball might have been a back-to-front one, but once we were deep into enemy territory, the good footballers in our team were encouraged to put their foot on the ball and start to play. Indeed, I had more of the ball than I'd expected, and the best part of this for me and Leeds was that, because of our method of attack, it was more often than not in areas where I could do the most damage.

The bottom line for me in what I learned from Howard is that I became more practical. That, inevitably, stood me in good stead when I became a manager. We all dream of producing brilliant footballing teams but, for the vast majority of us, the starting point – if not our approach throughout our entire managerial careers – has to be much more basic. The fact is that our jobs do not usually depend on the football our teams play – they depend on their results.

In those days, the money necessary for a manager to develop a team like Leeds was nothing like as prohibitive as it is today, and there is no doubt that once Howard had steered Leeds back to the First Division the team's individual skill level got higher. But he had to start from somewhere, and as his methods brought such good results, my attitude towards them changed considerably.

In terms of exploiting my ability in the Second Division, it did me no harm at all to operate in arguably one of the most physically intimidating midfield units in English football.

While recognising that this macho aspect of the game can be taken too far, I have always appreciated the importance of teams having one or two men with so-called hard man reputations. Quite often, these figures can create space for others to play just through their presence.

At Aberdeen, nobody could unsettle the opposition quite like big Doug Rougvie. When Aberdeen beat Ipswich in the Uefa Cup, the player who got most of the credit was Peter Weir; in our 3-0 win in the second leg at Portman Road, he ran Ipswich ragged in the second half. But what I remember most about the tie was the commitment of Doug, and the two challenges by him that, in my view, did much to give us the upper hand psychologically. The first was a rash two-footed challenge on Paul Mariner, and when the ball broke to Frans Thijssen, Doug took him out as well. Both Ipswich players were on the ground and as they were receiving treatment, John Wark said to me: 'He's a nutter.'

'Yup,' I said.

Not long afterwards, Doug went into a challenge with Mick Mills. Initially, it was a 70-30 ball in Mick's favour in my view, but Mick put the brakes on and it ended up being a 30-70 challenge for him. Not that I would criticise Mick for that – knowing how pumped up Doug was, I would have done the same.

Needless to say, I did my best to let everybody know that Doug was one of my biggest mates. At Manchester United, it was Norman Whiteside and Remi Moses. And at Leeds? During the second half of our Second Division Championship-winning season, our midfield included David Batty, Chris Kamara and Vinnie Jones. How's that for a trio of enforcers to look after you and put the frighteners on the opposition? I had to laugh when, at half-time during a match at Oldham, Howard – unusually animated – said to me: 'When are you going to start making some tackles?' Even Howard was struggling to come up with an effective reply when I pointed out: 'Looking at who I am playing with, I am amazed you think that is really necessary.'

People were staggered that Howard signed Vinnie. He was a better player than a lot of them gave him credit for in my view, but as far as ball-winning ability was concerned, he was not the best timer of tackles. He was okay when people were running straight at him, but if he had to suddenly change direction, that could be a problem to him. For any match against Vinnie, after he left Leeds, the best advice I could give colleagues was similar to the guidance I was given when I suddenly saw an alligator during a round of golf in Florida in 1994. Later, as I was discussing the experience with the club pro, I said that I was preparing myself to beat it off with my 9 iron. 'No,' he said. 'Alligators move in a straight line and long as you are moving in a zig-zag fashion, you can get away from them.'

To this day, every time I see an alligator at a zoo or on television, I think: 'Vinnie Jones.' No doubt, it is the same with those who had the misfortune to be on the receiving end of his combativeness.

In view of his disciplinary record, it was inevitable that his arrival at Leeds would prompt the fear that it would lead to the club's image dropping as low as it did in their early days under

Don Revie, and that he would spend much of his time being forced out of the team by suspension. This worry seemed perfectly justified during a pre-season match against Anderlecht in Belgium, shortly after Vinnie joined Leeds, when he was involved in an off-the-ball incident – not seen by the referee – which left his opponent with blood pouring from his nose. Afterwards, Howard and I both told him that this was not what he had been signed for or what we wanted from him. 'If you want to put the fear of death into people, do it by talking to them,' I said to him.

He settled down after that, although what I told him about rattling opponents verbally was perhaps not the best advice to give him because we already had a man of a million intimidatory words in Chris Kamara, who seemed to me to commit more fouls than even Vinnie. Chris's commitment was frightening. During a match there was not a single blade of grass that he did not cover, and everywhere he went he was winding up opponents all the time. 'Do us a favour and shut up,' I remarked to him once. 'Even our ears are getting sore.'

Chris, Vinnie and David Batty were absolutely fearless. In David's case this was always underlined for me by his willingness to stand in our defensive wall for free kicks – one of my pet hates – and the fact that, when the kick was taken, I never once saw him flinch or turn his body away from the ball. On one occasion, I even saw him block a ferocious kick with his chest and then hold the position of his body to do the same with the follow-up shot. One of the other lads looked at me and started shaking his head and laughing. 'That Batts – he's off his head, isn't he?' he said.

David, the best of the three on the ball, came across as the most 'controlled'. This, though, could be misleading. His father used to have a seat just behind the Elland Road dugout, and during one game against Hull, the pair of them had a

furious row over the studs David was wearing. They must have
been arguing about it before, because when David slipped his
father shouted: 'I told you about those studs.' Angry words
were exchanged and David was so furious that immediately
afterwards, as he was chasing an opponent into the box, he
brought the player down to concede a penalty.

It could be said that I was rather hypocritical where David,
Vinnie and Chris were concerned. If I had been playing against
them, I would probably have been looking down my nose at
them. Being in the same team as them obviously made my view
of them more liberal. Though it was impossible to condone some
of their more excessive combativeness, I had no compunctions
about using their reputations to our advantage.

I would often mention Vinnie in conversation with opponents
before or during a game. 'Oh, better keep away from him,' I'd
tell them. 'He's in a terrible mood today. Off his head.'

One incident I often refer to when discussing motivational
methods concerned my fib to David and Vinnie before a match
against Middlesbrough. As I was heading for the dressing room
to get changed, I'd caught sight of Middlesbrough midfielders
Mark Brennan and Trevor Putney, two lovely lads who just said
hello and asked how I was. However, I gave a different version
of the conversation when, having noticed that the atmosphere
among our players was a somewhat flat, I decided that the ideal
way to lift it would be to tell Vinnie and David that Mark and
Trevor had insulted them.

I said: 'I have just seen Mark Brennan and Trevor Putney,
and they told me: "We can't wait to face Jones and Batty.
They're no more than two hammer-throwers. If we can't play
well against them we can't play well against anybody."'

Suddenly, Vinnie and David were like two caged lions. Even
more disconcerting was that, in psyching themselves up to make
Mark and Trevor pay for what they had 'said', they were

growling like lions and slapping and punching each other. I thought: Hang on, this is a bit over the top, isn't it? What have you done?

In the match itself, Vinnie and David were kicking lumps out of Mark and Trevor (and everybody else in a Boro shirt). Deep down I did feel embarrassed, if not a little ashamed of myself, especially during a break in the play near the end. We were 2-0 up and Vinnie, standing next to Trevor and calling him all the names under the sun, tapped him on the head and shouted to me: 'Hey, skip, what was it this ****** said about me?'

Trevor looked at me as if to say: 'What's he talking about?' I just mumbled something and turned away.

Of all the players in this mould in England, Vinnie was the one that opponents least wanted to play against. As I've said, there was more to Vinnie's game than people thought. He was a tremendous striker of a ball – some of the goals he scored were outstanding by any standards – and had excellent leadership qualities.

Bearing in mind that even his own team-mates were rather wary of him, my influence as the Leeds captain owed much to his support of me. It could easily have been different because Vinnie, having been captain of Wimbledon, made it clear that he wanted to fill the same role at Leeds. I just said to him: 'Look, it's fine by me if you want to take on greater responsibility. Just because I have the job officially, that does not mean you cannot be the captain as well.'

He was happy with that, and he quickly became one of my most important dressing-room allies. If I made a point which someone disagreed with, Vinnie would be the first to back me up. 'Can't argue with the wee man,' he'd say. 'He has achieved too much to argue with him.'

Unfortunately – perhaps inevitably – Vinnie was among the

first casualties of Howard's quest to improve the team technically following our Second Division Championship success. For
our first season back in the top flight, the midfield was boosted
by Gary McAllister, who was signed from Leicester for £1 million, a deal which led to Vinnie moving to Sheffield United.
Chris Kamara also left – for Luton – as a result of the emergence
of Gary Speed from the club's youth system. For the 1991/92
season, our attacking ability was further developed through the
signings of Tony Dorigo and, for the vital last lap of the
Championship race, that of a then little-known Frenchman by
the name of Eric Cantona.

As for my own return to the First Division, it did worry me
that I might not be able to hack it at that level again. Towards
the end of my spell at Manchester United, I had been told that
Fergie suggested to certain people in the game that I was past my
best as a top-flight footballer – not just for United but generally.
I had no way of knowing if he really had said that, but for all the
praise I received for helping to steer Leeds out of the Second
Division, it was still difficult to dismiss totally the thought that
such a view might be right.

Maybe it would have been if I'd not had someone like Gary to
help take some of the weight off me.

Gary, who later also joined me at Coventry, of course, has
become one of my closest friends in football, which I am sure
will be looked upon as a surprise among those who were with us
at Leeds. One of the commonest sounds on the pitch and in the
dressing room was that of us two moaning at each other.

Initially, we clashed over his attitude to other players not
being on his wavelength. In his early days at Leeds, Gary found
it hard to get his head around the fact that not everybody was
blessed with his ability. When moves broke down through
players not being able properly to anticipate or control his
passes, he tended to allow his frustration to boil over. However,

Gary learned to curb this. Though he continued shouting and growling at people – that, after all, was part of his make-up – it was not taken to a level where it affected his relationship with them. Thus, with Gary getting greater respect and support from the players, his performances for Leeds just got better and better.

The argumentative aspect of my relationship with Gary stemmed from the fact that we looked upon each other as rivals as well as team-mates. I think both of us wanted to be seen as the best. One might have thought that this would cause us to become too individualistic, but in fact it had the opposite effect. We both appreciated that in order to get the best out of ourselves, it was necessary for us to combine properly with each other. I needed his help to produce my best form and vice versa.

The upshot of Gary's presence at Elland Road in the 1990/91 season, apart from my 1991 Footballer of the Year award, was the team's unexpected success in finishing as high as fourth. It proved to us that we could handle the demands of the First Division; and, of course, it provided the momentum for Leeds – still maybe not the most skilful team in the country, but certainly the hardest working and best organised – to win the title the following season for the first time since 1974.

For most of the season, it was a two horse race between Manchester United and Leeds and United looked like winning it when they were top, with three games in hand, at the start of April. But United, the team under the greatest pressure to get their hands on that Championship trophy – an honour which had eluded them for twenty-five years – crumbled under it. With us having forged a point ahead, the title was clinched in our penultimate match through a 3-2 win at Sheffield United – a crazy game settled in our favour by a bizarre Howard Gayle own goal – and United's defeat by Liverpool later that day.

No player deserved greater praise for this than Lee Chapman, Leeds' top scorer for the second successive season. Lee, who had played for Howard at Sheffield Wednesday, might not have been among the most polished of centre-forwards, but he was absolutely perfect for Leeds' style of play in those days. Less so was Eric Cantona, even though it is difficult to dispute that we would not have won the title but for his signing from Nimes in February, and the touches of individual magic he brought to the side, especially as a substitute.

In addition to his extraordinary skill on the ball and his vision, I do not think people fully appreciate how big and powerful Eric was. For all this, it was good management on Howard's part to use Eric sparingly. We were a more regimented team than he had been used to and I am not sure that he – and Leeds – would have been as effective had he been in the starting line-up for every match. I also have to side with Howard concerning the stick he took from Leeds fans following his decision to sell Eric to Manchester United in November 1992 – a move, of course, that led to United winning the title that season. Indeed, such was Eric's impact at Old Trafford that he is widely regarded as having been the most influential player of the whole decade in British football.

The fact of the matter is that, Eric, through his need to be the focal point on a big stage, the main attraction of a glamorous, free-flowing team, was much better suited to Manchester United than he was to Leeds.

It is well documented that Eric was not the easiest of players for any manager to handle and that part of his growing dissatisfaction with Howard's methods at Leeds concerned his difficulty in accepting Lee Chapman's prominent part in the Elland Road setup. Eric was able to put all this to the back of his mind when Leeds were winning but when we weren't – as was the case the season after our Championship triumph – it was a different matter. He could not relate to us and we could not relate to him either. The gap between us just grew wider.

In that post-Championship season, when Leeds sunk to the other end of the table and could no longer afford to have even someone of Eric's ability not rolling up his sleeves and battling, the rift between him and Howard became wider than ever following our two European Cup second round defeats by Rangers.

Eric had generally not been very good away from home and Howard really gave him a hard time after our 2-1 defeat in the first leg at Ibrox on 21 October. Eric, expecting to be dropped, was still in a sulk about it when he travelled to London for the match at QPR three days later. Howard planned to use only one striker, and as Lee Chapman was not playing well at the time, he was undecided about who it should be. As Howard and I were discussing it on the coach journey to London, he said: 'I think I will go for Eric.' Howard then decided to discuss it with Eric, but each time he tried to catch his attention, Eric ignored him. Upon our arrival at our hotel, as we were getting our bags off the coach, Howard tried again. He went straight up to Eric and said: 'Eric, can I have a word with you.' Eric just looked at him for a moment, then turned and walked away. 'Sod it,' Howard said to me. 'Chappie [Chapman] is going to play.' The friction between the two got worse at our team meeting just before we were due to leave for the ground. At the start, all the players were sitting there, in shirts and ties – but there was no sign of Eric. Then, as Howard started talking, he came in, wearing a T-shirt and torn jeans, and sat right at the front, staring coldly at Howard. Howard suddenly exploded. 'Right you,' he told Eric. 'You can get your passport and **** off back to France.'

Though Eric played in our next three or four matches, it was no surprise when Howard sold him.

As for Leeds, it did seem strange, to say the least, that we finished as low as seventeenth that season – but not, in my view, when you consider that this was the season in which the change in the back-pass rule was put into operation for the first time.

I have always maintained that the change, whereby keepers were no longer allowed to handle such passes, was one of the best things that have happened in the game during my career. It forced defenders into closer contact with their keepers, as opposed to pushing up to squeeze the play, and gave everybody more space to settle on the ball and use their skill. But it caught Leeds out in a big way. Our central defenders, Chris Whyte and Chris Fairclough – outstanding ball-winners – found it difficult suddenly to adjust to a situation where they were also called on to involve themselves in the creative play as well. It also presented problems to Lee Chapman, in that the ball did not come through to him as early as it had before, and he had to hold it longer. The rule change was great for Manchester United. Quite apart from Eric Cantona, they also benefited from having two central defenders who could use the ball as well as Steve Bruce and Gary Pallister. Generally, they had better footballers than we did.

Fairclough, Whyte and Chapman left Leeds at the end of that season. My own sell-by date arrived two seasons later. I played in most of Leeds' 1993/94 matches, but although we finished fifth, I knew that my influence on the team had started to wane. Having gone on as a regular first-team player considerably longer than most other players, I had no problem accepting that it was time to take a back seat.

Over the first half of the 1994/95 season, my first team league appearances were limited to six, the last being the 2-0 home defeat by Liverpool on 31 December. The rest of my time with Leeds was spent as player-coach of the reserves, a role I really enjoyed. With our matches at places like Halifax, often in front of the proverbial three men and a dog, it was a different world from the one I had been accustomed to. But this made no difference to me. I still loved playing and I also loved the challenge of helping to make youngsters like Noel Whelan and Ian Harte better footballers.

The experience whetted my appetite for a career on this side of the game. In March, I was given the chance to start it at Coventry.

# CHAPTER SEVEN

# THE LIFE OF BRYAN

It is often said that managers are only as good as their players. You could also say that managers are only as good as the men who employ them.

Certainly, on the road leading me to one of the biggest jobs in British football at Celtic Park, I have to acknowledge the part that my respective Coventry and Southampton chairmen, Bryan Richardson and Rupert Lowe, played on my journey. As with Ron Atkinson and Howard Wilkinson, I found the pair very different. However, I learned a great deal from both; and I also have a lot of time for both as people, although I found Bryan the easier of the two to work for.

My move to Coventry took place immediately after Coventry's 3-0 defeat at Leeds on 18 March 1995 – Ron Atkinson's fifty-sixth birthday. Ron had only been Coventry manager for a few weeks and both he and Bryan had agreed that the club should also appoint someone who could help him with the coaching and whom he could groom as his successor. According to Bryan, he got out two pieces of paper and suggested they both write down the names they each favoured. In both cases, I was the No. 1 choice. As Coventry's manager myself, from November 1996 to September 2001, I think I must have knocked a few years of Bryan's life. Yet, despite the erratic nature of our results and performances, and the fact that he was eventually compelled to sack me, we have remained very close. So much so that, since he himself was forced out of Coventry, in a boardroom coup in January 2002, we have often talked about the possibility of one day joining forces again somewhere else.

In the 2004/05 season, it might have happened at Manchester City. Bryan was then leading a consortium attempting to gain control of the club; and as this also coincided with reports that City's manager, Kevin Keegan, had made up his mind to take a break from the job himself, Bryan indicated that if the takeover bid was successful – and I was still free – he and his partners would want me to succeed Kevin. The plan became more complicated towards the end of the season when Kevin left City and Stuart Pearce took over from him. But as that appointment was made initially on a caretaker basis, I was encouraged to keep waiting in the wings. It was partly for this reason that I kept myself out of a job in football a bit longer than I had originally intended.

There was obviously a limit to the amount of time I could afford to be in this position, and Bryan and I eventually agreed that if his plan did not come to fruition by a certain date, I should consider it the end of the matter. It so happened that the deadline passed at about the same time that I was approached by Celtic.

You often hear managers moaning about not getting enough support from their chairmen but there is no way I could ever make that claim against Bryan at Coventry. I reckon it would be impossible for any chairman to back his manager more than he

backed me. He gave me a great deal of freedom and responsibility and I would think that my rapport with him was as strong
as you could find in any manager–chairman relationship. This
was one of the reasons why I turned down the chance to return
to Leeds, as George Graham's successor, in September 1998.

After Leeds sounded me out about the possibility, I saw no
point in talking to Bryan about it until I'd properly considered
the situation myself. However, as the media had picked up the
story, and seemed to assume – wrongly – that I'd said 'yes' to
Leeds, Bryan asked me for clarification.

'I know Leeds want you – what do you want to do?' he asked.
'Well, what do you want me to do?' I replied. Bryan then said
that he did not want me to go, but that because of Leeds' potential he would not stand in my way if I decided to do so. 'So you
really want me to stay?' I said. 'Of course I do,' he reiterated.

That was the end of it. I decided I was staying.

In hindsight, I have my doubts that this was the right decision
for me. The reality of clubs like Coventry is that they are career
stepping stones. So it could be argued that if ever there was a
good time for me to maintain or improve my status as a manager after Coventry finished eleventh in the table (a Premiership
club record) and reached the FA Cup quarter finals in the
1997/98 season, the opportunity presented by Leeds was probably it.

The 1997/98 season was one of the few in which Coventry
had not been involved in a relegation battle, and it was only natural that everybody connected with the club should feel that
this could prove the impetus for a more sustained period of success. However, because of our financial setup, and the problems
in holding on to our best players, it was always on the cards that
we would struggle to maintain our change of fortunes, and that
my reputation as a manager would deteriorate as a consequence.
That's the way it turned out.

Money has become more important than ever in professional football. While it is still possible for clubs to belie their financial positions, as Wigan, Bolton and Charlton have indicated recently, the extent to which they can do so has become more limited. Teams can no longer get by simply on physical power, determination and the right tactics as much as they did when I was a player. At the top level, it all boils down to how much individual technical quality you have – how much you can afford.

Both Coventry and Southampton had seasons in which they exceeded expectations when I was there – for Southampton, it was the 2002/03 campaign when they also finished in their highest ever Premiership position (eighth) and reached the FA Cup Final. But in terms of not getting ideas too far above their station, it is significant that the most lucrative bonus clauses in all my contracts at both clubs related just to keeping them in the Premiership.

All clubs want to push themselves to new levels. Nonetheless, for many of them – and I am particularly referring to those who do not compete regularly in the European Champions League – there comes a point when the amount of money they would have to fork out in transfer fees and wages to give themselves the best chance of stepping into a different category and maintaining it, is often more than they can reasonably hope to get back.

I do have sympathy for club chairmen on this because realism can easily be interpreted as lack of ambition. We managers might not always like the transfer market budgets we have been given. We always tend to want them to be bigger. But as few of us have the full picture of our club's financial situation and are not financial wizards, I do not think we can be too dogmatic about it. By and large, as long as I have trust in the chairman's desire to do the best he can for the football side of the club, and he appreciates what is reasonable to expect under his financial guidance, I am not one to stick pins in a wax effigy of him if I cannot get my own way.

In that respect, the most frustrating time for me was the summer of 2003, before my last season at Southampton.

One of the players I wanted to bring to the club was Emmanuel Adebayor. I first saw the towering Togo-born striker when he was playing for Metz at nineteen. Dennis Rofe and I had gone over to France to watch another Metz player on the recommendation of our European scout, Terry Cooper, but it was Adebayor who caught our eye. After Terry had run the rule over the youngster and confirmed our view of his potential, Rupert Lowe invited him over for discussions about his personal terms. The next thing I knew, the proposed deal was off.

'We are not going to sign him – I don't like his attitude,' Rupert explained. 'He was demanding too much money.'

'What did you offer him?' I asked.

'Well, he's only a young man,' Rupert replied. '£5000 a week.'

Rupert added that he'd been taken aback by Adebayor's reaction to the offer and that the player told him he was going to Monaco.

'That's not surprising, Mr Chairman,' I said. 'No wonder he took the huff with you. How can you offer him five grand a week when he will be playing in the Premiership with players getting double or treble that?'

Rupert did have a point about Adebayor's attitude, as was underlined in the 2005/06 season by reports of his clashes with Monaco's coach and missed training sessions. Even so, our assessment of his ability was spot on. In addition to his European Champions League performances for Monaco, he played a prominent part in Togo's surprise qualification for the 2006 World Cup Finals and, of course, in January 2006 he was bought by Arsenal.

Another post-FA Cup Final disappointment at Southampton was the loss of our England left back Wayne Bridge to Chelsea. Most clubs would have found it difficult to turn down the £7 million Chelsea were prepared to pay for him, but I felt that Wayne's departure at that time would cause more problems than Rupert realised. It was not just a question of us finding someone to replace Wayne; because of his ability and style of play, we had to change virtually the whole left side of our team. While moving to Chelsea was a tremendous move for Wayne, I was sure that, had Rupert told him he would have to stay at Southampton, at least for the time being, it would not have had an adverse effect on his performances for us. I said to Rupert: 'Wayne might be angry about it initially, but knowing him as I do, he will just get on with it.'

Allied to this was Rupert's reluctance to try to buy the two players who I felt could make the biggest difference to the team – Steed Malbranque and Louis Saha of Fulham. To me, the attacking flair of the two Frenchmen, their ability to do something out of the ordinary to unlock defences, was exactly what we required to improve the side significantly. 'If we can get those two, we'll be away,' I said. Fulham had paid £5 million for Malbranque and £2.1 million for Saha and, although the latter was sold to Manchester United midway through the 2003/04 season for nearly £13 million, we had been led to believe that we might be able to get the pair for £11 million. Rupert, however, took the view that the overall cost to Southampton for these players was too high.

Another reason why he was unwilling really to push the boat out to land Malbranque and Saha, despite the club's income from the FA Cup and the sale of Wayne, was that Fulham were also in the Premiership. Rupert did not like handing big transfer market cheques to fellow Premiership clubs. He did do so in July 2001 when he forked out £4 million (still a record fee for

Southampton) for Rory Delap from Derby, and another exception, of course, was Peter Crouch from Aston Villa for £2
million in 2004. But generally, Rupert's attitude was: 'Why make
our rivals financially stronger and ourselves financially weaker?'

All this led me to the view that I had possibly taken
Southampton as far as I could, although I have to stress that this
was by no means the only factor in my decision to take a break
from the job when my contract expired at the end of the season
and that there was no real animosity between Rupert and me
over these issues. While I found it difficult to agree with Rupert's
stance – as I feel many non-businessmen in the world of football
would have done – I could understand it.

That is still the case. Even in the light of what has happened
to Southampton since my departure, I still have an open mind
about whether it would have been a different story if the club's
transfer market policy had been less conservative. There are a
number of clubs which, having played above themselves in one
season and invested heavily in new players to keep progressing,
have ended up with egg on their faces.

Every season, the bar – the overall standard – gets raised. The
smaller the club, the more the challenge of raising it resembles
that of trying to climb a greasy pole. It was like that at Coventry.

To this day, Coventry's greatest claims to fame, apart from
their surprise FA Cup success in 1987, concern the number of
late relegation escapes they have experienced and the fact that
they managed to spend as long as thirty-four years in the top
flight. In no fewer than ten of those seasons they had to wait
until the last day to be sure of keeping their place. Because of the
nature of the club, its culture and financial limitations, I think it
is fair to say that the odds will always be heavily stacked against
anyone dramatically changing their image.

But it was impossible not to admire Bryan Richardson's
enthusiasm and determination in striving to beat those odds and

bring Coventry a greater measure of respect. Bryan's 'think big' philosophy was immediately apparent when, upon my signing for Coventry, he arranged for Lesley and me to start our lives in the area in a palatial suite at Coombe Abbey, one of England's biggest and most luxurious hotels. Set in five hundred acres of parkland, it is probably the most imposing place I have ever stayed in. What I remember most about it was the massive four-poster bed we had. It was so big that I virtually had to take a short run at it in order to get into it.

Unlike most club chairmen, Bryan has been a professional sportsman himself. He is a former county cricketer, like his older brothers, Peter and Dick, both of whom played for England, and has an innate appreciation of the pressures on performers at this level. He spoke the same language as us. But the major difference between him and Rupert was that he was more of an entrepreneur by nature – he initially made his money in a publishing business specialising in in-flight airline magazines, whereas Rupert did so as a City banker – and was more prepared to take financial gambles.

I could possibly have done with a bit of Rupert in Bryan at Coventry because, when it came to nominating potential signings, I did not do as much homework on some of the players as I should have done. I needed to be challenged on them more. Then again, I could have done with a bit of Bryan in Rupert at Southampton. I have often thought that if you could cross Bryan Richardson with Rupert Lowe, you really would have the perfect chairman.

Bryan was so enthusiastic about raising the profile of Coventry City that, when it came to signing players, I occasionally worried about the money involved more than he did.

'Be careful,' I'd tell him. 'Are you sure we can afford it?'

'Don't concern yourself with that,' he'd say. 'It's not your problem.'

That was his attitude when we signed Robbie Keane from Wolves in August 1999. Keane was nineteen and the £6 million Coventry had to pay for him – a record transfer fee for a teenager moving between British clubs – is still the highest fee ever paid for a player by Coventry. It proved one of the shrewdest signings of all time, as almost twelve months later we received £12.5 million for Robbie from Inter Milan. However, at the time Coventry landed him, my reaction was partly one of guilt at having set the transfer in motion through my praise of him to Bryan.

At Manchester United, Fergie had gone on record as saying that Robbie was only worth £500,000 – which I think was basically an example of Fergie mind games to force the price down – while at the other end of the scale John Gregory at Aston Villa had bid £5.5 million. As far as I was concerned that in itself made us non-runners in the race to sign him, let alone Wolves' determination to hold out for the extra half a million. Most clubs felt it was too much for someone of Robbie's age and inexperience, but not Bryan.

As he has said: 'We had done badly again the previous season, and I'd had enough of it [battling against relegation].' The subject of Robbie initially came up when Bryan asked who I considered to be the player who could do the most to improve our team.

'Robbie Keane,' I said. 'I would really love him but we could never afford him.'

'Never mind about that,' Bryan replied. 'Let's see what happens.'

A few nights later, when I was ill in bed at home and asleep, I was woken by a telephone call from Bryan. 'Right, we are going to do it – we are going to go for Keane,' he said, and put the phone down.

The following day I thought I must have been dreaming. I

remarked to Lesley: 'I am sure the chairman rang me and said he was going to go for Robbie Keane. Can't be.' But a couple of hours later, he rang again to say: 'It's on.'

I was gobsmacked, which no doubt was also the reaction of Wolves' chief executive at the time, John Richards, when Bryan approached him about Robbie. Bryan's account of it is that he telephoned Richards on a Tuesday morning and arranged to have a sandwich with him in his Molineux office at lunchtime. When he arrived, he said: 'John, I want to talk to you about signing Robbie Keane.'

Richards then explained that Wolves had already had offers of between £4.5 and £5 million but there was no way they were going to let Robbie go for less than £6 million.

'Okay,' Bryan said.

'What do you mean "okay"?' Richards asked.

'We will give you six,' Brian told him.

When Brian telephoned to let me know about the deal, my reaction was almost one of panic. Even after he explained that the payment for Robbie would be made in instalments over three years, I remember saying: 'Oh s**t. You do not have to do this, you know. I am sure we can get by without it.'

It is no secret that Coventry fell into debt during Bryan's period at the helm. Though some reports have indicated that it was by as much as £60 million and that the club came close to bankruptcy, Bryan has always vigorously denied this. He has claimed that the club's financial position was exaggerated by some of his opponents on the board. I do not have enough knowledge about the subject to comment on it, but having worked with Bryan so closely behind the scenes, I can present a different picture of him from the one that has been portrayed in the media.

Though I am sure Brian will concede that he made some mistakes, he deserves considerably more praise for his work at

Coventry than he has been given. Coventry made a transfer market profit over my five years as manager. The fees for our buys amounted to £55 million, but sales brought in around £71 million. In addition to the £12.5 million for Robbie Keane, others sold for more than we paid for them included John Hartson, Darren Huckerby and George Boateng, whose transfers brought us respective profits of £5 million, £4.5 million and £4.25 million.

As Bryan appreciated that Coventry were essentially a selling club rather than a buying one, the ability of people like me to improve the market value of the players was crucial. Of the established players I inherited at Coventry, I was particularly proud of the way that Dion Dublin blossomed. Signed by Phil Neal from Manchester United for £1.9 million six months before my arrival, Dion, having struggled to make an impact as a Premiership player, became an England international and was sold to Aston Villa for £5.75 million. But for his determination to go to Villa, as opposed to other clubs who were interested in him, the fee would have been even higher. In the business sense, you could not help being impressed by some of Bryan's work behind the scenes.

The best example – and one that I think sums up the wheeling and dealing expertise of a lot of club chairmen – was the remarkable saga concerning the Croatian international defender Robert Jarni just before the start of the 1998/99 season.

Bryan spent two days in Seville negotiating a fee for Jarni with the president of the player's club, Real Betis. Having finally settled on £2.6 million – to be paid in one £1 million and two £800,000 instalments over three years – and reached agreement with Jarni on his personal terms, his next step was to bring Jarni to Coventry for his medical. The pair arrived on a Friday night, on the eve of our last pre-season friendly at home to Español and, while they were both watching that game from the

Highfield Road directors' box, Bryan became aware that Jarni was having a heated argument with his wife on his mobile.

'Is there a problem?' Bryan asked. 'No, problem, no problem,' Jarni replied. Bryan, though, suspected otherwise and he was proved right when it quickly transpired that Real Madrid now wanted Jarni; that Real Betis wanted to rip up their provisional contract with Coventry in favour of selling him to them for more money; and that his wife was putting him under a lot of pressure to remain in Spain. We knew there was no point in hanging on to Jarni, but Bryan was determined that we would at least be well rewarded financially. To avoid giving Real Betis any possible loopholes through which to get out of their provisional agreement with us, he waived the clause relating to Jarni's physical examination and immediately sent the club the first payment of £1 million. Then a couple of days later, as the dispute over Jarni escalated, he sent them the extra £1.6 million. They actually refused to accept the money and we refused to take it back. It was farcical. Then, when Real Betis had been forced to accept that Jarni was our player, Bryan also came into conflict with Real Madrid over the fee we wanted for him. Bryan, though, continued to stick to his guns.

The result was that we received £3.35 million, giving us a profit of £750,000. Not bad going for a player who had only been attached to Coventry for about ten days, and not kicked a ball for us even in training. In that close season, Bryan also brought Coventry a £750,000 profit through the sale of the Romanian international centre-forward Viorel Moldovan to Turkey's Fenerbahce – just five months after he'd been signed from Grasshoppers Zurich.

In view of these sorts of transactions, it might seem strange that Coventry were not in a stronger financial position. That was mainly down to the contracts players were given.

To improve our performances and results, we needed better

quality players – and because of the image of the club as perennial strugglers, the only way we could persuade such men to come to us was to offer the most attractive salaries. I am not ashamed to admit that this was partly why I chose to come to Coventry myself. I was one of the highest paid people at the club when I joined. But, through Bryan's eagerness to move the club forward, the overall wage bill shot up to the point where I became one of the lowest paid. It was particularly strange to be in that position when I was player-manager. There were even some players who were not in the team – who were in the stand watching me run my guts out on the pitch on a Saturday – who were being paid more than me. They were getting so much in basic wages that they never even asked about their possible bonuses.

Looking back on it now, I feel that was wrong. The manager should be the best paid employee at any club in my opinion. At the time, however, I was rather laid back about it. The situation did not really bother me because I was conscious of being at the bottom of the managerial ladder in experience and I took the view that, irrespective of what others were being paid, I could only benefit in the long run by working with better players.

Financial experts have stated that it is generally advisable for clubs' wage bills to be no more than 50 per cent of their turnover. They argue that the absolute limit – and this applies to clubs with the greatest commercial power – should be 70 per cent. In our last season in the Premiership, when our average gate of 19,000 brought in just £5.3 million – the amount Manchester United raked in on gate receipts in only two matches – and our overall income was £22 million, the ratio was almost 80 per cent. It was difficult enough to cope with this in the Premiership; when Coventry were relegated, it became impossible.

The other major problem – and Bryan has long argued that it was even more of a financial blow to Coventry than relegation –

concerned the delays on his plans (and the eventual scaling down of them) for a new stadium for the 2001/02 season. Of course, in cases where grounds have not provided much scope for development, especially for non-football income sources such as corporate hospitality and catering, a number of clubs have benefited enormously from selling their traditional homes and relocating to more modern premises. For most of them, the step has been crucial to their very survival. Ironically, in addition to Arsenal's change of address in 2006, the other most recent moves among Premiership or Championship clubs have been those of Southampton in 2001, shortly before I joined them, and Coventry in 2005.

I should imagine that Coventry's eventual switch from their antiquated 23,000-capacity Highfield Road ground, some three years after Bryan's departure from the club, will have been quite emotive for him. It was a pity he was no longer involved with Coventry when their new Ricoh stadium was unveiled, given his initial groundwork.

As impressive as the Ricoh Arena is, the state-of-the-art stadium Bryan originally had in mind – it would have been the first in Britain with both a retractable roof and pitch – was mind-boggling. It was perhaps typical of Bryan to come up with a stadium blueprint as ambitious as that, and whatever one might think about the practicality of the dream I cannot help but admire him for it.

Not surprisingly, the same applies to his willingness to stand firmly in my corner in situations in which a lot of chairmen would have isolated themselves from me.

During the periods in which I was at my lowest ebb, Bryan did much to keep me going.

One such occasion was the 3-0 home defeat by West Ham in the opening weeks of our 2000/01 relegation season. I had become used to being up one minute, down the next – that comes with the territory at clubs in the lower half of the table – but we were so bad against West Ham that I was convinced I'd lost the plot and would be doing everybody a favour – including myself – if I called it a day. Bryan, realising how depressed I was, asked his children to take his wife and guests back to his house, and came straight over to my home to try and cheer me up.

'I am not sure that I can still motivate the players,' I told him. 'I think you might be better off getting someone else.'

He was having none of it. 'There is no doubt in my mind that you are a good manager and that you can be one of the best,' he told me. He added that he felt I had allowed myself to get too close to the picture. 'All you really need to do is simply to take two or three days off,' he said.

This did not have much effect on Coventry's results. Even so, the closer they got to losing their Premiership place, the more Bryan seemed to stick his neck out for me. In one newspaper interview near the end of that season, he said: 'People knocking Gordon now have short memories. I remember Gordon in his first eighteen months here as a player and how he kept us up single-handed. They were the most influential performances I have seen by one man – when he was on the pitch, he made the average players in our team much better. We would not be in the Premier League now if it wasn't for him.'

This backing for me when Coventry were at the bottom of the table brought him criticism not just from the fans but some of his fellow Coventry directors. I was not privy to what went on in the Coventry boardroom – I have never been one to take any interest in that side of football – but Bryan has said that the consensus of opinion there was that he was too close to me. One or two directors poked fun at him over this. On one occasion, I learned that when someone in the boardroom asked where he was after a match, he was told: 'He's probably in the dressing room holding the manager's hand.'

A lot of people involved with Coventry might well have felt that Ron Atkinson had a lot to answer for, if only because I am not sure I would have decided to go there but for his presence at the club. I was far from unhappy in the job I was doing at Leeds and felt I could afford to wait for another opening either there or somewhere else. The fact that Ron was Coventry manager was also the main reason why I started playing first-team football again in that 1994/95 season – at the age of thirty-eight – and ended up going on until I was forty. It had certainly not been my intention to make a comeback. As far as I was concerned, I joined Coventry as first-team coach and nothing else. It had been three months since my last league appearance, for Leeds, and I was convinced that my body had done all it could. Indeed, if anybody else but Ron had asked me to play again, I would have said no. I have the feeling that from the day I joined Coventry, it was always his intention to get me back playing again. When I was taking part in training matches, he would often tell me: 'You are the best player at this club.' It took him and Garry Pendrey six weeks really to put the thought of a comeback in my mind, and even then I was more or less cajoled into it.

I surprised myself. I was no Wayne Rooney, but because of my determination not to let Ron down and the long break I'd had from playing in the Premiership, I was able to revive myself. It was a bit like the last spurt of energy from a dying man. I was in the starting line-up in five of the last six matches that season, a period in which Coventry dropped from twelfth to eighteenth (one place above the relegation zone) and finally finished sixteenth through a 3-1 win at Tottenham and a goalless draw at home to Everton. The game against Spurs, which ensured that we remained in the Premiership, was unquestionably the most memorable of the six for me, partly because it was Jürgen Klinsmann's last match for Spurs at White Hart Lane. As for the result, I set up our first and third goals by Peter Ndlovu and

Dion Dublin, both with crosses, and it was from a foul on me by Justin Edinburgh that Peter Ndlovu scored our second from a penalty.

From then on, most of my other Coventry appearances were as a substitute. I played in a total of twelve Premiership matches the following season, when Coventry only ensured their Premiership survival on the last day, on goal difference; and nine in the 1996/97 season, when another win at Tottenham enabled us to pull off arguably the most famous of all Coventry final-day relegation escapes.

By that time I had become Coventry's manager and the encouragement for me to extend my Premiership playing career – notably in the five matches leading up to that nerve-wracking Tottenham game – came from Gary McAllister. Gary, signed from Leeds before the start of the season, was inevitably finding it increasingly difficult to cope with the huge responsibility on his shoulders, in a struggling team, and felt that it was essential to have someone who could take some of the weight off him. 'I could do with some help from you here,' he told me.

Though everybody knew that I would take over from Ron, the fact that it happened about a year earlier than had first been mooted, and that it came when Coventry were second from bottom – after a dreadful run of one win in the opening twelve matches – made the situation somewhat embarrassing for me. While Ron was very supportive of me, I do not think he was entirely happy about being forced out of the job, into the position of Director of Football, at the time. The circumstances made it seem more like a sacking than a job change. It was a blow to his pride.

I was not entirely happy about it either. It worried me that I might be accused of having engineered our change of jobs – which, though I had been finding my coaching role too restrictive, was far from the case.

However, I suspect that, for all his disappointment at being moved upstairs, Ron, who had become the longest-serving manager in the Premiership, was relieved about it deep down.

If anyone needed a break from the front line, it was Ron. It was a really bad time for him, in more ways than one.

Ron had been under enormous stress on the football side. Though he spent almost £17 million on new players, including what I considered to be good British buys like Kevin Richardson, David Burrows, Paul Telfer, Paul Williams, Richard Shaw, Noel Whelan, Eoin Jess, Liam Daish and McAllister, his total of Coventry wins was just fourteen in sixty-four matches. He was also under a lot of pressure in his personal life through the long, serious illness of his father, to whom he was exceptionally close. The strain on him showed. Both Garry Pendrey and I noticed that he had changed, that he was not the same Ron Atkinson we had known before. He was not as sharp with the one-liners, and he just looked older and more careworn.

It was not long before the same could be said about me.

## CHAPTER EIGHT
# WHELAN AND DEALING

The experiences of a manager can be nothing if not bizarre. I had only been in the job five minutes when I was given my first example of that.

It happened on a Sunday afternoon at Ron Atkinson's farewell bash as Coventry manager, at a countryside pub recommended by a member of the coaching staff. Having promised to take Lesley and the kids to a fireworks display that evening, I only had two or three half pints of lager. But by about 5 p.m., I felt as if I had drunk the pub dry. I felt so ill that I had to be taken home. I immediately went to bed and slept from 6 p.m. right through to eight the next morning.

I cannot be sure why I ended up that way, but I have a strong suspicion that someone spiked my drink. Knowing what I do about the mischievious conduct of professional footballers when they are letting their hair down, it would not surprise me if it was one of the players; and if forced to select the likeliest one to have played such a joke on me, I would probably plump for Noel Whelan.

After I'd left the party, Noel had a bust-up with Dion Dublin – apparently, believe it or not, over Noel's attempt to land his fellow striker in trouble with his partner by giving him a love bite. That evening he was caught drink driving, for which he was banned for twenty months.

What a welcome to the world of football management.

I thought I was pretty streetwise as a player, but some of the things I had to deal with when I crossed over to the other side of the fence, and my responsibilities became far more wide-ranging, did affect me.

During my spell as Coventry's coach, Ron Atkinson felt – rightly – that I tended to allow my frustration over players not producing the performances I expected, to get to me too much. 'I used to advise Gordon to calm down,' Ron has said. 'He would be quite excitable and go over the top.'

One incident to which I am sure Ron was referring was my altercation with our keeper Jonathan Gould in a pre-season friendly against Gothenburg behind closed doors. At thirty-nine, I was also playing in that game because we were short of numbers, and after one of the goals Gothenburg scored – in my view as a result of Jonathan staying back for a cross – I immediately said to him: 'You should have come for that.' He then turned on me, mentioning a mistake I had made in giving the ball away. 'My career is finished anyway,' I said. 'We are talking about you here.' Unfortunately, it got more and more heated.

'If that is what you feel about me, then get rid of me,' he said.

'Well, Ron and I try each day to get rid of you, but nobody wants to sign you,' I retorted.

I realised straight away that this was below the belt. I later explained to him that it was no use him turning on me in front of the other players; as the coach, there was no way I could allow him to have the last word in a dispute in such a situation and have me lose face. However, what I said was totally uncalled for. I apologised to him and I also apologised to his father, Bobby, the former Coventry, Wimbledon and Wales manager who was at the game. But I felt badly about it for some time.

Once I was in Ron's position, I found that his comment applied to my reaction to all the other common frustrations of management.

Although I am still not exactly the most laid back manager in the world, I do think that I have mellowed. I have had to – in order to remain relatively healthy in mind and body (note that word 'relatively'); there is no way that I could have carried on blowing fuses as often as I did at Coventry.

For obvious reasons, I found it particularly difficult to be Mr Super Cool when I had the added pressure of playing. I still cringe about what I said to Arsenal's captain, Tony Adams, during our 1-1 draw at home to the Gunners towards the end of the 1996/97 season. It started with Adams clattering me near the touchline; as I was chasing a ball towards the corner flag (a bit daft, I know, for a forty-year-old), he came across to boot it away and then followed through and caught me on the chest.

'The next time, I am going to knock you into the stand,' he warned. 'Don't start that, Tony,' I said. 'You have had many years to do that to me and you have not been able to do it once. Even though I am now forty, you've no chance.' Instead of dropping the matter, he kept chuntering on about it. About a minute later, when we were close to each other in the middle, he was still telling me about the harm he was going to inflict on me. 'Look,' I said. 'Why don't you just **** off and go for a drink, and let the rest of us get on with the game.'

Not surprisingly, as soon as I mentioned that word 'drink' – the most sensitive of subjects to Tony because of his much-publicised battle against alcoholism – I knew I was in trouble. His eyes were popping and in no time at all his big Arsenal mates were gathered menacingly around me. They did not want my autograph, that's for sure. It was just as well that the match was being shown live on TV because otherwise I am sure I would have got thumped. As it was, all I could see were angry Arsenal faces and I was thinking: 'Where's my help? Where are the other Coventry boys?'

Although Tony had started it, I knew that I had been out of order and that I could not possibly let him leave our ground without an explanation and an apology. We came face to face in the dressing room corridor, and when I asked if I could have a word with him, he said: 'Well, I was just coming to have a word with you.' We then went into my office, and I told him: 'I have great respect for you as a footballer. But you have to remember that I am under a lot of pressure here [as a young manager trying to keep Coventry in the Premiership] and you set the whole thing off. I felt I had to hit back at you in some way, but I accept that I should not have said what I did.'

'No problem,' he said. 'All forgotten.'

I am not sure if he truly meant it, but fortunately for me the fact that I packed in playing at the end of the season meant that I was never in a position to find out.

I have always been touchy about any form of oppression – little guys being picked on by the big guys, for example – so being with a club as low in the pecking order as Coventry was probably quite appropriate for me. Such was my determination not to allow anybody to abuse or make fun of us that I even had words about it once with the West Ham tannoy announcer. Near the end of the Coventry–West Ham FA Youth Cup Final second leg at Upton Park, with the Hammers leading 9-0 on aggregate, he made a sarcastic remark to the effect that after the final whistle the trophy would be presented to the winning team – 'whoever that may be'.

The guy did not mean to cause offence. To him, and probably most others, it was just a bit of harmless fun. But me being me, the remark grated.

It was at Coventry, where my inexperience and the team's position sometimes made me feel that the whole world was against us, that I was liable to get particularly het up over bad refereeing decisions.

Because of the extent to which the decisions – or mistakes – of referees and other match officials can influence results, and the emotional nature of the game, I would say that it is virtually impossible for any manager to avoid clashes with such figures. This, indeed, is arguably the most common aspect of management. While I am not proud of some of the comments I have made about referees – I know my criticism has been beyond the acceptable limit occasionally – I can at least claim to have been in good company.

No individuals are capable of causing a manager to burst a blood vessel quite like the men in black. This does not stem simply from our perception of the standard of referees, but also from the way in which some of them conduct themselves.

I never cease to be irritated by the referees who give the impression of wanting to be celebrities. They all say: 'I do not want to be in the spotlight – I just want to do my job with the minimum of fuss and bother.' This, though, is not always the case. They can change, in the same way that one or two of the businessmen who become football club chairmen can change. The publicity they get is like a drug to them. Before I joined Coventry, I had only been sent off once in a competitive match – during a Leeds defeat at QPR, when I told the referee that he had cost us the game (well, that's the cleaned up version of my comments to him anyway). That, though, was tame stuff compared to some of my brushes with officialdom when I was Coventry's coach and manager.

Early in the 1996/97 season, three months before I took over from Ron Atkinson, there were two such clashes in the space of just six days.

The first came in Coventry's 2-0 defeat at Chelsea, our third Premiership match. I thought that the referee, Paul Danson and his assistants had failed to spot a handball by Dan Petrescu which had led to Frank Leboeuf putting Chelsea ahead.

The nature of our protests caused both Ron Atkinson and myself to be charged with misconduct by the Football Association; and, before we were due to appear before the Disciplinary Commission in Birmingham to answer them, we – and especially me – landed in hot water with these gentlemen again.

It happened the following week, when I was sent off while playing in a reserve match against West Bromwich Albion, but refused to leave the field. I had been booked in the opening five minutes for a remark to the referee, Tony Green, about him allowing an opponent to get away with clobbering me. Later, when the ball ran out of play for a throw-in, a player I was chatting to said: 'Where do they get these ***** refs from?' Green had his back to us, and when he turned around, he said to me: 'Right you are off,' and showed me the red card.

Despite other players confirming that the remark had not come from me, he remained adamant that it had. 'I am not going,' I told him. He replied that, if I did not go, he would. 'OK, see you later,' I said. Green and his assistants did leave the field but 10 minutes later, with me having decided – reluctantly – to accept the sending-off and fight against it afterwards, they returned to resume the match. All of which brought me a second misconduct charge.

Fortunately, Ron and I got away with just a warning over the first one. As for the second, I was fined £2,000 and Ron, for his comments to Green in support of my action, was fined £750.

I have always been sensitive about the officious manner in which some match officials talk to you. They make you feel like a schoolboy being lectured by a teacher, which for somebody with my personality and temperament is always bound to be difficult to handle. The match officials with whom I have had the most fractious relationship have been Steve Dunn and Mike Tingey.

My biggest bust-up with Tingey concerned his part – as the referee's assistant – in me being banished from the touchline during Coventry's 2-1 defeat at Chelsea in January 1999. The incident arose when our midfielder George Boateng went down injured and the ball ran out of play – to where I was standing in the technical area – for a Chelsea throw-in. I picked the ball up, thinking that the referee, Jeff Winter, was going to allow George to receive treatment; and as he signalled otherwise, I let it go. In doing so, I unwittingly stopped Chelsea taking the throw as quickly as they wanted; two of their players had run towards me to take the ball off me, only to find I had already thrown it back on to the pitch.

Thinking – wrongly – that this was time-wasting on my part, they started shouting at me. The technical area then resembled a battle zone with players from both sides and stewards – all to the right of me – involved in an angry mêlée and Jim Blyth standing between them and me to make sure that I did not come to any harm. Once some measure of order had been restored, Winter, having discussed the incident with Tingey, came over to me and said: 'I am sending you off.' When I asked why, he said: 'I'm not telling you – just get off.'

To my amazement, when we received the FA report the following week, I discovered I was being accused of 'inciting violence'. At my disciplinary hearing, my lawyer Peter McCormick, a Leeds director when I was a player at Elland Road and a close friend, asked Tingey if he had seen the incident. He replied that he had seen everything that had happened and that, in his opinion, I had started the trouble. We then used a video of the match, from a Sky TV camera directly above the dugout, to show that this had not been the case and that Tingey, who'd also been on my right and had around twenty people between him and me, could not possibly have had a proper view of the incident anyway. The FA changed their charge to that of me stepping outside the technical area, which I thought was also farcical because I had to do this to avoid the flying fists and boots.

Managers have long memories for such clashes. Hence the fact that after my last Southampton match at Arsenal in February 2004, in which Tingey kept his flag down for a Thierry Henry goal which I had no doubt was three or four yards offside, I found it impossible to stop my innermost feelings about it to rise to the surface. As Tingey and I passed each other in the dressing room corridor, I blurted out: 'I suppose that was your way of paying me back for what happened at Chelsea?'

Rightly or wrongly, I was rarely happy about Dunn's refereeing performances in Coventry matches. I remember one game against Wimbledon at Selhurst Park when I encouraged Bryan Richardson to confront him. After the game, Bryan found me leaning against the wall in the dressing room tunnel, shaking my head.

'What a dreadful performance by the referee,' he said.

'I agree,' I said. 'Why don't you go and tell him?'

Bryan, even more charged up than I was, immediately burst into the referees' room. I do not know what he said to Dunn, but it was enough to bring him a £500 FA fine (which he still reckons I should have paid on his behalf).

Dunn was instrumental in my other sending off as a manager, when he was the fourth official for Southampton's home match against Everton in September 2002. It arose from the confusion over the rule relating to managers and coaches in the technical area during matches. During the close season, the guidelines on this had been amendeded and my understanding of the situation was that clubs could have more than one person standing in that zone (as long as only one was directly involving himself in the game). Therefore, when I came down from the directors' box to stand behind Gary Pendrey in the technical area during the Everton match, I was taken aback to find Dunn tapping me on my shoulder and telling me brusquely to sit down.

It was not: 'Would you mind sitting down', or 'Please sit down, Gordon', it was: 'Sit. Down.' He spoke to me as if I was a small child, which put my back up straight away.

'No,' I said.

'Sit down now, or I am going to get the referee [Steve Bennett],' he replied.

'Do what you want,' I said. 'It doesn't matter to me because I know the rules and you clearly don't.' Bennett came across, and as an insurance against again being charged with a 'crime' I had not committed, I took the unusual step of bringing over a police officer to act as an independent witness to our conversation.

'Why don't you sit down?' Bennett asked. 'He [Dunn] says you are being abusive to him.' I tried to explain the situation, but it did not make any difference. I had to go back to the stands. It worked out satisfactorily for me in the end as the FA decided that I did not have a case to answer.

One should not generalise; there are some excellent match officials, as well as what I believe to be inadequate ones. But football is a highly emotive game and when you have gone through the experiences that I have, generalisations (of the negative kind) are difficult to avoid. It is the same with players' agents, the other group of people who might have had a lot to answer for had I keeled over with a heart attack at Coventry.

I lost count of the number of faxes I received from agents.

They used the scattergun approach; the lists of players they put forward to us as potential signings were absolutely overwhelming and, given the obscure professional backgrounds of the vast majority of those players, I quickly discovered that any attempt to sift through all of them was too time-consuming. After a while, most of the circulars – at least those from the representatives I did not know and trust – went straight into my wastepaper basket. When I got to Southampton, I informed all the agents to send their circulars to Rupert Lowe.

At Southampton, my personal involvement with these men became more remote, which suited me perfectly. Just having to sit in on some of Bryan Richardson's negotiations with them at Coventry – and see at first-hand how dishonest and morally bankrupt a few were – was possibly the aspect of the job that I found the most difficult to come to terms with.

It did have its light moments, however. I remember one agent sending us a video of a Scandinavian goalkeeper he was hoping we would sign. Embarrassingly for him, the previous film on the video – of a pornographic nature involving him and a woman we took to be his wife – had not been totally erased. The first five minutes of the tape were infinitely more entertaining than anything we subsequently saw of the keeper.

Generally, my experience of the way a number of agents conduct their business was equally disconcerting.

For example, what can one make of the guy who falsified the figures on a player's draft contract? Once he and Bryan had reached agreement on the player's terms, Bryan – running late for a meeting elsewhere – wrote down the details and asked him to take the notes to the club secretary, Graham Hover, for him to incorporate them into a formal typewritten contract. As Bryan was in his car heading to his next appointment, he received a call from Graham telling him that, unusually for the chairman, some of his handwritten figures were not clear. It transpired that, after

Bryan had left, the agent arbitrarily changed the fives to sixes and the sevens into eights.

I could never get my head around the instances of agents screwing us to the wall on their clients' personal terms – which I could just about accept as being a valid part of their jobs – then demanding that we give them personal payments of up to £250,000 before the deals could be completed. On at least two occasions, we had two or three agents purporting to represent the same player and actually ending up having a fierce row – in front of Bryan and myself and their client – over how their cuts should be divided.

On another occasion, Bryan and I, after setting up the signing of a centre-forward, waited for hours in his Highfield Road office for the player and his representative to show up for the contract negotiations. The representative telephoned us a few times on his mobile to tell us that they had been held up in traffic and would be with us 'shortly', but they never arrived. The reason was that, unknown to us, they were on their way to another club and only intended to meet us if the other potential transfer fell through.

It was nice to be able to play agents at their own game – and win – occasionally. In my case, there was an interesting battle of wits and wills with Fergie's son, Jason, one of the best-known agents in England, concerning Coventry's midfielder Youssef Chippo.

Youssef was not as good or accomplished a player as his Moroccan colleague Moustapha Hadji, as was reflected by the difference in the transfer fees we paid for the pair (£600,000 for Youssef from Porto in June 2001 and £4 million for Hadji from Deportivo La Coruna the following month) and their Coventry wages – £6000 and £20,000 a week respectively. The latter did seem unfair in Youssef's first season. It was hard to believe he had been languishing in Porto's reserves – on even less money than we were paying him, I should add. Though he lacked Hadji's expertise on the ball, his drive and energy were tremendous assets for us; and not surprisingly, this led to him and Jason Ferguson justifiably pressing us to give him a new, improved contract.

We were prepared to go to £10,000 a week, but he and Ferguson – and maybe Ferguson in particular because I always had the feeling that Youssef could be quite easily led – saw no reason why he should not be on a par with Moustapha. This in itself did not bother me unduly, but I did get irritated by Ferguson's attitude at the meeting in my office – initially just between the two of us – to discuss the matter.

It seemed to me that Ferguson's approach was of a 'we want this, we want that – or else' nature. 'What do you mean "we"?' I said. 'I think you mean "me".' I must admit that, because of my previous conflict with his father, I was possibly touchier and more aggressive towards him than I might have been with anyone else in this situation. I thought: 'I have been bullied by one Ferguson; I am not going to be bullied by another.'

He told me that both Manchester City and Newcastle were keen to sign Youssef and that if Coventry did not give him what he wanted he would set his sights on a move. This prompted me to call Youssef into the room and get the Manchester City and Newcastle managers, Joe Royle and Bobby Robson, on the phone. I asked them if they wanted to sign Youssef. Joe said 'no', and Bobby said: 'Well, I might be interested later in the year, but not now.' At my request, Joe and Bobby immediately sent me faxes confirming what they had said. They were passed over to Youssef and Ferguson, and that was the end of the story.

As I have said, losing key players to bigger and more successful clubs was an inevitable part of life at Coventry. However, some outgoing transfers were harder to take than others.

The most controversial Coventry transfer during my time as

manager was unquestionably that of Dion Dublin, our top scorer for four seasons and the club captain, to Aston Villa in November 1998.

Though Dion had signed a new three-year contract a few months earlier, both parties knew that it was only a matter of time before he moved onto a bigger stage. One of the reasons he agreed to the fresh deal was the insertion of a clause allowing him (and us) to enter into negotiations with any club prepared to pay Coventry more than £5 million for him. At that time, the highest offer we had received had been £3 million from Crystal Palace, so when Blackburn bid around £7.5 million for him towards the end of October, just before our League Cup tie at Luton, we were obviously happy to accept it. Dion was also keen on the move at first – so much so that he refused to play against Luton on the grounds of avoiding an injury that might scupper the transfer.

The first I heard of it was through a third party on the eve of the game. 'Dion does not want to miss the chance of a big contract,' he explained. I went ballistic. Then, at my request, I received a call from Dion. When I pointed out that I could force him to play, he said: 'I know, but I feel that if the ball were to come into the box and there was a chance of me getting injured by going for it, I would pull out.' What could I do? Players' contracts stipulate that they must perform to the best of their ability at all times, but I felt that ignoring his comment was a gamble we could not afford.

After the match, which Coventry lost 2-0, there was another shock for us. Aston Villa, having been tipped off about that £5 million-plus transfer clause in his contract, came into the picture; and Dion, encouraged by the thought of not having to uproot himself and his family from their Midlands home, decided he wanted to go to them. Thus, he held all the aces and we were forced to sell him to Villa for £5.75 million. Dion, who had been ordered to train with the reserves after the Luton tie, also got his own way in overturning the fine of two weeks' wages that Coventry imposed on him. His case was heard at a Premiership enquiry, and was based partly on the claim – denied by Bryan – that the chairman told him he could go to Blackburn to discuss his personal terms with them on the day of the Luton game. As for the explanation that Dion had given to me about not wanting to play against Luton, a member of the tribunal told me: 'A stronger manager would have made him play.'

Determined not to give in, Bryan appealed against the ruling, but it was upheld. This, of course, was not the happiest of ways for the fruitful professional relationship between Dion and myself at Coventry to end, although once my initial resentment over his attitude subsided, I was able to view it more philosophically. I think life is too short for one to be too judgmental about people. I do not necessarily condone what Dion did but bearing in mind the level of insecurity among professional footballers – not to say managers – I could still appreciate his point of view.

All players should want to better themselves and, though they do not always go about it in the proper manner, I think we are all entitled to one or two mistakes. Certainly, in Dion's case, I felt it would be wrong to allow one short, dark period in our four years together, to spoil the memories of our good times. And, of course, the point was underlined at the end of January 2006 when I signed him for Celtic.

Bryan, however, who did a great deal for Dion, has found forgiving and forgetting more difficult. The two men had two other clashes. One concerned Bryan's claim that Dion acted as a secret intermediary in Aston Villa's successful bid to sign another important Coventry player, George Boateng (an allegation which was refuted by Dion). The other was when Coventry's relegation fate was sealed – at Aston Villa – in 2001 and Dion, on coming face to face with Bryan in the Villa Park foyer, refused to shake his hand. As for their dispute concerning Boateng, I was convinced that the Ghanaian-born midfielder, who moved to Villa eight months after Dion, had been tapped by someone, even if it was not Dion.

Signed from Feyenoord for just £212,000 midway through the 1997/98 season, it did not take George long to enhance his reputation in the Premiership and, like Youssef Chippo, to start feeling that he was worth a better club than Coventry. The first we knew of Aston Villa's interest in him was after our 1-0 win over them in the FA Cup fifth round in February 1998. Villa's chairman, Doug Ellis, telephoned Bryan to ask if we might be prepared to let him go, and was told 'no'. That was the last we heard about the matter – officially – but the following season, as his stock continued to rise, we began to notice a change in George. I remember a clash with him and his agent when he was unavailable for selection for a match and breached club rules by not being present at the game. Annoyed that he had not even asked our permission to be absent, I gave him a ticking off and he was fined. His agent then told me: 'George has been happy at Coventry, but if you shout at him, he could become unsettled you know.'

Without our knowledge, he spent a lot of his free time back in Holland – he just kept disappearing. If he was not required for training on a Wednesday, he would get a flight to Holland on the Tuesday night and come home early Thursday morning. On his return from one trip, a couple of days before our FA Cup fifth round defeat against Everton in February 1999, he actually fell asleep while I was conducting a team meeting. Much to the amusement of the other players, I stopped talking, crept over to him and shouted his name in his ear: 'I am not boring you am I, George?'

I thought he probably had a cold, but I eventually realised it was down to the tiredness from the travelling he was doing, and the clandestine talks regarding Villa's interest. Ironically, just a couple of weeks after that Everton match, George made Villa keener than ever to sign him. We won 4-1 at Villa Park (our first ever league win there) and George capped a wonderful performance by scoring twice. This, indeed, was looked upon as the game that truly sealed his move.

George asked for a transfer, on the grounds that he needed more money. 'But you are earning decent money here – you are on £10,000 a week,' I said. He then explained that he needed extra to help his family in Ghana, to which I pointed out that he had forked out some £70,000 on a car, and could probably raise all the money he needed just by selling that.

He then put his foot in it. 'If I played for Aston Villa, I would get £17,000 a week,' he said.

He seemed confused when I asked him how he knew this; and, knowing that he is a deeply religious person, I used that to force him to tell me the truth about his links with our Midland rivals.

At first, he denied that he had been approached by them.

'Are you a Christian, George?' I asked.

'Yes,' he replied.

'So you don't tell lies.'

'No.'

Getting increasingly wound up, I repeated the questions, and he gave me the same answers.

But this time, when I added, 'Have you been tapped by someone from Villa', his conscience got the better of him and he said: 'Yes.'

I was as angry as I think I have ever been. I had become so animated that I was virtually doing a tap dance on my desk. But at least it provided some entertainment for the youth team coaches who were having a meeting in the office directly under mine, and could hear everything that was said – or, in my case, screamed. I did go over the top, although in my defence, I think it was a reflection of my anxiety over the thought of what I would do if we lost George. I was still sensitive about Dion's departure and I feared that George, who could both win the ball and play as well – a rare combination – would be equally difficult to replace.

I was still feeling sorry for myself that evening, as Lesley and myself were driving to Stratford-on-Avon to see a film and have a meal out. This turned out to be somewhat unfortunate for a group of boys who were sitting at the back of a bus immediately in front of us and doing their best to wind me up. With one of them making an obscene hand gesture to me, and the others laughing over it, they succeeded. Lesley, reading me like a book, said: 'Just don't bother about it – give it a miss.' But after the sort of day I'd had with George, it was the straw that broke the camel's back.

'No,' I said. 'This is what is happening in Britain now and everybody seems to accept it. After the episode with George, I felt I had to stand up to something and this was it. When the bus stopped, I drove past and turned sharply in front of it to stop the driver moving off. I got out of the car and asked him if I could reprimand the youngsters. 'Be my guest,' he said. I might have changed my mind had I known how big the lads were – as I was giving the one who made the gesture a ticking off, and threatening to write to his school about his behaviour, I realised that he and his mates, who must have been about 16, were all taller than me. So George would clearly have had a lot to answer for if it had turned really nasty.

As with Dion – and indeed all the players I have crossed swords with – my annoyance with George did not last very long. Just before his transfer to Villa was completed, I went around to his house for tea and a chat. He had done a good job for me, and Coventry, and I was grateful for that – just as I know he was grateful for the help he'd received at the club. Some months later, when his first child was born, he even sent me a short note and a picture.

I remember a newspaper interview in which George talked about his impoverished life in Ghana before leaving at the age of ten to live with his father and stepmother in Holland. He recalled: 'In Africa, I'd walk a mile to get water and you had one bucket for a shower. Every summer, my wife and I go back and are faced with the poverty. Once we saw a girl with a basket of fruit. My wife gave her £10 for an orange and the girl started crying. The whole basket was worth less than that and she could not believe someone would do such a thing for her. You come back here [to England] and think, why do I deserve a life like this? But then, after a few months, you get sucked back in and take the luxury for granted.'

It has stuck in my mind because, to a degree, I think the latter point applies to a lot of players.

I once said that, when you become a coach or a manager, it's a bit like taking a sort of oath – in this instance, to make footballers better. All of which brings me back to Noel Whelan.

Of the players I inherited when I took over from Ron, Noel and Gary McAllister were the ones I knew best. Like Gary, Noel had been with me at Leeds; and, as with Gary, I had a big influence on Ron's decision to buy him for Coventry for a then club record fee of £2 million. Noel, who was a few days short of his twenty-first birthday in December 1995 – five months after my own arrival at Highfield Road – had been a graduate of Leeds' youth setup; in my last season at Leeds, he was one of the youngsters I worked with in the reserves.

I had no doubt that he could make a big impact at Coventry. He had the ability to succeed at any club because he had a good touch, he could beat people, he was decent in the air and he had tremendous stamina. The other side of the coin – and this was something I felt I could change – was that Noel, like so many talented players, did not apply himself as well as he should have done.

Nothing is more frustrating to a manager or coach than seeing a player not making the most of his ability. This was particularly difficult for me to handle in Noel's case because, having known him since he was sixteen, and become fond of him – he was an immensely likable lad in a lot of ways – I felt I had a responsibility to look after him. We were a bit like father and son; I sometimes thought that I wanted him to do well more than he did. The challenge for me in helping him to work harder in training and eradicate his irresponsible lifestyle habits was more like a personal crusade.

At Leeds, and for some time at Coventry, we were inclined to fight like cat and dog. I always felt he could be doing more to make himself a really top-class player. The more I could see this slipping away from him, the more uptight I became about it. It was driving me crazy. Apart from his tendency to want to cut corners in training and occasionally in matches, I was even more concerned about what he was getting up to off the field.

He was a hyperactive lad and, being single and living alone, he could attract trouble like a magnet. He was once quoted as saying: 'When you are put into a situation where you are missing half of your life because of football, you feel you still want to go out with your mates and behave normally. You forget who you are. You want to go out and have a few beers with the lads, and situations will crop up and you just don't think.'

The tabloids must have loved him. During one night out in the summer of 1997, while he was recovering from a right ankle problem, he caused further damage – a torn right Achilles tendon – through losing his temper and kicking through a plate glass window. It put him out of action for the opening four months of the 1997/98 season, and brought him a club fine of £8000. Early the following season, he was involved in a brawl at a party in Nottingham, and ended up in hospital with a fractured cheekbone and other facial injuries. His face was in a terrible state – I have never seen a mess like it in my life. When I visited him in hospital, I told him: 'The best advice I can give you is to look at yourself in a mirror.'

Noel, who claimed that he had been attacked with a snooker cue, had been arrested but not charged. Later, one of the police officers involved pointed out: 'If he gets into this sort of trouble again, he could well end up in jail.' That's when I decided that the best way to get Noel on the straight and narrow would be for him to move in with Lesley and me for a while.

He spent about six weeks living at our house, where we made sure that he ate the right food and had plenty of rest. Though he was able to go out and have a social life, he had to be back home at what I considered a reasonable time. He was on his best behaviour, although he did try to pull the wool over our eyes from time to time. One night he asked if he could meet Paul Telfer and watch a video with him at his house. 'Okay,' I said. 'But be back here by 10 p.m.' Shortly after he left, Lesley and I decided to take Craig and Gemma to the cinema; and as we were walking down the aisle towards our seats, just before the film was due to start, who should Craig spot sitting on the right – with a blonde female? Noel Whelan.

The girl, who looked familiar, saw me and tried to get his attention, whereas he just kept staring at the screen, as if pretending that this was not really happening. I told Lesley to take the kids to our seats and went over to where Noel and the girl were sitting. She was still nudging him and whispering and he was still staring at the screen. So I sat beside her and said: 'May I say that you are looking lovely tonight – PAUL.'

'Oh hello, gaffer,' Noel said, doing his best to look as if he was pleased to see me. He then explained that he and Paul had bumped into the young lady at the video shop, and, as she was on her own, he thought he would keep her company. I thought: 'Lying b*****d.'

At any event, when I rejoined Lesley and the children, she said Noel's companion was Coventry goalkeeper Magnus Hedman's girlfriend. 'Oh no,' I thought. 'I don't need this either.' I was anxious to talk to Noel about it, and made sure that we were back at home before his 10 p.m. deadline. However, when he came through the door – at about twenty past – he hot-footed it straight to his room. I said to Lesley: 'This is like having another kid in the house.' As it turned out, the girl he'd been with and Magnus had split up a couple of weeks earlier and – again much to my relief – I also learned that the relationship between her and Noel was platonic. When Noel moved to Middlesbrough in August 2000, I was delighted to receive a letter from his parents thanking me for the help I had given him. Because of my fondness for him, that meant a lot to me. I have mixed feelings about it now because the help was just not enough as far as I am concerned. I still feel that Noel, who has since played for Crystal Palace, on loan, Millwall, Derby, Aberdeen, Boston United and, most recently, Livingston, has not had the success that he should have had.

However, I cannot really complain about what he did for me at Coventry. But for people like Noel, we would have gone down long before we did.

# CHAPTER NINE

# SNAKES AND LADDERS

When a manager arrives at a new club, I feel it is important that he quickly has a meeting with his most prominent or longest serving senior professionals. In striving to get all the players to understand and accept your methods, consultation with these figures tends to be the most effective first step. On becoming Coventry manager, my lieutenants were Steve Ogrizovic, Paul Telfer, Richard Shaw, Kevin Richardson and Gary McAllister, and the support they gave me was excellent. They were all in my first Coventry team in November 1996; and more significantly, they were all in it when we pulled off that extraordinary relegation escape on the last day of the season at Tottenham.

Paul Telfer is one of four players with whom I have been associated at more than one of the three clubs I have managed; the others are Dion Dublin and John Hartson (both Coventry and Celtic) and Paul Williams (Coventry and Southampton). But he is the only one I have signed for more than one club. It was Ron Atkinson who brought Paul to Coventry, in July 1995 (four months after my own arrival). I signed him for Southampton, on a free transfer from Coventry, in October 2001, and for Celtic, from Southampton for £200,000 in July 2005.

There are many players with whom I have found it a pleasure to work. For every player who undermines the image of professional footballers, there are countless others who set the right example. Paul is one of the latter. I once said to him: 'Wherever I go, I would want to take you with me. I would take you anywhere.' Indeed, I look upon Paul in the same way that Brian Clough looked upon John McGovern, the midfielder Clough signed for four of his five clubs.

Like McGovern Paul has tended to be underrated. Part of this is down to his contentment in doing things in the best interests of the team, rather than for himself – which does not make him particularly eye-catching – and the fact that he does not truly appreciate how good he is. He is his own biggest critic, which means that if he is not having a good game he will never look for excuses. There was a good example of that when Celtic were beaten 2-1 by Clyde in the Scottish Cup in January 2006. Paul was one of a number of Celtic players who did not do themselves justice that day, but he was quoted as saying: 'After a game like that, the first thing you do is look at yourself and when you have played so poorly, it is hard to even look at anybody else.' The Clyde defeat was followed by our signing of another full back, Mark Wilson from Dundee United, and the youngster replacing Paul for our league match against United a few days later. Here again, Paul's reaction was to concentrate on getting his own house in order and making sure that he did well in his next game. It's a pity that more players are not as honest with themselves as he is. If anything, he is too honest.

I once had to take him off at half-time – not so much because he was below his best but because it seemed to me that he was torturing himself over it. It was one of Paul's archetypal 'I am not a good player' days. As the other players went out for the second half, I waited behind to explain the decision to him and give him some words of consolation. But before I could speak, he just said: 'Don't say a word. I know I was s\*\*\*e. Just leave it at that.'

It is very rare for him to produce a performance that can even remotely be described as such. He is a very well-rounded player. His passing, shooting and heading are good. On top of this, he is one of the fittest players I have ever known and he has a tremendous footballing brain. That's why, though he is at his best as a right back or right-side midfielder, I have played him in all manner of different positions and roles. Not once has he complained about this. No matter what you ask him to do, he gets on with it with the minimum of fuss and bother.

Oggy is the best goalkeeper, and one of the most remarkable players in any position, that I have known. A member of Coventry's 1987 FA Cup-winning team, he broke every club appearance record during his sixteen-year playing career there, which is why it was so difficult for me to drop him in the 1997/98 season. Oggy, who had only been dropped on one occasion previously, was not playing badly. But the team was looking stale and, bearing in mind the strain Oggy had been under in all but carrying the side on his shoulders for so long, I felt that replacing him with Magnus Hedman – who had been signed in the close season and been outstanding in training – would help freshen it up.

As I was explaining the decision to him, you could tell what a blow it was for him because his hands were shaking. As he had inevitably feared, this marked the beginning of the end for him as a Coventry first team player. But I was determined to give him a memorable finale. His selection for his last match – our final home game of the 1999/00 season against Sheffield Wednesday – at the age of forty-two was my way of making sure that the curtain did not come down on his Coventry career without the supporters getting the opportunity to show publicly their appreciation for what he had done for the club.

Having been out of the first team for some time, he was nervous about it. I think part of him was hoping that I would change my mind. 'I don't want to be remembered as a keeper who let us down,' he said. 'No, you will be fine,' I told him, and he was. We won 4-1.

Richard Shaw is another long-serving Coventry stalwart. Signed by Ron from Crystal Palace in November 1995, he was still playing for Coventry – at thirty-seven – in the 2005/06 season. I was delighted to help arrange for Celtic to play in Richard's testimonial match in April 2006. It was the least I could do after what he and his former central defensive partner, Paul Williams, had to put up with from me when I was Coventry manager. I still do not understand how these two have remained friends with me, because it always bothered me that they were not particularly tall for players in their positions – Richard is five foot ten and Paul six foot – and I was never reticent about telling them this. I used to say to them: 'Look, if I can find two guys who are as good as you, but taller, I will sign them.'

I think I might have unwittingly done a 'Fergie' on them, in that my comments on the subject probably fired them up and made them more determined to prove me wrong. They were close friends as well as a team-mates and such was the bond between them that every time another central defender came into the first team to threaten their partnership, they seemed to grow stronger together. If either had to operate alongside someone else, I am not saying that he did not try to help his partner, but the chemistry was not the same, and though I tried a number of alternative pairings, I always ended up coming back to Richard and Paul.

The faith I had in them also applied to Gary McAllister and

Kevin Richardson in midfield. We must have had the oldest mid-field trio in Britain at the tail-end of the season, when my comeback as a player included me coming on as substitute to join Gary and Kevin in the remarkable 2-1 win at Liverpool (one of the outstanding results in Coventry's history) and Kevin and me coming on to join Gary in the 2-2 draw at Southampton. I was only on the field for the last seven minutes at Liverpool, to help calm us down, whereas at Southampton it was for most of the second half, when we had to chase the game through being 2-0 down. It did seem a bit incongruous, considering that I was forty and Kevin and Gary were thirty-four and thirty-two respectively. We were like Dad's Army. But in that situation, because of their experience and the sort of mentally tough characters they were, I was probably happier playing with them than anyone else.

Gary would be the first to concede that his move to Coventry was a culture shock for him and that it took him time to adjust – at least in terms of his role as the orchestrator of our attacking play. That was why he asked me to start playing again at the end of the season. However, though he did not initially reproduce the form he had shown when we were together at Leeds, he was still contributing to the team.

Nobody was more accurate with free kicks and corners than Gary. This in itself was important to us. All teams do a great deal of work in training on set-piece moves, but without having people who can deliver the ball properly – in a match – they become a waste of time. In that win at Liverpool, after we had gone behind, both our goals – scored by Noel Whelan after seventy minutes and Dion Dublin in the last minute – came from corners by him. People think it is easy to deliver good dead-ball kicks, but I have always maintained that the reverse is true. You have so much time to think about what you are going to do – it is one of the very few actions on a football field that is not instinctive – and therefore the pressure on you to get it right is so much greater. This is particularly the case when your team is a goal down, with a minute or two left.

Kevin was Coventry's captain and highest paid player when I arrived at the club. He deserved to be because, while he did not have the natural technical ability of people like Gary, he had won two Championship medals, with Aston Villa and Arsenal, and, through his work on his game, he just seemed to get better and better. I liked being in his company, talking about football, because he knew the game and had the knack of being able to get his views across without being too dogmatic or aggressive. He was good to play with as well. He never had a lot of pace, but this did not matter as he was so intelligent and could think his way around the pitch. Added to this, he was a good passer of the ball. I am not referring to long passes, but the simple ten- to fifteen-yard balls in-between opponents – which, in fact, are not as simple as they look. Indeed, in my experience, it is passes over such distances that players have the most problems with, especially if they are short on confidence. I often mention this as an example when talking about players not being brave enough. You could never say that about Kevin.

Looking back, it still seems strange to me that Coventry came so close to the drop in my first season. I think that at least six of the players I started with at Coventry were better than those I started with at Southampton, where the team – also second from bottom when I became manager – eventually finished eight points above the relegation zone, in eleventh place.

I have to concede that the more desperate nature of Coventry's battle might have stemmed to some extent from my inexperience. It is often said, with much justification, that managers need to serve an apprenticeship at a lower level before stepping into the Premiership, and my case at Coventry possibly supports that view. As a player or a coach, you think you know the game. But really, insofar as the management side of football is concerned, you only know 30 per cent of it.

An odd aspect of my managerial career is that, whereas the appointment of a new boss often has the effect of giving a team an immediate lift, I appear to have the opposite effect. I reckon that the next club I join would be well advised to send me away on holiday for their first few matches. Apart from my start at Celtic, where that defeat by Artmedia Bratislava was followed by a 4-4 draw at home to Motherwell after we had been 1-0 and 3-1 ahead, my opening matches at Southampton produced a draw and three defeats. It was even worse at Coventry.

My first match was a League Cup replay at home to Gillingham, which we lost 1-0 – and deservedly so. It was Gillingham's first-ever win over a top-division team. This was followed by a more encouraging Coventry performance in the league at Wimbledon, where a great performance by Steve Ogrizovic and goals from Noel Whelan and Dion Dublin enabled us to fight back from two goals down to draw 2-2. But then we suffered three 2-1 defeats, two of them at home against Aston Villa and Tottenham and the other against Derby. This increased the club's run of Premiership matches without a win to ten and put us twentieth in the table – rock bottom.

It was during that run that I made my first Coventry signing – Scotland assistant manager Alex Miller. Immediately after it, striker Darren Huckerby became my first player signing. Both were to prove crucial in helping to keep us afloat. When teams are in trouble, the starting point for managers and coaches in their attempt to improve matters is nearly always their defence – hence my decision to bring Alex on board. I am sure that Alex, now assistant manager at Liverpool, would hate anybody describing him as a 'defensive' coach, but this is an area in which I feel he has excelled.

In training, while Garry Pendrey and I worked on our attacking play, Alex involved himself with the goalkeepers and back four players. It was only to be expected that we would find ourselves singing from different hymn sheets occasionally – as we did when I played in the 3-1 win over Chelsea in April.

On Alex's initiative, we operated with three central defenders and two wing backs that day, and, as the right-side midfielder – aged forty remember – I quickly noticed that the player immediately behind me, Paul Telfer, was not as adventurous in making runs alongside or beyond me as I expected him to be. I remember getting the ball and shouting to Paul: 'What's your problem? Get yourself up the wing – I need your support.' He started to explain that Alex had told him to stay back, but I said: 'I don't care what Alex says. I am struggling for my life here and we need to win games. Get your arse forward.' As he was doing so, he was looking at Alex and shrugging, as if to say: 'Don't have a go at me – it's the gaffer you should be moaning at.' Generally, though, Alex and I complemented each other well.

The signing of Darren Huckerby from Newcastle, prompted by Coventry having scored no more than ten goals in 16 league games, was even more important to us. This had to be one of the best signings of my managerial career. Darren was, and still is, one of my favourite players.

I have to laugh over one or two of the falling outs we had. He once took umbrage with me for describing him as 'a scorer of great goals rather than a great goalscorer'. He came in moaning about it, which was more wearisome than you might think because, when Darren had the bit between his teeth, he never seemed to shut up. It took me ages to convince him that I meant it as a compliment.

Indeed, nobody in English football has scored more spectacular goals than Darren; in that department, I rate him on a par with the likes of Paul Gascoigne and Wayne Rooney. Some of

the things he can do with the ball – notably the way he can go
past two or three defenders and get in a shot or cross – are awesome. I do not think people appreciate how powerful he is.
Another striker I had at Coventry who loves to attack the space
behind defenders is Craig Bellamy. The difference between the
two, though, was that Darren could take a knock better than
Craig. The latter always had to be on the move to stop people
getting close to him because he did not have the body strength to
hold them off. This was less of a problem for Darren. The fact
that he has the courage and confidence to keep trying to beat
opponents can work against him, in that it inevitably increases
the chances of him losing possession. In putting himself into situations that other players would avoid, he is liable to look
brilliant one week, awful the next. Unfortunately, people have
tended to expect him to produce the goods all the time, which is
impossible.

It is well known that Darren performs mainly by instinct, and
that even his own team-mates can have problems anticipating
what he is going to do next, let alone the opposition. For all his
wonderful raw talent, I did find him a difficult player to coach in
facets of the game such as his movement in relation to other
members of the team and his decisions on when and where to
hold the ball.

He frustrated me so much sometimes that I could have cried.
We often made a joke about it and even he had to smile when I
expressed my frustration with him after one training session by
throwing myself on to the ground, straight into a puddle. We
worked him to death in training and he did get better. However,
there came a point when we felt that we could not improve him
further, which was why the £4 million that Leeds offered in
August 1999 was difficult for us to turn down. I still wonder,
though, if this really was the right decision. He is a great crosser
of the ball and, noting the number of chances he has created at

his present club, Norwich, by going on to the left flank and playing the ball into the box with his right foot, it occurs to me that I could have tried him in the sort of role that Marc Overmars filled at Arsenal.

For all his unpredictability, he has done a wonderful job for Norwich, just as he did for Coventry. I will always be grateful to him for his work there. At the time he joined us, he had virtually no background as a Premiership player. He had made only sixteen league appearances for Lincoln (then in the old Third Division) before his transfer to Newcastle in November 1995 and his chances of further development were hampered by the club's decision to scrap their reserve team. He played only two first-team matches for Newcastle, both as substitute. But even in his first season at Coventry, when he was still adjusting to the demands of the Premiership, he immediately gave our attacking play the pace and ingenuity it had lacked.

Nobody benefited more than Dion Dublin. He was having a poor time when I took over from Ron Atkinson. The crowd were getting on to him and if we had received a decent offer for him, I am sure we would have let him go. He scored his first goals of the season after my appointment (making a total of three in twenty matches) but it was after the arrival of Darren that he truly seemed to come alive in that respect. He scored another ten in his nineteen other games to become our top scorer again.

He and Darren did not always play together up front that season. Dion had a few matches at centre half, with Darren being partnered by Noel Whelan. One of those games was Darren's Coventry debut – ironically, at home to Newcastle – when his flair and determination to prove a point to his old club brought me my first win. It might only have been my fifth match as manager, but I was so stressed that it felt like the 500th. It was a midweek match, and instead of going home after our morning training session I stayed in my office for the rest of the day and actually fell asleep in my chair. For obvious reasons, I will never forget the match itself, especially Darren's contribution. He scored our first goal after only six minutes, from Kevin Richardson's pass, and set up Gary McAllister for our second fifteen minutes before half-time. Dion could take a lot of the credit for the success as well because, apart from the Alan Shearer goal in the second half, he had an excellent game against the then England centre-forward.

That win was a tremendous fillip for us because Newcastle were second in the table and this was only their fifth defeat of the season, and it showed over the next few weeks. By winning our next three matches against Leicester, Leeds and Middlesbrough, and drawing against Sunderland, we moved up to twelfth. Then, with only one more league win in eleven matches (six of which were lost), we were back in the relegation zone, third from bottom. It was not the happiest of periods for Dion; sent off against Sunderland and also in the following 4-0 defeat at Blackburn, he was suspended for seven first-team games. The same could be said for Darren, as our other 4-0 defeat was at Newcastle.

It meant a lot to Darren to do well against them, especially at St James' Park. I could understand this, except that I felt he put unnecessary pressure on himself by placing too much emphasis on it in his pre-match media interviews. The more he talked about his aim of putting one over on Newcastle, on their own ground, the more I felt he was digging a hole for himself. On his first return to St James' Park, his embarrassment about his poor performance and the result was compounded by my decision to take him off. Significantly, our most heated dispute in all the time we worked together at Coventry was sparked by another occasion when I substituted him at Newcastle – during our 4-1 defeat there in February 1999. Our argument as he came off the field and headed for the dressing room became so heated that it led to the intervention of a police officer.

Looking at our position at the tail-end of the 1996/97 season, and the teams we had to face in our remaining matches – Liverpool (a), Chelsea (h), Southampton (a), Arsenal (h), Derby (h) and Tottenham (a) – it was tempting to suggest that I could have done with the help of an entire police force in order to keep us in the Premiership. My decision to return to first-team action, and the results we achieved, made this spell unquestionably one of the most stimulating – and certainly the most nerve-wracking – of my entire career. It is always difficult to combine the roles of player and manager at any level, not least when you are as old as I was. However, there were one or two advantages in it for me. Being on the field during a match provided a great outlet for the frustration I was experiencing; I still loved playing, and as I was still fit enough to do so this was the one area of my new career in which I could be guaranteed to enjoy myself. Not only this, I was able to put into practice all the knowledge I had acquired at Coventry. It is often said that you become a better player when you stop. In other words, while you learn a lot as a footballer, you gather considerably more knowledge as a coach or manager. I was lucky in that through my Coventry playing comebacks, I was able to use that knowledge in a more direct way than most others of my age.

Having come on as a substitute in that momentous win at Liverpool, I made my first full appearance of the season in the 3-1 home win against Chelsea – then sixth and due to face Wimbledon in the FA Cup semi-final – three days later. That result also gave me a lot of satisfaction, if only because this was probably the club towards whom I tended to feel the most hostility. That attitude towards Chelsea has become pretty widespread in recent seasons, as a result of the ascendancy that Roman Abramovich's money and José Mourinho's brash management style has given them. But even throughout my playing career in England, Chelsea – because of where they are situated and their trendy, glamorous image – were one of the teams that those from more basic provincial football environments most relished beating.

It is amazing how much comparatively minor, inconsequential experiences can influence one's perception of clubs. I still remember a Manchester United match at Stamford Bridge when I went out to have a look at the pitch before the kickoff and met a staff member whom I assumed was their groundsman or one of his assistants. He was coming on to the pitch as I was walking off it back to the dressing room, and, as we were about to acknowledge each other with a handshake, he suddenly pulled his hand back and thumbed his nose at me.

'You are very funny, you are,' I said, sarcastically. I was not laughing. I hate that sort of joke. To me, it is bad enough when a child does it, as happened when a five-year-old Liverpool mascot embarrassed Steven Gerrard in that way before the match against Chelsea in February 2006. It is even worse when an adult conducts himself in this manner.

As reflected by my most notable brushes with match officials, games against Chelsea had a habit of accentuating the belligerent streak in me. For my first match against them as a manager, when Ruud Gullit was in charge of them and their team included Frank Leboeuf, Roberto Di Matteo, Gianfranco Zola and Gianluca Vialli, I even had a dispute with them over their kit.

Having made the mistake of turning up with only their first-choice blue strip, which they could not use as it clashed with Coventry's, they suggested to referee Dermot Gallacher that the simplest solution would be for us to play in a different colour. Determined not to be seen to give in to Gullit I said no, and refused to budge. This led to the kickoff being delayed for fifteen minutes and Chelsea having to don our red and black second-choice strip. It clearly angered some of them, which was the reaction I had hoped for. I thought: 'Well, if we can wind them up before the kickoff, that has to be to our advantage.' As it happened, Chelsea took the lead, very much against the run of play near the end of the first half, through Paul Hughes. But, at the start of the second, we hit them with three goals in nine minutes from Dion Dublin, Paul Williams and Noel Whelan.

At that stage we were three places above the relegation zone and draws in our next two matches against Southampton and Arsenal kept us there. However, instead of going on to get the win that would have guaranteed our Premiership survival, against Derby in our last home match, we suffered the kick in the teeth of a 2-1 defeat. The result, from a game in which Derby had only had a total three shots, put us third from bottom, with the knowledge that the outcome of our bid to avoid the drop in our final match at Tottenham the following Sunday was no longer entirely in our own hands.

That Derby match, which proved to be my last first-team appearance, was hardly the happiest ending point for me. The first Derby goal early in the second half stemmed from my irritation over one of their players being allowed to get away with encroachment at a Coventry free kick. Having been booked for dissent – which did nothing at all to calm me down – I then conceded a free kick for a foul on Chris Powell. The kick, taken by Gary Rowett, was deflected into our net by David Burrows. Then, after I had gone off with a hamstring injury, Gary McAllister equalised from a penalty – only for Dean Sturridge to take advantage of Gary Breen's hesitancy in dealing with a long Mark Poom clearance to put Derby ahead again. One of my most vivid recollections of the afternoon concerned Sturridge's ecstatic celebration of his strike. Of course, he had every right to rejoice – I would have done the same in his position – but at the time, because of what the goal meant for Coventry and me, I couldn't help but feel resentful and angry about his reaction. This was even more the case immediately after the match, when we learned that the other teams facing relegation had all won.

At that moment, the picture in my mind of Sturridge's goal celebration turned him into the easiest hate figure in the whole world for me.

Nottingham Forest were already relegated and on the last day we were one of five teams in a position to go down with them. However, the anxiety was particularly intense for Middlesbrough and ourselves, the other teams in the bottom three – level on points – and Sunderland, immediately above, two points ahead. Of the three, we had the second worst goal difference, behind Boro. Even though we were all playing away from home (Sunderland and Boro were at Wimbledon and Leeds respectively), it was difficult to visualise our positions changing. As far as Coventry were concerned, the bookies' odds of 9-1 against us staying up said it all. I might have made positive noises about our chances publicly, but privately I really did feel we were goners.

At our hotel on the day of the game I had breakfast with Gary McAllister. In normal circumstances, our chat would only have lasted for about half an hour, but on this occasion we talked so much about the prospect of relegation – where we felt we had gone wrong during the season and how we were going to try to put it right – that we sat there from 9.30 to 11.30 a.m. As for the match, it would have been understandable had the general feeling of doom about Coventry's immediate future had an adverse psychological effect on the team, but this was not the case. It would be difficult to imagine any side being more charged up for a game than we were that day. I was exceptionally proud of our performance, not just because of the determination and doggedness in our play, but also of our team discipline. We opened the scoring after just thirteen minutes, thanks to Dion Dublin's header from Gary McAllister's cross. After thirty-nine minutes, Paul Williams's shot from Gary's corner made it 2-0, and though Paul McVeigh pulled one back for Spurs just before half-time, I still felt we were in control.

One reason why the match will always be remembered by everybody involved was the emotional turmoil we all went through in the last fifteen minutes. Some people felt we were given an unfair advantage through the decision to put the kick-off back from 4 p.m. to 4.15 p.m., because of the delay in Coventry supporters getting to the ground following an accident on the M1. But though this meant that we knew the results from the matches involving the other relegation-threatened teams before our game had finished, I disagree that the knowledge helped us. Quite the opposite, because it was in the last fifteen minutes – when we knew that Sunderland and Middlesbrough had dropped points and that we would remain in the Premiership if our score stood at 2-1 – that we started to panic. It was in that agonising quarter of an hour that Oggy brought off his best save of the game to deny Neale Fenn an equaliser.

Since then, the most common question put to me by Coventry followers concerned my decision not to play in that game, not even for the last fifteen minutes.

I left myself out of the starting line-up partly because of the fear that my exertions in the previous matches might have started to catch up with me and partly because I thought it was important for me to concentrate just on my main responsibilities – as a manager – in a match of this importance. As for not coming on as a substitute, both Garry Pendrey and Alex Miller urged me to do so in those last fifteen minutes, to help us keep the ball better. Indeed, when I left the dugout and sat on the ground a few feet in front of it, it was not just to get a better view of what was happening on the pitch; I also did it to make it more difficult for me to hear what Garry and Alex were saying. On the premise that they were trying to make me feel bad about myself, their comments about the team needing me on the pitch was the last thing I wanted to hear, because my concentration on the play and the emotional energy I had expended had left me feeling totally drained. I was not sure that I had the energy even to tie my bootlaces and do a warm-up.

Not surprisingly, some of the players were running out of fuel as well. At one point, as I walked into the technical area, Gary or Alex shouted: 'Huckerby is knackered – you will need to go on for him.'

I looked at Darren, and asked: 'How are you?'

'Absolutely knackered,' he replied.

His face was a picture when I shouted to the dugout: 'He says he is okay.' He looked as if his eyes were popping out of his head.

At the final whistle, some of the players were in tears. For all of us, the sense of relief was indescribable.

Being the manager of a football club is often like playing a game of snakes and ladders. The up and down nature of the job is reflected in the careers of virtually all the men filling this role. If you are fortunate to be with one of the most powerful clubs, as I am now at Celtic, there is hardly any variation in your position from week to week, month to month and season to season. But for most of the others, it is a different matter. It's an occupational hazard.

In the season after Coventry's relegation escape at Tottenham, we were as high as eighth after our sixth match, and as low as seventeenth after our twentieth. We eventually finished eleventh, a considerable improvement on our record in previous seasons and one that was further emphasised by our reaching the FA

Cup quarter finals. From then, though, I landed on more snakes than ladders. Over the next three seasons, our respective Premiership positions were fifteenth, fourteenth, and nineteenth and we had only moderate success in the cup competition. The slide continued after our relegation; at the time I left Coventry, we were eighteenth in the First Division.

In the 1997/98 season, despite the Dion Dublin hat-trick which gave us a 3-2 opening-day win over Chelsea, after we had twice been behind, our number of league victories after twenty matches totalled no more than four. The first real sign of the transformation that was to follow – which was to give me my best ever spell at Coventry – was when we came from behind to beat Manchester United 3-2, our first win over United for nine years. Then, after picking up only one point from our next two games, we had a run of five successive Premiership wins against Bolton (5-1), Sheffield Wednesday (1-0), Southampton (2-1), Barnsley (1-0) and Crystal Palace (3-0). Even better was that it formed part of a club record seven straight wins in both league and FA Cup matches; and a run of fourteen matches in which our only defeat was against Sheffield United in the Cup on penalties.

Among the most satisfying aspects of that season for me was that our team included another Strachan – Gavin.

For obvious reasons, the situation of a manager having a son on his playing staff, is never easy for either party. Gavin had joined Leeds, as a 15-year-old member of their Academy as I was coming to the end of my career there and I brought him with me to Coventry because I wanted to keep the family together. I had to feel sorry for him sometimes. I am sure that he heard some horrible comments about me from other players (which, to his credit, never got back to me through him); and, because of my determination not to be seen to be favouring him in any way, I was probably harder on him than I was anybody else. In one of his reserve matches, I remember turning on him at half-time just because I felt his hair was too long. I can see now that there was no real need for me to treat Gavin in this way, but I think this it is a trap that all managers in this position fall into.

Gavin's introduction into the first-team that season, for the first time, stemmed partly from the absence of Gary McAllister for much of the campaign because of injury. Although the new central midfield pairing of George Boateng and Trond-Egil Soltdevt enabled us to overcome this – thanks to their tremendous drive and energy – I still felt we needed someone who could help us retain possession and control games a bit more. In practice matches, it was obvious that Gavin could control and pass the ball as well as anyone but I was still not sure that he could do the job I had in mind in first-team matches. I'd only seen him in youth and reserve-team games and I found it hard to look beyond that.

Garry Pendrey and the other coaches kept nagging me to try him, but it was Gary McAllister who probably did the most to open the first-team door for Gavin. I played Devil's Advocate with him. 'It's time you gave Gavin a game,' Gary said. 'He can't get around the pitch,' I replied. 'He is not like Trond [Soltvedt] and George [Boateng]. He is just not made that way.' Gary just shook his head and said: 'Maybe not, but look at how well he can use the ball.' He was right. Gavin proved an ideal figure for us to bring on when the physical intensity of a game had dropped. After making his debut as a substitute in the 3-0 defeat by Aston Villa in December, he played in all of those five successive Premiership victories.

Though Gavin was with Coventry until March 2003, he did not make many further appearances for the club. However, in view of the high number of footballers who never get anywhere near Premiership level, he has a lot to be proud of.

It sometimes bothers me that Gavin, and Craig might have

found it difficult to come to terms with not having had the success in football that I have achieved. But Lesley and I did not produce sons in order to establish some kind of Strachan soccer dynasty. When I look at the way they have turned out as people, I think: 'I am not sure if you ever have ever wished you could be like me, but I certainly wish I could be like you.'

Of all Coventry's matches in that 1997/98 season, the one which stands out in my mind the most was the victory at Bolton that sparked our record run. It was as good an example as any of how unpredictable this game can be. It was Coventry's biggest away victory since 1959, but nobody can have envisaged the eventual score line in the first half. Bolton had taken the lead and although Noel Whelan equalised, we were getting battered. The fact that it was 1-1 at half-time was farcical.

How did we manage to turn it around? That's a good question, and one that most managers will have asked themselves from time to time. I remember discussing this once with Kenny Dalglish, when he was Liverpool manager. 'Do you ever get games where things are going wrong, and you are struggling to find the answer?' I asked. 'Many a time,' he admitted, adding that he had posed the same question to Bob Paisley, the most successful of all Liverpool managers and got the same reply. The match against Bolton was among those in that category for me.

It would have been great for me to be able to attribute our 5-1 success to my powers of motivation, in the sort of team talk that once prompted me jokingly to ask the players at Southampton if they thought I sounded like Martin Luther King. But I do not think this was the case. Even Martin Luther King would have had difficulty thinking he could make the players believe they could beat Bolton, let alone me. I could not even attribute the win to me wearing one of those 'lucky' items of clothing that many managers (including the ones who keep trying to tell us what tough characters they are) are inclined to put their faith in.

We just started causing Bolton problems from set pieces – which undermined their confidence – and it seemed that everything we hit ended up in the back of the net. It was the classic 'game of two halves', especially for Dion Dublin and Darren Huckerby. From being comparatively subdued in the first forty-five minutes, they suddenly burst into life and each went on to score twice.

Strikers are by far the most important players in any team as far as I am concerned, not just because of their goals – pricelesss commodities in themselves – but the psychological effect their records can have on the other players in their sides and the opposition. If any footballers can make or break a manager, it is these – as I know to my cost. It is a difficult subject for me to discuss, in relation to my time at Coventry, because I have always been wary of giving the impression of making excuses for my failure to keep the club in the Premiership. Even so, I do think I am on safe ground with the view that Coventry's inability to hold on to their best strikers was possibly the biggest factor in that. It was no coincidence that the period when I had my best run of results at Coventry was the one in which Dion Dublin and Darren Huckerby were on fire. By the end of the 1997/98 season, they had scored eighteen and fourteen goals respectively. The only Premiership partnership with a better scoring record was that of Chris Sutton and Kevin Gallacher at Blackburn.

If the truth be told, we were an ordinary team at the back and in midfield, but an excellent one up front. Dion and Darren were the classic striking combination, with the former operating as the target man and the latter feeding off him. Dion, always a handful for defenders in the air, would usually be the one to come short for balls to be played to his feet, while Darren would go in the opposite direction, looking to attack the space behind defenders. Dion had good feet for such a big man, something not very widely appreciated when I first started working with him. It can be easy to stereotype players on the basis of their height and build, as Liverpool's Peter Crouch has found. When you have a big centre-forward, trying to exploit his ability in the air can be an obsession. Therefore, part of our work in getting the best out of Dion involved making other players understand that it was not just about hitting high balls to his head all the time, but encouraging Dion himself to get into positions that would invite – if not force – them to give him a different service and to hold the ball longer. The one problem for him was that he did not have a lot of pace, which meant that when he came deep to join in the build-up play and the ball went wide, it was some-times difficult for him to get into the box again for the cross. Because of his intelligence, though, this was not as much of a headache for him as it would have been for other players.

Dion was the joint top scorer in the Premiership that season, with Sutton and Michael Owen. He also played for England for the first time and was unlucky not to get into the squad for the World Cup Finals in France. I remember as we were walking to our cars following Coventry's last match at Everton he came over to me and asked if he could have a word with me. 'I just want to thank you for all you have done for me,' he said.

It was a great moment for me. I thought: 'This is why I became a manager. This is what makes all the hard work and stress worthwhile.'

After a season like that, it was probably only to be expected that Dion would want to move on. He did not make the best of starts to the following season, which was also the case with Darren, and even more so with the team as a whole. Dion only scored three goals in his ten league matches before his departure, and, with seven defeats in those games, we were second from bottom. John Aloisi, the man we signed from Portsmouth to replace him, did not do a bad job, but, even so, Noel Whelan was the only Coventry player to push his league goal total into double figures (he scored ten) and it was not until our second match from the end of that season, the goalless draw at Derby, that we made ourselves totally relegation-proof.

We did not have anybody among the top Premiership scorers in the 1999/2000 season either. But because of the sort of attacking football we produced, which at one stage prompted Sky TV pundits to describe us as 'The Entertainers', I got as much enjoyment from this campaign as I did from the 1997/98 one. The tag was particularly pertinent in our home matches. The crazy thing about that season was that while we won twelve league matches and scored thirty-eight goals at Highfield Road – our best season there in the league since the late 1970s – we did not get any away wins at all, for the first time in the club's history, and our goals total on our Premiership visits was no more than nine.

Coventry's unusual position of being acclaimed as one of the most exciting teams in the country was not surprising in view of some of the new faces at the club that season – notably Moustapha Hadji and Robbie Keane. Moustapha, Morocco's 1998 World Cup star, is not only among the most skilful footballers I have worked with, but he is also one of the best people. He became our highest-paid player when he joined us in the summer of 1999 and he deserved every penny he got.

I have mixed feelings about the view that foreign players can be too temperamental for British football. This might have been true with a number of the average-to-good players but there are rarely any problems with the very top ones. Of the ones I've worked with, Sweden's Roland Nilsson was certainly in that category. So too, is Moustapha.

When he came to Coventry, I told him I wanted him to operate in a floating role just behind the strikers in a 4-3-1-2 shape. He would have been absolutely perfect in that setup.

Unfortunately, I found it difficult to get other players to fit into the system, so I had to keep going with a 4-4-2 system with Moustapha wide on the right or left of midfield or up front as one of the strikers. 'I'm sorry about this,' I said to him. 'I have not done what I promised you. All I can say is that if it does not work out well for you, I will tell everybody that you are not playing in your proper role and take full responsibility for it.'

Players in that situation are generally happy enough with such an arrangement, but I had the feeling that Moustapha would have gone along with me anyway. He told me: 'The club pay me a lot of money and I am a football player. You tell me what you want me to do and I will do it.'

Before a match at Everton, he could not train all week because of a foot injury, and it was still so swollen and black and blue on the eve of the game that there seemed no way he would be able to play. In fact, I asked him: 'Do you think you will be okay for next week?'

'Oh no,' he said. 'I think I will be okay for tomorrow.'

When I asked how he felt this was going to be possible, he just said: 'Oh, don't worry. I will play.'

On the Saturday, just before I announced the team (without him in it), I thought I would just make one last check on him. 'You won't believe what he is doing,' the physio remarked. He was right; I didn't. Moustapha had bought a piece of fillet steak – not to eat, but to place on top of his foot, inside his boot, to protect it. He did play, and was superb.

Robbie Keane, meanwhile, was the most talented nineteen-year-old striker I have known. Every time I saw him playing for Wolves, or talked about him with his Wolves manager, Mark McGhee, I felt a bit depressed that Coventry would not be able to sign him – or so I thought. As with Darren Huckerby, whose transfer to Leeds in August helped us raise the money for the Robbie deal, he is another striker I would classify as a scorer of spectacular goals rather than a prolific scorer. The main difference between the two is that Robbie finds better positions in which to get himself on the ball. I remember seeing him playing for Wolves in a pre-season friendly against Barcelona. In terms of his movement off the ball, the way he created space for himself, it was one of the best performances I have ever seen. Even as a teenager, he had so many strings to his bow – wonderful ball skills, strength, imagination. Having someone like him in our team made everybody connected with it feel better about the side. Some of the tricks he pulled off in training had the coaches looking at each other in amazement. Occasionally, all the other players would just stop and applaud him. I once asked him who had taught him to do some of the things he did. 'Nobody,' he said, adding that he just picked them up from watching other players and giving his own interpretation. He only needed to see something once to be able to do it. It takes some players months and even years. The bottom line for me was that when Robbie came to Coventry it was as if I had signed a fantasy player. My first thought was: 'Now we have a real chance of winning matches.'

In addition to Moustapha and Robbie, another important component for Coventry in the 1999/2000 season was the central midfield partnership of Carlton Palmer and Gary McAllister.

The signing of Carlton, from Nottingham Forest in September 1999, at the age of thirty-four, was very much a personal gamble, one that I would not have taken earlier in my managerial career. Indeed, I could easily have worked with Carlton at Coventry sooner than I did because Ron Atkinson wanted to sign him when I was Ron's coach. I was in a difficult situation when Bryan Richardson asked for my opinion about the signing because, while Ron was looking to me to back him on it, I felt duty bound to be totally honest. Ron knew Carlton much better than I did – he had signed him for no fewer than three of his previous clubs – West Bromwich Albion, Sheffield Wednesday and Forest. However, I had also worked with Carlton before, at Leeds, and as I knew I would be taking over from Ron as Coventry manager, I did not think I had the ability at that stage to handle a player of his temperament and personality. I did not tell Bryan that we should not sign him; I just gave him all the pluses and minuses about it, from my point of view, and in the end the decision not to bring Carlton to Coventry was down to Bryan. It was easy to see why Ron had so much faith in him. Carlton, at six foot three and thirteen stone, and with those telescopic legs that prompted people to refer to him disparagingly as 'Bambi', was never going to be the most skilful or elegant of footballers. But successful teams embody all manner of different qualities and attributes and the contribution that Carlton could make though his ball-winning ability, the amount of ground he covered, and his tactical awareness was as valid as anyone.

But the Carlton Palmer package also included a lot of baggage in terms of problems in his personal life – especially with regard to his drinking habits – and a tendency to believe that he knew more about the game than any of his managers or coaches. Ron, referring to Carlton's strong views, once said: 'I'm a big fan of Carlton and wherever we have worked together, I have always expected to have more dressing-room barneys with him than any other player. But I like that – I don't want shrinking violets. I like to work with guys who have an opinion.' I endorse that. I have never been one to discourage players from questioning my decisions – as long as it is done in the right way. This is where Carlton and I clashed.

When I signed him, I thought he was at an age where he would be more understanding of the problems of managers. He may well have been, but he was also at an age where he was preparing to be a manager himself, so his desire to assert himself in that area at Coventry was probably stronger than ever.

Ironically, far from this being the best time for me to be his team manager, it was possibly the worst. It was a shame because there were a lot of things I liked about Carlton and I wish that I could have worked with him on a more level playing field.

He is no mug where football is concerned, and we used to spend hours discussing the tactical side of the game. Perhaps our main point of conflict concerned his opinion that we should switch from 4-4-2 to 3-5-2. Unlike him, I did not accept that having five men in midfield was absolutely necessary for us to gain control of that area; I felt this could be achieved just as easily by having a four-man midfield operating more narrowly. He had a bee in his bonnet about being outnumbered, which I interpreted rightly or wrongly as a sign of fear on his part over the fact that his athleticism was on the wane. In the circumstances, it was natural that he should want as many team-mates in close contact with him as possible.

We never did see eye to eye on this; we just agreed to disagree. Unfortunately, Carlton's tendency to say whatever was on his mind, without considering the consequences, became more pronounced. It was typical of Carlton that, after one disagreement between us, when a team-mate made a comment about his former Nottingham Forest manager, David Platt, Carlton – with me in earshot – said: 'Yeah, but at least Platt listens to his players.' It reached the point where I felt my authority was being undermined, and that the help I tried to give him with his problems outside football was not working. However, despite the deterioration in our relationship, which led to Carlton dropping out of our first-team picture in our 2000/01 relegation season, I like to think that there are no hard feelings on either side today. For my part, I can never forget the job he did for me in his first season at Coventry, when his presence in the side from September, after we had gained only one win and suffered five defeats in our opening eight Premiership games, brought us four wins and three draws in the next seven – our best run.

Gary McAllister had even more cause to be grateful to Carlton than I did, because the way they complemented each other was a major factor in Gary having his best season at Coventry and, indeed, getting the chance to move to Liverpool. Because of the presence of such strong attacking midfielders as Moustapha Hadji and Youssef Chippo, I had started the season by trying to turn him into more of a holding-type player. But Gary, because of his attacking instincts, struggled to come to terms with the job – hence the signing of Carlton. Thus, instead of Gary having to curtail his attacking instincts, he found himself with as much freedom as ever.

As one might have expected of such strong characters, he and Carlton used to wind each other up something terrible. 'Just you do the running and winning the ball for me,' Gary would tell him. But Carlton could really get to Gary as well and that helped Gary produce his best form. Gary's remarkable lease of life also arose from his decision to stop playing for Scotland, which helped Gary and Coventry in the same way that Alan Shearer's decsion to bring down the curtain on his England career helped both him and Newcastle.

Gary, with eleven league goals and two in the League Cup, was the Premiership's highest scoring midfielder in the 1999/2000 season, so losing him to Liverpool in the summer was a big problem for us. We had originally paid over the odds for Gary, a common occurrence in British football in those days, and during his four years at Coventry he had probably been one of the highest paid players in the Premiership. By the time of his Liverpool move, he was getting about three times what I was getting. Therefore, in our negotiations with him on a new agreement, we took the view that, as he was thirty-six, he could hardly have cause to think we were mean in offering him the same terms. I remember that when Bryan Richardson asked for my opinion on what Gary should be offered, I said: 'Offer him a one-year extension on his contract, on at least the same money.'

'We can only afford to give him the same money anyway,' Bryan pointed out.

I was convinced that this would be enough to keep Gary at the club. The first indication that this would not be the case came in April. 'I have a sniff of Liverpool' was the way Gary put it to me. I can't deny that I was sceptical – I was sure Gary was not lying, but I thought that his agent might have been making more of Liverpool's interest than actually existed. Wrong again. Liverpool, in fact, were prepared to pay Gary double what he had been getting at Coventry and, of course, the footballing aspect of joining a club of this stature – the most exciting challenge of his career – was even more appealing to him. All I could say to him – all any manager in my position could say to him – was: 'On you go – best of luck.'

What made the situation even worse was that just eighteen days before our opening match we also lost Robbie – our top league scorer with twelve goals – to Inter Milan.

I appreciated that there was no way we could turn down the £13 million that Inter were willing to pay for him, especially in the light of the fears then about a transfer market recession. But for this concern, I think we could have held out for £15 million for Robbie. That's how highly I rated him. What surprised me about the situation was that, when I broke the news to him of Inter's bid, he genuinely did not know anything about it. Because of the vast network of agents and middlemen in professional football – not to mention the intense media spotlight – it is very unusual for a player to be so much in the dark about a club's interest in him, especially in a proposed transfer of such magnitude.

I should imagine that Robbie had a big problem preventing himself from bursting out with laughter as I was explaining the Inter situation to him. I know I would have done had I been in his position. Having told him that he would get around £40,000 a week if he went to Inter, and would be rubbing shoulders with world superstars like Ronaldo, I added: 'I would love you to stay with Coventry for another year to develop further. It's up to you. Just think about it and get back to me.' Not surprisingly, that was the last I saw of him. I said to Lesley: 'I gave him the choice of living and working in Coventry or Milan. What a tough decision, eh?'

It was really no laughing matter for me, because the loss of Robbie and Gary – or to put it another way, the loss of twenty-three goals a season from a team with a 1999/2000 league total of forty-seven – was the signal for our drop into the Football League, and my eventual sacking.

CHAPTER TEN

# OFF WITH MY HEAD

George Boateng is a good tennis player. I once challenged him to a match, and though I got about the court quite well and could out psych him, his superior stroke play enabled him to get the better of me.

I remember that almost every time he won a point George put his hands together and gave thanks to God.

'It wasn't fair,' I remarked to him the following day, as he was telling everyone how he had beaten me. 'I was playing singles and you, with God on your side, were playing doubles. I would have thought that God had better things to do than help you beat me at tennis.'

Unlike George, I am not a religious person, which is probably just as well because had I tried to follow George's example in Coventry's 2000/01 relegation season – the worst of my entire career – I would have taken up more of God's time than anyone. There are many far worse things in life than being the manager of a relegated team. However, it is not easy to put such setbacks into proper perspective when you pour so much energy into your job – your heart and soul in a lot of cases – and take so much flak when it does not pay off. I had never been associated with a relegated team before, and because of the club's pride in their thirty-four-year survival in the top division, I felt as if I was viewed almost as the anti-Christ in the city.

A lot of things went wrong for Coventry that season, but the biggest headache – at least before the arrival of John Hartson towards the end of it – was our lack of scoring power. We won only eight league games and scored just thirty-six goals. The previous season, our Highfield Road goal total had been thirty-eight; this time it was fourteen.

This was exactly the sort of situation I had feared when we lost Gary McAllister and Robbie Keane. Indeed, because of my anxiety over their departure, I probably did not give the signings we made to compensate for their absence – midfielder-cum-winger David Thompson from Liverpool and striker Craig Bellamy from Norwich – as much consideration as I might have done, or, indeed, should have done, in normal circumstances. That is not to say that David and Craig were not good players. They were excellent. But whether they were really right for Coventry at that time is another matter.

David filled a different role from that of Gary, but he could do everything – his ball control was great, he could go past people, he could shoot; his talent was incredible. Gary confirmed this when I asked him what David was like in training at Liverpool. Having also spoken highly of his attitude, Gary added: 'The only problem is that he sometimes tries to do too much and does not hold his position enough.' I thought: 'That's okay – we can work on that.'

However, it was more difficult than I thought. David seemed to believe that if he was not in the game for two or three minutes on the right side of the field, then he was having a bad time and would have to go looking for the ball in the centre or even the other flank. This meant that he did not make it easy for other players to know where to find him when we had the ball and, of course, they had to keep covering for him when the opposition gained possession. I am not knocking him for this because he worked hard and the truth of the matter was simply that we didn't have the all-round ability to be able to accommodate someone like him successfully. He needed to be in a better team although, ironically, he was magnificent in the First Division in the season that I left Coventry.

I also felt that David was never totally comfortable living in the Midlands. Birkenhead born and bred, he had spent all his early years as a player at Liverpool and I always detected a longing on his part to return to the north – which he eventually did when he joined Blackburn. I was delighted for him when, shortly after his move to Ewood Park, he was called up into the England squad.

I have reservations about the timing of the signing of Craig Bellamy because he had missed almost all the previous season at Norwich with a knee injury. He had only started playing first-team football again in April. I did not truly take on board the time he would need to recuperate fully and get back to his best. In hindsight, I should have waited for two or three months before making a decision on him, and plumped for somebody else in the meantime, although other clubs were interested in Craig then and it is likely that had we not stepped in for him when we did, we would have missed the boat.

Top strikers can be quite self-centred at times, and I would say this was true of Craig. He loved working on his game – he would have been happy to be out there all day if necessary – but was less enthusiastic if he had to involve himself in training work designed to help the defenders. He did not throw any tantrums over it, but his body language indicated to me that he did not feel it was right for him to turn his attention to this aspect of our play.

I found him similar to Carlton Palmer in that, whatever was on his mind, he had to come out with it. I think everybody who has known Craig will confirm that he moans a lot and can be very lippy. Some footballers use physical violence as an outlet for their frustrations, whereas with Craig it is mostly violence of the tongue. I remember talking to him about all this and making the point that, in order to fulfil his potential, he would need to learn to give his colleagues greater help and respect. I said: 'If you do not do that, they will not give the same help and respect to you. That means that when you are in difficulties, their attitude will be: "Let's see how good you are now", and leave you on your own.'

I am not sure if Craig has ever fully grasped this but I have to stress that this side of him was never that much of a problem to us. If he took his dissent to the extreme, we would just laugh and tell him to shut up. He was okay with that.

You could not help admire his honesty. He always seemed to be missing training because of illness in his family – or so he said. On one such occasion, I said to him 'How many members of your family are still alive? You are telling me a lie, aren't you?'

'Yep,' he replied.

I then told him I was fining him two weeks' wages. 'Okay,' he said. That was it.

You could not help but like what he had to offer as a striker as well – as Celtic fans will readily acknowledge after seeing Craig help the team compensate for the departure of Henrik Larsson to Barcelona in the summer of 2004. It was a pity that we were not able to keep him at Celtic Park when I became manager there, especially in view of his rapport with John Hartson – the sort of rapport that I honestly believe would have saved Coventry from relegation had it not taken us so long to bring the two Wales strikers together there.

Up to John's arrival from Wimbledon in February, I had to feel sorry for Craig. It had been a real struggle for him because, in addition to him having started the season handicapped by his comparative lack of strength and sharpness, we were not able to give him a great deal of team help, especially up front.

Our other strikers were Cedric Rousell, John Aloisi, Ysrael Zuniga (the Peruvian player signed in February 2000), Jay Bothroyd (who came to us from Arsenal in July 2000) and Noel Whelan. But none truly emerged as the perfect foil for Craig. Cedric and John Aloisi seemed the best bets, but Cedric's form declined because of personal problems and John was hampered by injuries.

The member of this group with the most potential was Jay Bothroyd. He only cost £100,000, which was peanuts for an eighteen-year-old striker with his physique – six foot three and thirteen stone – and wide range of ability. But, of course, Arsenal did not let him go for nothing. To me Jay was the classic example of a player spoilt by too much adulation too soon. When he came, he said: 'I do not know how Arsenal can have left me out of the team because I am a better player than Kanu.' He was possibly right in some ways. But, in common with so many other players who have been outstanding in schoolboy and youth football, he had difficulty getting his head around the fact that he was not yet the finished article and needed to do various things better.

He had only been at Coventry a couple of months when a clash with one of the coaches brought him a club fine of two weeks' wages. It then got back to me that he had told another member of the coaching staff: 'It does not bother me – I've got enough money', so we decided not to allow him to play in any match for a month. That really did get to him, however – every week, he would knock on my door asking me to change my mind. In fairness to him, he buckled down well in our reserves and over his two seasons with Coventry he did get better. It is no surprise to me that, after a spell with Perugia in Serie A in Italy, he recently returned to the Premiership with Charlton.

It says much about Coventry's struggle to find the right striking blend in our relegation season that at one stage we had as many as five different partnerships up front in the space of ten matches, and we sometimes had to use Craig in wide positions. I must admit that I have to take some of the blame for all this – because I probably had too many front men to choose from. Craig, in being expected immediately to make the same impact as Robbie Keane, was under a great deal of pressure, which was not very fair on him. After we beat Tottenham 2-1 at home in October (only our third win in the opening nine games), I said to him: 'We are going to struggle this year, but you have the ability to be a top player so don't allow yourself to be dragged down by this.'

It was only when John Hartson arrived from Wimbledon to take some of the weight off his shoulders – and I challenge anyone to name a centre-forward anywhere who can have done that job better than this awesomely powerful figure – that Craig was able to start to blossom.

It was once said of John Hartson that, had he been a race-horse, he would have been shot some time ago. This, of course, is a reference to his injuries – especially to his knees – and the fact that when he was at Wimbledon proposed transfers to clubs like Rangers, Charlton and Tottenham all fell through because of his failure to pass the medical examinations he had to undertake in order for them to get him insured. I had wanted to sign John some weeks before I did, but with Wimbledon continuing to hold out for a big transfer fee for him, we were baulked by the insurance problem as well.

However, because of Wimbledon's financial difficulties, and the need to get John off their wage bill, we were eventually able

Give this man a medal! Me with my Coventry chairman, Bryan Richardson – before the effects of working with me began to show. (COLORSPORT)

What an advert for my porridge and banana diet! Playing again for Coventry, and taking on Arsenal's Dennis Bergkamp, at the age of 40. (OFFSIDE)

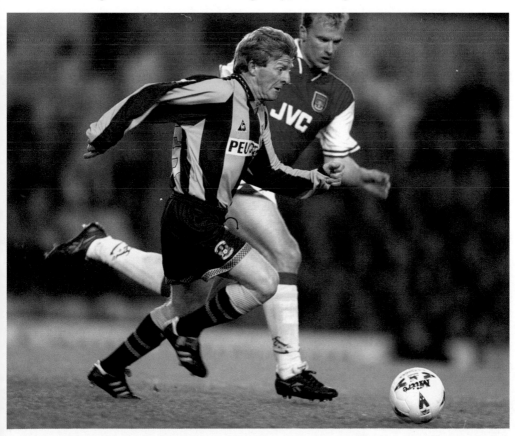

My assistant Garry Pendrey plays a blinder in stopping me clashing with a match official. (EMPICS)

This time, at Southampton, I even enlisted the help of a policeman as a witness to my discussion with Steve Bennett. (COLORSPORT)

A Coventry fan sees his prayers (and mine) answered through the last-gasp 2-1 win at Tottenham that kept us in the Premiership in 1997. (OFFSIDE)

From hero to zero — as Coventry head towards the Premiership exit, a fan thrusts his shirt at me in disgust. (EMPICS)

Dion Dublin and Darren Huckerby. Their scoring partnership was the major factor in my best spell at Coventry. (COLORSPORT)

Paul Telfer, a dressing room lieutenant for me at Coventry, Southampton and Celtic. (COLORSPORT)

Brett Ormerod and James Beattie, the Southampton front men after their demolition of Watford in the FA Cup semi final in 2003. (COLORSPORT)

Football management does not get much more exciting than this. Arsenal's Arsene Wenger and I lead our teams out for the 2003 FA Cup Final. (ACTION IMAGES)

The goal that destroyed our dreams. Trust Robert Pires, the player we were the most concerned about, to get it. (COLORSPORT)

A warm welcome by the Celtic fans at Parkhead for my unveiling as manager in the summer of 2005. (EMPICS)

The ultimate nightmare that followed shortly afterwards. I'm in shock as Celtic crash 5-0 against Artmedia. (SNS GROUP/WWW.SNSPIX.COM)

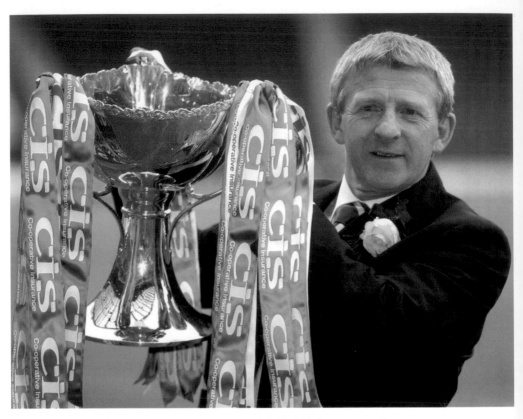

My first Celtic silverware – the 2006 CIS Insurance Cup. (EMPICS)

The highest point of my managerial career. Parkhead erupts as we are crowned Premier League champions. (ACTION IMAGES)

to strike a sort of hire purchase deal for him which involved the payment to Wimbledon of just £200,000 after he had completed twenty first-team appearances plus the first £1 million of any fee we received by selling him. I am sure a lot of people felt that John was finished as a top-class player, but I didn't. For all his injuries, he had still played a fair number of matches, and scored a number of goals. John had never been able to run about as much as other strikers, but had reached a stage in his career where he had learned how to handle his heavy build. Nobody could hold the ball up better than him. His touch and his awareness of the game were outstanding. The irony of his comparative lack of mobility – the fact that he needed to be in a central position most of the time – was that this was a great help rather than a hindrance to Craig. It gave Craig more space to work in; he could make any runs he wanted either side of John without having to worry about getting in his way. That was important to Craig because, as I have said, he did not have the body strength to be able to cope with having defenders tight on him. With just twelve matches to go when he was signed, and Coventry second from bottom, it was asking too much even of someone with John's physical and mental strengths to lift us out of the relegation zone. But he certainly had a reasonable stab at it. Following a Coventry run of four successive defeats, he immediately made a big difference to our attacking play on his debut in the 1-1 draw at West Ham, one of his former clubs. He scored six goals in the next 9 matches, which produced three wins and two more draws. Unfortunately, this came too late to make a significant difference to our league position and our relegation fate was sealed in our penultimate match at Aston Villa.

Of all the performances that contributed to our downfall, the one I remember the most was the 3-1 home defeat by Everton in January. It was a dreadful Coventry display against a team that had gone seven matches without a win and was considerably understrength because of injuries and suspensions. In its way, it was as embarrassing as that Celtic performance in Bratislava. Everton, in fact, were 3-0 up after thirty-one minutes, and that score line at half-time was Coventry's worst at this stage of a home match in some twenty years.

This was the game that effectively marked the parting of the ways for Carlton Palmer and me. It was also the game at which I experienced the first – and possibly the most disturbing – of the demonstrations against me by the Coventry crowd and it produced my first major crisis point in terms of keeping my job.

As far as Carlton was concerned, we got into a dispute on the eve of the game over my decision to name him as a substitute. We had just brought him back from a loan spell at Watford, because of injuries, but I elected to select Mo Konjic in the starting line-up instead of him simply because I was worried about the aerial power of Everton centre forward Duncan Ferguson. We knew that Ferguson had been in and out of the Everton team because of recurrent injury problems, but I felt that he would play against us and that Mo was better equipped to handle him than Carlton.

As it turned out, Ferguson was left out of the Everton side; and Mo looked so ill-at-ease that we had to bring Carlton on for him after just twenty-six minutes. Not only this, but the match sponsors – Audi – voted him the game's best player. Unfortunately, this seemed to make his sense of injustice over my decision to leave him out of the side even stronger, as I discovered the following Monday when I learned of the remarks he had allegedly made about me, and also about Bryan Richardson and members of the coaching staff, when he joined the sponsors' representatives to collect his award after the match.

My own sense of injustice over this at that time was fuelled by the belief that we had been exceptionally supportive of him with his problems in his personal life. He seemed at a particularly low ebb during this period but I do not think anybody can have shown him greater understanding and tried to help him more than I did. Thus, when I heard about his latest outburst, my first thought was: 'This is not fair.'

Of course, I was not going through the best of periods in my own life either. The abuse directed at me by Carlton was nothing compared to what I was having to take from the Coventry fans.

There had already been a lot of hostility building up against me before the Everton match, so much so that Andy Harvey, anticipating the danger of my car being damaged if it was parked in its normal place at Highfield Road, persuaded me to allow him to park it in a less conspicuous spot. Later, as Lesley and I were driving home – somewhat shell-shocked by the stick directed at me from the stands – I said: 'If things carry on like this, I shall have to use an ice cream van as cover.'

The crowd's abuse started at half-time and at the final whistle all hell was let loose. I was aware of some scuffles breaking out around me, and a couple of fans who had come on to the pitch even tried to attack me physically. Fortunately, they were prevented from doing so by the stewards and also Archie Knox, who provided further protection by forcing himself between them and me. I am not sure that I could have done much to protect myself because I was like a zombie. All I could think of was Lesley and her safety. I knew roughly where she had been sitting and as I headed for the dressing room tunnel I just kept looking back in the hope that I could see her and get confirmation that she was all right. As it happened, Lesley, whose nerves can easily get the better of her when watching matches in which things are not going well for me, had left her seat and was in the boardroom toilet.

Later, knowing what a bad state I was in, Andy Harvey and two other members of my backroom staff, Jim Blyth and George

Mackie, came over to our house with their wives to give Lesley and me some moral support. We ended up going to a local pub together, and for the first and only time in my managerial life I tried to forget my problems through alcohol. I must have had five or six pints of lager, which ensured that I got a reasonable night's sleep. But when I woke up the next morning the pain was still there, and although we still had guests – Jim and his partner, Karen, had stayed the night – I knew I was not in the frame of mind to talk to them or anyone else. Before they got up, I told Lesley I was going for a walk. It was only intended to be a short stroll, to clear my head and help me to become a human being again, but I was so uptight that the stroll took me fourteen miles from home. It had started raining and I did not have any money to return by taxi or public transport, so it was a relief to find a previously discarded mobile phone in the old jacket I was wearing, and that I was able to use it to call Lesley and get her to come and collect me.

Later that week I was made aware of moves by some members of the Coventry board – whom I assumed to be Geoffrey Robinson MP, the former Paymaster General who had bought around 30 per cent of Bryan Richardson's 60 per cent shareholding and was the key figure in providing much needed extra funding for new players, and Mike McGinnity, the Coventry vice-chairman who was to replace Bryan as chairman – to force me to accept Stuart Pearce as my assistant, at the expense of Garry Pendrey. When I had taken over from Ron Atkinson, earlier than had been intended, there had been reports that this move had been forced on Bryan by a suggestion from Robinson that his vital financial commitment to the club would be curtailed or withdrawn if it did not happen. I suspected that Bryan also had his arm twisted in the same way over the idea about bringing in Pearce.

I was not aware of this development at the start of the

week – all that I could think about was whether I would be sacked. Following the crowd reaction to that performance against Everton, I thought: 'If the club are going to sack you, this is the time to do it.' A board meeting had been scheduled for 12.30 p.m. the following Thursday, at Highfield Road, and having been asked by Brian to make myself available to attend if the other directors deemed it necessary, I feared the worst. I think everybody at the club did.

On the Thursday, while I was waiting in my office at the training ground for Bryan to let me know if I should come across, I arranged for a member of our kitchen staff to bring up a bowl of soup and some sandwiches. As she was putting the food on my desk, she burst into tears. 'You are the best manager we have ever had,' she told me. I did not know what to say to her – I just mumbled something like: 'Oh, that's all right', and left it at that. Then came the call from Bryan summoning me to what I expected to be my execution.

When I arrived at his Highfield Road office, he said: 'Gordon, there is only way I can save you.' He then explained that other board members felt I needed someone other than Garry to help me and had decided that Pearce – then playing for West Ham and starting to prepare himself for a managerial and coaching career – would be ideal. The inference was that while Garry would remain at Coventry, he would be pushed to one side and effectively demoted.

I was determined not to allow that to happen. I had nothing against Pearce. You had to admire his playing record and leadership qualities. He had started his league career at Coventry, of course, and I have no doubts that his return to the club would have been warmly welcomed by the supporters. But I had never worked with Pearce; and Garry, who had been Ron Atkinson's assistant, was doing an excellent job as far as I was concerned. With his knowledge of the game, and wonderful temperament, he was invaluable to me; as my subsequent decisions to bring him with me to Southampton and Celtic have shown, he always has been.

Unfortunately for Garry, his background with some of Coventry's closest rivals – notably Birmingham, where he was captain and then manager – made him an easy target for our disgruntled fans. This made me even more determined to resist the boardroom attempt to give me another partner. I told Bryan: 'Garry and I started this job together and we are going to leave it together.'

Bryan suggested that I should consider it at home, and though I insisted that I would not change my mind, we agreed to have another meeting there later that afternoon. In the meantime, I became increasingly resentful about what I was being asked to do. So much so that when I caught sight of McGinnity sitting in his car as I came out of the stadium, the temptation to let him know that the sack did not bother me was impossible to resist.

He was looking at the glove compartment – pretending that he had not seen me, I think – as I approached the vehicle. I then tapped on the window, and as he wound it down I said: 'Don't worry about it, Mike. It's just business', and walked away.

I will never forget Bryan's reaction when I reaffirmed my stance, as we were sitting together in my kitchen, a few hours later.

'Well, what are you going to do?' he asked.

'I haven't changed my mind,' I replied.

I was expecting him to reiterate the other directors' position. Instead, he just stood up, rubbed his hands together and said: 'Fair enough, we'll just have to put it to one side and get on with it. I'll deal with the rest of the board.'

My sensitivity about Gary's position was not the only reason why I was opposed to the idea of bringing in Stuart Pearce. I am sure the men who came up with the idea had been influenced by what was happening at Middlesbrough following the appointment of Terry Venables to help Bryan Robson the previous month. The move, which was apparently initiated by Bryan himself and meant Venables effectively becoming the joint manager, seemed an inspired one. Boro, at the bottom of the Premiership with only two wins from seventeen matches at the time of Venables's arrival, immediately improved and got themselves out of the relegation zone in just a few weeks.

However, with respect to Venables, I did not altogether agree that his prominent role in team selection, coaching and tactics was a good thing for my old Manchester United colleague. I couldn't help thinking that it undermined his credibility – a point which Bryan has since acknowledged himself – and that he was good enough to have lifted Boro out of trouble under his own steam. My misgivings about the situation were borne out at the end of the season, when Boro's 2-1 win over West Ham, which lifted them to fourteenth, drew an ovation from their crowd for Venables but some boos from a section of it for Bryan. Venables then left the club, and Bryan was sacked the following month.

It was not long before I, too, bit the dust. But at least I had the satisfaction of knowing that I had done the job my way.

Not surprisingly, with Coventry going down and then making a disappointing start to the 2001/02 season, the fans' reaction to me did not get any less fractious. Usually, because you are starting with a clean slate again, there is an air of optimism around clubs at the start of a new season. But the reverse was true with Coventry. Part of this was due to the fact that John Hartson, Craig Bellamy and Moustapha Hadji – the players considered to be our big-hitters – had all left in the summer, for Celtic, Newcastle and Aston Villa respectively. I felt quite confident that we would be in reasonably good shape, having signed midfielder Keith O'Neill from Middlesbrough, and strikers Julian Joachim and Lee Hughes from Villa and West Bromwich Albion. But, with Julian being ruled out of action through an injury in a pre-season game, and Coventry following a 2-0 win at Stockport on the opening day of the season with a 1-0 defeat by Wolves in our first home match, it was obvious that most of the fans would not be happy until they saw the back of me.

It was a catch-22 situation for me. I was determined to stay put. My attitude was: 'You have already gone through the worst experiences [the crowd abuse at the Everton match and relegation] and whatever the fans do now cannot possibly hurt you more than you have been.' I knew I was strong enough to handle it. But at the same time, I also knew that the atmosphere at our games was affecting the players.

During the Wolves match, an irate fan walked up to me in the dugout and thrust his replica jersey at me. In the next match, the 2-1 defeat at Bradford, the hostility seemed even more scary because all the Coventry followers were packed into a corner of the ground, in a section which seemed little more than a cage. I thought: 'I would hate to come across one of you in a dark alley.'

Not all of those who wanted to see me disappear expressed it with such hostility and aggression. After we had been held to a goalless draw at home to Nottingham Forest – despite Forest having been reduced to nine men and Coventry having created a hatful of chances – I was approached by a middle-aged gentleman, who said: 'Mr Strachan, you have done a good job in the past, but I do not think you are the right man for us now.' He had waited some time outside the ground for the chance to have a word with me, and as he had put forward his view in a reasonable manner – unlike the group who had earlier been screaming for my blood – I had no compunction about giving him the respect of listening to what he had to say. 'Well, I hear what you are saying,' I told him, 'but I am not a quitter.'

Three days later, when Coventry's disappointing run continued with a 1-0 home defeat by Grimsby – another game in which we had the chances to have won with plenty to spare – the Strachan-baiting was ratcheted up a notch. One newspaper report of the match, referring to my walk to the dressing room tunnel past a 'venomous' crowd pressing forward as close to me as they could get, stated that I looked like 'a prisoner being led to his execution'.

To this day, my clearest memory of that walk is of the extraordinary behaviour of a man in a part of the stand usually reserved for the guests of club directors and corporate hospitality clients. I have long felt that, due to the availability of plenty of drink before and after a match, and at half-time, these spectators can be more unruly and outrageous than anyone.

This particular person, who did not strike me as being the type of dyed-in-the-wool fan who spends hundreds of pounds a year travelling all over the country to watch his team play, seemed to encapsulate the whole thing. The fact that he was what I would call a privileged spectator made his foul-mouthed attack on me even harder to accept. He must have been in his late forties, and, in appearance, he struck me as being a cross between Engelbert Humperdinck and the late Ronald Allen who had played the part of the dashing hotel manager David Hunter in *Crossroads*. Like Humperdinck, he had a deep tan; and like Allen (or Hunter), he wore a bright yellow shirt with a white collar. He could only have been about ten yards from where Lesley had been sitting and it was while looking for her that I had the misfortune to clap eyes on him.

The tirade he directed at me was appalling by any standards. His face was contorted with rage and, indeed, he was so worked up that as he was screaming at me he was virtually spitting.

I immediately hated that guy with a vengeance. I still do. Whenever I think of that man – and even that awful shirt – I can feel my hackles rising. The following day, that guy, and all the others who felt I should go, got what they wanted.

I'd gone to the training ground to watch one of our Academy teams in action, and while I was having a cup of tea I saw Bryan Richardson's car approaching the centre. It was rare for Bryan to be at the ground on a Sunday, so I knew what was coming. You could see it on his face as soon as he walked through the door, and asked to have a chat with me in the privacy of my office.

'I am afraid there has to be a change now,' he said.

I really felt for him. Knowing him as I do, I reckon it was exceptionally difficult for him to do what he did – what I think he had to do. 'I cannot argue with that, Bryan,' I replied. 'I don't have a leg to stand on.'

We agreed that Bryan would delay announcing the decision until 9 a.m. the next day, to give Lesley and myself plenty of time to get away and make it more difficult for the media to contact me. I did not feel I had anything to say to newspapers, television and radio reporters, and the last thing I wanted was to make any comments that could be interpreted as excuses. That night, Lesley and I went to Jim Blyth's house for a drink with him and Garry Pendrey, and at four o'clock the next morning we set off by car to my parents home in Edinburgh. Our intention was to stay with them that night and fly to Tenerife on the Tuesday for a holiday.

We got to the Borders at about 9.30 a.m. and it was then that I received the first call of the day on my mobile, from the company from which I was leasing my car. There were still three weeks to go before my next payment, but the guy on the other end of the line, having obviously heard the news about my sacking, seemed to think that I was going to suffer some kind of breakdown and drive the vehicle to the other ends of the earth.

He was not among the most sensitive people I have come across. Once he had introduced himself, he said: 'About the car.'

'Yeah?' I said.

'We want it back right away,' he said.

'No, I have another three weeks to go with it, which I have paid for.'

'Well, we think the car should be back anyway.'

'What do you mean?'

'Well, we don't want you running about in it, using up all the mileage. Where do you want us to pick the car up from? Will you bring it back?'

How's that for making someone feel better about himself after getting the sack? No prizes for guessing that my reply was unprintable.

It was the same when Bryan's departure from the club was followed by Mike McGinnity attempting (unsuccessfully) to stop payments due to me on my agreement. I had been given two contracts during my five years there. I signed a four-year deal when I joined in 1996 and in 1998, in recognition of my work as manager, I was given a new four-year agreement. Though my reputation had grown, nobody can say that I put a gun to Coventry's head over my money. In fact, when Bryan and I started discussing the terms of the fresh contract, I said to him: 'I will leave the money side of it to you – just pay me what you think I am worth.'

My basic salary was low compared to that of other Premiership managers, but this was offset by incentive packages. One of these concerned an annual loyalty bonus, to be paid in full at the end of my contract or upon the club terminating it. I could have taken the money each year, but I thought it would be a help to the club for them to use the money for their running costs and just let me have the accumulated sum at the finish. It amounted to £600,000 when I got the sack, but because of

Coventry's financial difficulties I was happy to waive the stipulation of it being paid to me immediately and take it in two annual instalments.

After I had received half the money, though, McGinnity, on the premise that things had gone better for me than one might have expected following my departure, tried to get the club out of this obligation. It was disappointing, given how hard I had worked there and my willingness to do all I could to make it easier for Coventry to handle their financial commitments to me. For the sake of my self-esteem alone, I was glad that I stood my ground on the matter. The upshot was that, again to help Coventry, I agreed to take the rest of the money owed to me over six years.

That self-esteem could not have been lower than it was when I left the club. At the finish, I had become so sensitive about the change in my professional fortunes, and the way I felt I was perceived, that just being in a public place – any public place – was inclined to bother me. It got to the point where I dreaded people recognising and approaching me. Even if I was just walking down a street, or helping Lesley with the shopping, mere eye contact with members of the public, let alone conversation – was to be avoided as far as I was concerned.

While I was trying to come to terms with what had happened to me, I did go to watch matches. But generally I would pick games at clubs such as Northampton Town and Rushden & Diamonds, where I would be less likely to bump into people I knew. Here again, I felt the need to avoid drawing too much attention to myself. Lesley and I would sit among the ordinary fans – like them, we paid for our tickets – and my attempts to get lost in the crowd extended to the wearing of a big woolly hat pulled down as low as possible without it covering my eyes. Of course, this form of disguise was never going to work 100 per cent for somebody with my appearance, notably my distinctive nose, which is why being a hundred feet in the air in the Canary Islands, with only Lesley and the birds for company, proved so enjoyable.

Up there, nobody could get to me. Nobody could rant and rave at me. Nobody could insult me, and make me feel worse about myself than I already felt.

# CHAPTER ELEVEN

# TAKE THE LOWE ROAD

On the occasions I got uppity with Rupert Lowe his response would be: 'Now, now Gordon, I was the only one [on the Southampton board] who wanted you here.' He said it so often that, as he started, I would finish the sentence off for him. 'I think I've got the message now, Chairman,' I'd tell him.

Of course, I will never need anybody to remind me – least of all Rupert – how much I owe him.

When I was sacked by Coventry I never thought I might land another manager's job after only six weeks; and I certainly did not expect it to be back in the Premiership. The opportunity Rupert handed me, which to me was rather like getting back behind the wheel of a car for the first time following a bad road accident, came earlier than I would have preferred. But nobody likes to be branded a failure, least of all a football manager, and as I had no way of knowing when or if I would get the chance to rehabilitate myself, there was no way I could turn the Southampton offer down. It could not have worked out better for me. But, had the reverse been true, I rather think it would have marked the end of the road for me in this role. I doubt that other clubs would have been falling over themselves to take me on and I am not sure I would have had the confidence to try again somewhere else anyway.

So I can never lose sight of the way that Rupert stuck his neck out for me in giving me the job, and also what I learned from him.

A lot of the stick he has taken from the fans as a result of Southampton's slide in recent seasons has been unfair in my opinion. People have short memories – they forget that it was Rupert who filled the lead role in Southampton's crucial move from The Dell to St Mary's and that it is mainly down to him that the club, despite their failure to remain in the Premiership, have remained in comparatively good shape financially. As a businessman, he is one of the toughest and most astute people I have known.

I am sure Rupert will concede that he has made mistakes on the football side. But as I have said to him: 'There is a limit to how much you can blame yourself. There is no way you deserve to have all the blame heaped on your shoulders.'

He is a remarkable character, and, though there were tensions between us, I found it impossible to dislike him. To my knowledge, it was the same with everybody else who occasionally moaned and groaned about him at Southampton. You certainly had to admire him for the way he handled the gripes. I remember one occasion when he invited all the coaching staff and myself to a meeting in my office to air any complaints about him to his face. He arranged for us to sit in front of him in a semi-circle, and he said: 'Come on then – say what you think. Let's have it out in the open.' We verbally battered him, but he had an answer for everything and nothing we said seemed to upset him. In fact, as he sat there, with his arms folded and his rosy cheeks getting redder by the minute, he even started laughing. 'I'm enjoying this,' he told us.

I don't think I have ever had a club chairman – either as a player or a manager – as different from me in his social background and mentality as Rupert. As he is constantly reminded, he is not what most people in the game would call a real football man. He had only ever seen one or two matches before becoming involved with Southampton – his favourite sports were and possible still are hockey and Rugby Union – and one of the other reasons why he has been looked upon as being different from the norm is that one of his chief forms of relaxation is duck shooting. Someone once remarked: 'If he was not a football club chairman, he would probably be an estate manager.' His image was perhaps best summed up by a comment attributed to Graeme Souness, the first of his Southampton managers. Graeme, by way of an explanation for his apparent difficulty in establishing a rapport with him, was quoted as saying: 'How many people do you know in professional football with the name Rupert?'

All this, though, is part of the reason why I am fond of him – I like people who are unconventional and, in the world of professional football, he is certainly that. Though he got on my nerves sometimes, just as I must have got on his, we could make each other laugh. I really did get a lot of fun out of working with him.

It was always liable to get particularly entertaining when he was in the company of his mate Andrew Cowen, Southampton's managing director. The two men go back a long way – they were in the same class at prep school – and are very much kindred spirits. I still laugh when I think of Andrew's words to me when I bumped into him in the dressing room tunnel before my first Southampton match. 'Are the boys ready to bite the boils off a bear's arse?' he asked. The players loved that one when I told them. What a double act he and Rupert made. They were like two Harry Enfields. On one occasion, when the three of us were talking about a player causing a few headaches for me off the field, the conversation – with me unable to get a word in – went like this:

Rupert: 'Oh, there's a danger of him going off the rails.'

Andrew: 'Off the rails and right through the barrier.'

Rupert: 'Through the barrier and over the cliff.'

Andrew: 'Off the cliff and into the sea . . .'

Rupert: 'And never to be seen again.'

For the early part of matches, I would sometimes sit with Rupert and Andrew in the directors' box. That experience could also be somewhat amusing (if that's the right word). Rupert was fond of comparing football situations with those he experienced as a hockey player. For example, it bothered him that Southampton did not score more goals from corners. He was particularly irritated once when a corner landed at one of our player's feet, only for him to blast it over from eight yards out. 'Should he have done that, Gordon?' he asked.

'No, Mr Chairman, of course he shouldn't have done that.'

'Did he practise his shooting?'

'Yes, Mr Chairman, he did practise his shooting.'

Andrew, who, like Rupert had not previously been a football follower, tended to make the same sort of comments. In one ear I would be hearing: 'Oh, what a terrible pass', and in the other, it would be: 'Doesn't he work on this?' Hence the fact that when I left them to join Garry Pendrey in the technical area, Garry would joke: 'I know why you are here – bet those two are getting on your t**s again.'

I know that I could be a source of much amusement, if not bafflement, to them as well. I am sure that Rupert still laughs and shakes his head in amazement over the memory of my one and only appearance at a Southampton board meeting.

I had never attended board meetings at Coventry. I avoided them like the plague because I have never been a political animal and have always found that a lot of club directors talk in a language which tends to go over my head. Bryan Richardson appreciated that I could be quite sensitive about some of the comments that directors are liable to come out with at times – as Mark McGhee once remarked to me: 'You can get one or two who deliberately try to catch you out to show how clever they are' – so any boardroom ideas or decisions that involved me at Coventry were discussed by Bryan and myself over a pot of tea at my house.

To Rupert's dismay, I was not willing to attend Southampton board meetings either. When I told him this, he said: 'Well, if that's the case, it would be good for us [the directors] to at least be able to have an informal chat with you after a game.' That idea did not grab me either. I explained: 'Look, I know what it is like. You lot are drinking from 12 a.m. to 5 p.m. and whether our result is good or bad, you can be sure that somebody is going to make a comment to me that I won't be happy with and that, because of my immediate post-match emotional state, I will be liable to go off my head.'

'Okay,' he said. 'But you do need to come to the occasional board meeting. Why not just come to one and see what it is like?' I think even Rupert was happy to wave the white flag on this issue when it almost led to a fight between me and a board member.

For some time, I had been pressing for the board's permission to allow us to do more of our first-team work during the week at the stadium because, in bad weather, I did not feel that our two pitches at the club's Marchwood training centre were suitable. I had actually seen the board member discreetly watching us work there one day – from behind a bush, would you believe – in order to get a clearer idea of what we did. That was fair enough, except that he did not properly grasp our programme.

At the board meeting, Rupert – who was sitting beside me – asked me to explain our procedure, and as I was telling him that we always did our warm-up on a bit of land behind the pitch, I could see the director shaking his head.

'What are you shaking your head for? I asked. 'Are you calling me a liar?' I then realised that what he had thought was the warm-up – which I do not think he could have seen – was, in fact, the final stage of our preparation in another area before we went on to the pitch. He was still shaking his head as I was trying to explain this to him, which made me even angrier.

The next thing I knew, as I started to get off my seat to confront him, Rupert was pinning me down by clamping his hand on my knee.

Rupert then quickly moved on to the next item on the agenda, and upon being told I could go, I was out of there like a shot. It is reasonable to believe that, had I attended board meetings on a regular basis, as he had urged me to do, I probably would not have lasted at Southampton more than about six months.

The aspect of working with Rupert that required the biggest adjustment from me was that his control over my decisions concerning potential signings was considerably stronger than Bryan Richardson's had been. I felt that Bryan trusted me more on this than Rupert did. My opinion on a player's ability, and the job he could do for Coventry, was good enough for Bryan – he did not feel the need to ask anybody else. It was different with Rupert. If I said: 'We need Player X', the final decision would usually be taken through a poll involving Rupert, me, our European scout Terry Cooper and chief scout Ray Clarke. Occasionally, if it was 2-2 (which was always on the cards given that Terry had a particularly close relationship with Rupert and Ray had a particularly close relationship with me), members of the coaching and training staff like Dennis Rofe and Steve Wigley would be brought into it as well.

Whereas Bryan looked upon me as the team manager, Rupert, who like many other modern-day chairmen in Britain is a great believer in the setups of continental clubs, viewed me more as the team head coach.

As I have said, as I occasionally did not give potential signings enough thought at Coventry, the Southampton system was good for me in some ways. However, it did take some getting used to; and having to battle to get the players I wanted could be quite wearying, especially as Rupert became more assertive with his own opinions on them. The situation could get quite compli-cated, with me thinking: 'If I let him have his way on signing Player A, he might let me have Player B.'

Rupert held all the aces in these matters. If he wanted to bring in a player I did not want, there was not really much I could do about it. I could threaten to keep leaving the player out of the team, but then Rupert could easily knock that idea on the head by telling me: 'If that's your attitude, I will make sure that any player you want is not offered the wages he is looking for.' This, indeed, was the scenario behind the signing of goalkeeper Antti Niemi – Rupert's choice – rather than the Croatian international Stipe Pletikosa – my choice – in July 2002.

I have to stress that I liked Niemi, too. In fact, I had tried to sign him for Coventry. However, I'd had rave reports about Pletikosa from our goalkeeping coach, David Coles; and having reached a stage in my relationship with Rupert where I felt I needed to make a stand on these issues, I looked upon this one as the ideal opportunity to see how far I could go. My bloody-mindednesss did not get me very far because, although I had been led to believe that Pletikosa would cost us considerably less in wages than Antti, Rupert claimed that Southampton could not afford him. Of course, this wrangle with Rupert turned out to be somewhat embarrassing for me because Antti was unques-tionably one of Southampton's best players during my time with the club. I knew he was good, but he proved to be even better than I thought. Rupert once told me: 'Football managers are not necessarily the best judges of football talent.' He illustrated the point by claiming that, although he had no background in livestock farming, one or two of his friends in that business thought he was a better spotter of good cows and bulls than they were.

'That's good, Chairman,' I said. 'If we need a couple of cows to play up front for us, you are the man to see, eh?'

'Don't be facetious, Gordon,' he said.

I could appreciate where Rupert was coming from. Generally, players, coaches and managers tend to be very dismissive about the football knowledge of most chairmen, let alone those with Rupert's background. The picture that the great Len Shackleton painted of these figures in his 1956 autobiography *The Clown Prince of Football* – in which one chapter was headed: 'The Average Director's Knowledge of Football' but consisted of a blank page – has never really faded.

The truth of it was brought home to me in a conversation with the chairman of one of the clubs who approached me during my spell out of the game. When he asked me my views about set-piece moves, I related something that Alex Ferguson had told me. 'You know Fergie?' he asked. He genuinely did not know that I had played for Fergie at Aberdeen and Manchester United. It amazed me that he had not previously done the small amount of research that would have given him that information. But not all chairmen are like that. Their overall image is misleading because, by the standards of people who have never played football at a high level or been professional coaches or managers, a lot of them do have a good knowledge of the game. Bryan Richardson was definitely in that category, and I would say this is also true of Rupert.

He once told me: 'You know, Gordon, I think I have cracked this game of football now. It is very much like hockey.' While I would question whether his experience in hockey is as relevant as he might have thought, his argument cannot be totally dismissed.

He is no mug on the general psychological and physical sides of sport. He is very much into various aspects of sports science and, as reflected by his radical decision to bring England's former World Cup Rugby Union coach Sir Clive Woodward on to the Southampton staff, his ideas on how football teams can maximise their performances can be refreshingly broad-minded and progressive.

I also found him extremely inquisitive. Some people at the club, and especially those on the football side, felt they had to be on their guard against him because he was forever trying to pick their brains about what was going on in the dressing room and on the training ground. When word got back to me about the questions he had been asking, I sometimes thought: 'Well, I am supposed to be the manager – why doesn't he just ask me?'

The up side of this trait in him, however, was that it gave him a greater insight into the game than that acquired by less intrusive chairmen. A little knowledge can be a dangerous thing, but to give Rupert his due the case of Antti was not the only instance of him showing that his football judgement should be respected.

There were a few players about whom he was spot-on. Take Peter Crouch, the player he went on about the most. Rupert suggested the centre-forward as a Southampton signing so often that it was like listening to a cracked record. We did not try to sign him from Aston Villa when I was manager because in addition to myself, none of the other members of our staff who were consulted on the idea by Rupert voted in favour of him being brought to Southampton either.

Crouch, always an ungainly looking figure because of his extraordinary height – six foot seven – and beanpole build, took some time to gain widespread credibility as a top player, to convince people that he had more to offer than just aerial ability. I could see he had a decent first touch and was a good finisher, but one of my doubts about him concerned the question of whether his body was strong enough to enable him to deal with strong physical contact and therefore consistently create the time and use these qualities.

Not only this, we already had James Beattie and I could not see how we could accommodate both Crouch and him in the same team.

Imagining the two of them together, I had visions of the other players just whacking the ball up to Crouch's head or knocking it into the corners for Beattie to chase. That was not the sort of football I wanted. I wanted us to be more imaginative than that, and was therefore looking for one striker to operate right up front, with the other dropping into the hole behind – à la Dennis Bergkamp – to help orchestrate the play. I did not think James or Crouch could do that.

Of course, Southampton did eventually sign Crouch after I left (and after James's departure to Everton) in July 2004 for £2 million. Twelve months later, he had become an England player and been sold to Liverpool for £7 million. Take a bow Rupert . . . but don't forget that not all the signing which could be attributed to you have turned out well.

It is doubtful that Rupert will ever totally live down the dubious distinction of being singled out, at least in some quarters, as being mainly responsible for the ill-fated £3.5 million signing of the Ecuador World Cup striker Agustin Delgado. The deal, which coincided with Delgado's excellent performances in Ecuador's 2002 World Cup qualifying matches, in which he played the leading role in steering the country to the finals for the first time, had been agreed before my appointment and was finalised shortly after it. When I took over, Rupert told me: 'Look, we are in the process of signing a guy for £5 million and

I cannot stop it because we have already paid the agent's fee. You will just need to trust me.'

How Rupert must have regretted those words. Delgado made only nine first-team appearances in my two and a half seasons as manager, mainly because of interminable knee problems exacerbated by his commitment to playing for Ecuador in the World Cup when not fully fit and also his failure to adhere to the treatment schedules we gave him. The club eventually released him on a free transfer.

The part that Rupert played in bringing him to Southampton has always been something of a grey area. My predecessor Stuart Gray claimed that the player was virtually forced upon him but Rupert has denied this. He has said: 'Terry Cooper, who had watched Delgado playing for Ecuador, advised Stuart Gray to buy him and Stuart sanctioned it.'

If that was the case, I was in a similar position when, just after I joined Southampton, Rupert recommended Delgado's Ecuador team-mate Kleber Chala to me. We were discussing the need to get someone who could give our play a bit more width, and Rupert said: 'I've got just the man for you [Chala]. Terry really likes him. He can play right side, left side, and he is a great crosser of the ball. We can get him for just £500,000.' I had not been at Southampton long enough to challenge the chairman's opinion so I was happy to go along with the transfer, especially as I thought Chala would help Delgado settle down. But, when I started working with him, it became clear to me that he lacked the ability I was looking for – which was a pity because I found him an absolutely smashing lad – and he was not able to have much influence on Delgado either.

Delgado was every club's worst nightmare. There is always a risk factor in signing a player from abroad – especially from outside Europe. In terms of their mentality, you generally know what you are getting with stars from Britain and most other parts of Europe, but this is less the case with those from further afield. I have always felt that South American players are particularly difficult to integrate into British football and my dealings with Delgado (which admittedly provided a somewhat extreme example) inevitably strengthened this view.

Indeed, the whole Delgado episode was like a farce.

In one training session he was involved in, we also had a Chinese player working with us. Both had interpreters with them, and the one helping the Chinese lad was a lady in a trouser suit and high heels. They had no problems in relaying my instructions to their players in the warm-up, but it was a different matter for the lady when she had to do it during the small-sided game that followed because the Chinese player had to do considerably more running and cover more ground than Delgado. She seemed to be running around in circles. It was crazy.

As a result of his injuries, I doubt that I was able to coach Delgado individually on aspects of his game such as his movement for more than twenty days. Because of the language barrier, we could not really give him any instructions on the occasions that he played, so we just had to keep him up the park, in the middle, and try to make his role as basic as possible. One of his matches was at West Ham, where his lack of movement forced us to substitute him with Anders Svensson.

I got his attention by shouting: 'Tino – Cambio per Svensson.' He nodded and came off. Cambio? After the game, Gary Pendrey asked: 'Where did you get that word from?' Not surprisingly, Gary seemed even more dumfounded when I explained: 'You see it all the time when you are on holiday abroad and want to change your money.' I wish we could have reached Delgado more often. Referring to his much better performance immediately before the West Ham game, in the 3-2 win over the champions, Arsenal, I said to Rupert: 'There is clearly a good player in there somewhere.' That was like music to Rupert's ears. 'I told you this, Gordon,' he said. 'Aye, Chairman,' I replied. 'But he is only a good player if he plays. You try and get him to do it.'

Initially, I felt a bit sorry for Delgado. He could hardly speak a word of English, and despite having Chala with him, he cut quite a lonely, isolated figure. Part of his problem in my view was the influence of his brother, Marcos, who was to become his agent. He seemed to me to dominate Delgado. Moreover, Delgado was under a great deal of pressure in terms of his involvement with his national team. He was Ecuador's biggest star, and it seemed to us that they exerted a greater measure of control over him – even when he was not playing for them – than we did. There was some conflict between us and them over our diagnosis of his injuries and what we felt he needed to get over them properly, which must have been very confusing for him. Though he was not fit to play for us when he joined us, we agreed to allow him to join the Ecuador squad for their crucial World Cup qualifying tie against Uruguay on the proviso that he did not take part in the match. We then discovered that he had played for half the game, and made his injury worse as a result. Why? 'They told me that if I did not play, they would not take me to the World Cup Finals,' he claimed.

But I think all this was only part of the story. I have never known a club to try so hard to help one player as Southampton tried to help Delgado. Unfortunately, he did not do a great deal to help himself.

It was not unusual for him to miss training, or a treatment session at the club, without informing anybody. Our physiotherapist, Jimmy Joyce, who had the unenviable job of trying to locate him, got so stressed out over Delgado that we kept having to try to calm him down. Even when Delgado was in the treatment room, it was very difficult for Jimmy to get him to do all the remedial work set out for him. For example, if Jimmy asked him to carry out an exercise involving weights, Delgado would point to his knee and say: 'Pain.' No matter how many times Jimmy tried to explain to him that it was only to be expected that he would experience discomfort, and that he needed to push himself through it in order to get over the problem, the message never really sunk in. 'He will start an exercise when you are in the room, but when you go out, he will stop,' Jimmy complained.

The reality with Delgado was that he had been used to being the centre of attention in Ecuador and could not handle the situation of being in a country where nobody knew him and, in the football sense, he had to start from scratch again. He seemed to think that he could do whatever he wanted. Even some of his interpreters lost patience with him. It was immensely frustrating for everybody involved, but we did get a lot of laughs over it.

The local *Daily Echo* newspaper had a field day with Delgado over his disappearing acts. One back-page headline, along with a big picture of his face which was cleverly edited to look like a police mug shot, read: 'Wanted – have you seen this man?' It stated: 'The *Echo* appeals for anybody with information as to Delgado's whereabouts to contact Saints.'

According to reports, one of his explanations for his displays of discontent was that I 'hated' him. Another was that nobody at Southampton acknowledged his birthday. He was actually quoted as saying that he was upset because none of us had sung 'Happy Birthday' to him. I cannot believe he really said that – I am sure something must have got lost in translation – but it did give us a laugh. The morning after his birthday, before we went out for training, I said to the players: 'Right, lads, I don't know when you were born, but before we start, I want you all to sing "Happy Birthday" just in case there is somebody here who is expecting it.'

My most bizarre experience with Delgado concerned not so much him but one of his interpreters.

I had no idea who he was when he and Delgado turned up for a training session – some forty-five minutes late – but once he started talking I immediately recognised his voice. 'Don't I know you?' I asked. He then reminded me about a telephone conversation we'd had a couple of weeks earlier – not the brightest of moves.

The guy, a 25-year-old Ecuadorian living in London, had left a number of messages for me. When I got back to him to find out what he wanted, he asked if Southampton could give him a trial as a player. As he had only played for local amateur teams, I explained that there was a limit to the number of players a club could look at and said that, because of his age, he would need to get himself to a higher level before we would consider doing so. Unfortunately, he clearly had problems accepting this. He was so persistent that I eventually had to tell him: 'Look, I am trying to help you, but you are not listening. Please do not call me again.'

When he and Delgado wandered on to the training field, I thought it was strange that he was in training gear as well. Not that he looked like a footballer. He was wearing the tightest shorts I have ever seen – I think they must have been cycling shorts – and black ankle socks. As it was about 11.15 a.m., and I had been working with all the other players since 10.30 a.m., I was also wondering how Delgado, who knew perfectly well what our training times were, had the nerve to think that he could join in.

The players knew what was coming, but obviously Delgado and his new mate didn't. As the pair came on to the field, at the opposite end to where we were working and headed towards me, I pretended I had not seen them. Finally, I said: 'Yeah?'

'We are ready to start training now,' said the interpreter.

'Are you?' I replied.

'Delgado wants to know where to go in the training session.'

'He does not go anywhere,' I said. 'He goes right back in the dressing room with you.'

This was followed by a lot of arm waving and muttering between the two. 'We are going to have to see the chairman,' the interpreter said. 'He [Delgado] is not right in the head.'

'I know he is not right in the head – just get off.' I then asked why he was in training gear. 'Well, I thought I could join in as well,' he explained.

He then got it in the neck, too. With that, off they went.

Even Rupert had to concede that the signing of Delgado had been a mistake. The start I made as Southampton manager, in the club's first season at the St Mary's Stadium, made me think that he might also have made a mistake about me.

# CHAPTER TWELVE

# REVIVAL

At the media conference for my Southampton appointment, I was asked: 'Do you feel you are the right man for the job?' I felt it was a daft question and I gave a daft answer. 'No.' But the question and answer seemed entirely appropriate after my first few matches.

Southampton had been second from bottom when I took over from Stuart Gray, having won only twice (away to Bolton and Middlesbrough) and suffered six defeats, in their opening eight matches. My first match was at home to Ipswich, who fought back from 3-1 down to hold us to a 3-3 draw. After losing the next three games, we were at the bottom. Then came our 1-0 over Charlton. It lifted us to fourth from bottom and sparked a steady rise which eventually saw us finish eleventh.

The goal that sank Charlton came through a Marian Pahars header from James Beattie's cross just after half-time, but Charlton were desperately unfortunate not to make it 1-1 in the last minute when Steve Brown beat Paul Jones with a wonderful volley, only for the ball to hit the inside of a post and fly back across the goal, without any other Charlton player managing to get a touch. I often think that, had the ball gone in, my Southampton story might well have turned out differently.

But prior to that game, had Rupert wanted to say goodbye to me, I would probably have got down on my knees and thanked him for putting me out of my misery. After watching Southampton lose 2-0 at West Ham immediately before my appointment I knew the job was not going to be easy. I had already been sounded out by Rupert on the possibility of replacing Stuart Gray if Southampton lost and, because of all the media speculation about Stuart's position, some people felt I shouldn't have been at Upton Park that day. However, I had not seen Southampton in action for some time, and as sensitive as I was about the pressure Stuart was under, I did not think anybody could truly blame me for wanting to see what might be in store for me if I did take over from him.

I did my best not to draw attention to myself. I went to the game with Gavin and Craig and, in an attempt to make sure nobody knew I was there, we all wore the same sort of clothes as thousands of other spectators – including woolly hats – and sat with the die-hard West Ham fans behind one of the goals, not in the main stand. I would have got away with it, except that I was recognised by a couple of guys alongside us when they started talking to us. I suspect that the news of my presence at the match in the media, which hardened the stories about me having been lined up to step into Stuart's shoes, arose from their tip-offs. My first impression of the team was not favourable. This is not meant as a criticism of Stuart Gray and his right hand man, Mick Wadsworth – I'm not sure that Southampton had all their players available and, at any event, it could be that I just happened to catch them on a particularly bad day. There have been plenty of matches in which some of the other teams I have managed have not looked too clever either. However, I could only go on what I had seen and in this instance I felt there was little variation of movement in Southampton's play – they played in straight lines and sort of plodded through the game. West Ham, who had made a disappointing start to the season themselves, were so much sharper and more fluent and imaginative.

The views of Gavin, Craig and Lesley on the possibility of me going into it were mixed to say the least. Gavin was saying: 'I would forget about it if I were you', while Craig's attitude was: 'Get right back in there.' Lesley put the ball into my court. 'It's up to you,' she told me. 'If you really want to do it, go ahead. I am happy to go along with whatever you decide.'

I continued to have doubts over the weekend. At the same time, I thought: 'Are you going to be a coward?'

Before the Charlton match I was thinking that I should have answered that in the affirmative. I really did believe that coming to Southampton was one of the worst decisions of my life. If anything, I felt even more uptight and depressed than I had towards the end of my career at Coventry.

It was during this period that I promised Lesley that I would take a break from football when my Southampton commitments had ended. My mindset was that I would honour the two and a half year Southampton contract I had signed – provided, of course I was allowed to do so – and that would be it. As the usual managerial cycle at most clubs is three years, I took the view that whatever position Southampton were in by the end of my agreement, it was probably going to be the best I could possibly do there anyway. Not surprisingly, I did not feel quite as strongly about the need for the break at the end of my second season, with Southampton having finished in their highest-ever Premiership position of eighth and reached the FA Cup Final for the first time in 27 years. I was on so much of a high then that if Rupert had done more to show that he wanted me to stay, it is possible that I would have changed my mind. As it was, when the subject of my contract was raised by him in May, during a meeting mainly to review the contracts of the players, he just said, almost in passing: 'We will give you a one-year rolling agreement.' That was virtually it.

I must admit that I was disappointed, not with the offer but the manner in which it was made. I expected a much longer, and broader conversation on my position than this. I accept that I was probably being over-sensitive, but at the time, it seemed to me that I was being taken for granted. I thought: 'You deserve more than that.'

I could have – and maybe should have – made that point to him. Instead, as it was still in my mind to leave, I just said: 'Don't worry about me for the time being', and left it at that. We agreed that I would think about the offer and that we would discuss it more fully at a later date. It was not until October that he broached the subject again – by which time, Southampton's form had dipped; and my inclination to take that break had got stronger again.

'We've got to discuss your contract,' he said to me.

'It doesn't matter,' I said.

'What do you mean it doesn't matter?' he asked.

'Well, I am keeping a promise I made to Lesley,' I explained. 'I will see out the remainder of my present agreement and then I am taking a break from football.'

I felt quite badly about it – it came as much of a shock to Rupert as it did to everybody else, and it was difficult to convince him that the decision ultimately had precious little to do with anything he had said or done. 'Have I missed something here?' he said. 'Is it the money? Is it me?'

The basic truth is that it was neither.

I had been in professional football virtually non-stop for around 30 years. Had I stayed with Southampton, I am really not sure that I would have had the freshness or enthusiasm necessary to do myself justice. As far as I am concerned, I left more or less on my sell-by date. It was the right time for everybody.

There were a number of reasons why we went on to lift ourselves into a mid-table position in my first season. It will come as no surprise to those who know me that, as at the start of my careers at Coventry and Celtic, the players were pushed harder in training. In that area alone, my first signings for Southampton – my former Coventry players Paul Telfer and Paul Williams – were a tremendous help in assuaging any dressing-room misgivings about my methods.

Both were signed on free transfers and, without wishing to appear prejudiced, I think they made a big difference to the team. Paul Williams did an excellent job as Claus Lundekvam's central defensive partner. Tahar El Khalej, the man he replaced, was a wonderful lad, but Paul brought a greater sense of composure and authority to that department.

At the start of the season, the right-back spot was being filled by Rory Delap. Though he is an extremely strong and versatile player, I was not 100 per cent sold on him in that position partly because he did not communicate with the other defenders. The other reason why I had mixed feeling about Rory as a full back was that when he burst forward in support of attacks – his greatest strength – he could be quite lackadaisical about getting back. He looked as if he was out for an afternoon stroll. So we put Rory in midfield, where his attacking drive could be utilised more effectively.

Rory's move enabled Jason Dodd, previously the regular right back, to re-establish himself in the side. Jason, the third longest serving Southampton player at the time, behind Matt Le Tissier and Francis Benali, is typical of many players who started their careers in non-league football and had to do ordinary jobs outside the game. His enthusiasm for the game has remained the same as it was when Southampton signed him from Bath City at nineteen in 1989. Jason and Paul Telfer on the right side of the midfield, made an excellent combination.

The other early Southampton team change after my arrival – and possibly the most crucial of all – was the switch of Chris Marsden from central midfield to the left side, to help left back Wayne Bridge fully exploit his attacking ability.

That was not happening at the time I joined Southampton because the four midfielders were stretched across the field and, therefore, whenever Wayne tried to get forward, his path was blocked. This was one of the things I noticed when I watched Southampton at West Ham; Kevin Davies filled the wide left role and was positioned directly in front of Wayne.

Our solution to that problem was to narrow the midfield and to convince Chris that he could benefit from his new job as Bridge's partner, in the same way that I had benefited from my right-side partnerships with the similarly vibrant attacking full backs I played with at Aberdeen, Manchester United and Leeds. I remember saying to him: 'I wish I was still playing, and could be in your position.'

When you ask a central midfielder to play on the right or left, they immediately think you are trying to turn him into a winger. It was understandable that Chris had such reservations initially because, while he was a strong runner, he did not have the burst of speed to take the ball past opponents consistently. His main asset was his passing. However, as we said to him: 'We do not want you to play like a winger. You do not have to make runs with the ball down that side of the field, because Wayne will be doing that. All you have to do is make sure you are far enough infield to give him the space he needs; use your passing skills to bring him into the play; and try to give him as much support as possible when he is in difficulty.'

Chris really blossomed, and I suspect that even he will have been amazed at some of his performances. Needless to say, Wayne blossomed as well. Their left wing partnership was one of the best in Britain.

On top of all this, we had two players with excellent technical ability for other midfield positions in Matt Oakley, like Chris a good passer of the ball, and Anders Svensson; and up front, in addition to Kevin Davies, we had James Beattie and Marian Pahars – our top scorers – and also the underrated Jo Tessem, whose electric pace and ability to play in other positions made him particularly valuable to us as a substitute. The next steps in our development came in December, when we signed Fabrice Fernandes from Rennes for £1.1 million and Brett Ormerod from Blackpool for £1.75 million.

However, just in case anybody was in danger of running away with the idea that we were approaching the super-team bracket, it was also in December that Manchester United hammered us 6-1 at Old Trafford.

The only other team to hand me a 6-1 defeat as a manager are Arsenal, who beat Southampton by that score just before we met the Gunners in the FA Cup Final the following season. That Arsenal win, which was the start of their amazing record run of forty-nine successive league matches without defeat, could be explained partly by our decision to leave out the likes of Claus Lundekvam, James Beattie and Brett Ormerod. To avoid giving too much away on how we intended to play against Arsenal in Cardiff, there were as many as five or six men in our starting line-up who we knew would probably not be in the Cup Final team.

But we weren't trying to hide anything against Manchester United. The only consolation was that with United in that sort of mood, the pounding we took – especially from Ruud van Nistelrooy, who scored a hat-trick – could have happened to anybody.

To me, it was yet another reminder that systems and tactics

are only important up to a point. I have to admit that managers do sometimes talk a lot of claptrap on this – they make the game sound much more complex than it really is.

In terms of touch and imagination, the most unstoppable football I have seen from any English team came from Arsenal in the first half of their 3-1 home win over Aston Villa in the 2004/05 season. In the opening forty-five minutes, when they scored all their goals, they produced more variations of attacking play than seemed possible in one game. The only explanation I could offer for Arsenal not maintaining it in the second half and getting a hatful of goals, was that they possibly ran themselves dizzy, let alone Villa. Manchester United have been different from Arsenal, in that there has been a more distinct pattern to the play of Fergie's Old Trafford teams. But that has not made United any easier to counter. There has been nothing out of the ordinary about their system – it's usually been a basic, straightforward 4-4-2 – but, of course, what is out of the ordinary is the quality of the players in it.

Indeed, if I had to choose between playing the best of Fergie's teams or the best of Arsène Wenger's, I think I would always plump for the latter. United seemed to me to be more ruthless than Arsenal – if Arsenal were two or three goals up, they would be more inclined to take their foot off the pedal. They would just want to tease you. United would want to annihilate you.

On the subject of how to stop United, one of the funniest comments I have ever heard came in a TV interview with the manager of a struggling team after they had managed to keep a clean sheet against them. United had produced so many shots and headers, it could have been 10-0. I think their number of goal attempts was as high as thirty-seven, which must have been some kind of record. However, in all seriousness, the interviewer told the manager: 'Well, you had the tactics spot on there.' I could imagine the manager standing up in the dressing room before the match and telling his players: 'Right, lads, you just keep them down to thirty-seven goal attempts and it will be a good performance.'

One of my remarks during a team talk for a match against United was even dafter. 'Right, lads, we have a plan which is guaranteed to stop them,' I said. 'Great, brilliant,' someone remarked. 'Aye,' I said, 'but I don't think we will be able to get away with it. It involves having fourteen of our players on the field at the same time.' During United's 6-1 win over Southampton, Garry Pendrey, trying to make sense of my gesticulations to the players from the technical area, asked: 'What are you doing?' 'I am just giving the players some hand signals to kid people that I know what I am doing,' I said. 'You can join in if you like.' I wasn't entirely joking.

With Southampton seventeenth in the table, our hiding at Old Trafford did not seem to augur well for our chances of getting much out of the games coming up for us. Our next match was against Tottenham, which we won 1-0. This was followed by a run of eight matches, in which we had to face all the teams in the top six, including Manchester United again and Liverpool twice. But it did not turn out as badly as one might have feared. Manchester United beat us 3-1, and there were also defeats at the hands of Leeds and Newcastle. However, we took eight points against Chelsea, Liverpool and Arsenal, and with a win over West Ham, our overall points total from the eight games was eleven.

If any match showed that we had the potential to do better, it was the 4-2 win at Chelsea on New Year's Day – one of my best ever results as a manager. Chelsea had only conceded six goals in their previous twelve matches and it was Southampton's record Premiership away victory. It was very much the Marian Pahars–James Beattie show. After Beats had given us the lead with a stunning thirty-yard free kick, we found ourselves 2-1 down at half time. In the second half, though, Chelsea were blown away. Marian, leaving John Terry for dead from a great through ball by Paul Telfer, made it 2-2 and, after Chris Marsden had put us ahead again, he supplied the cross from which Beats scored our fourth goal.

The two strikers provide an intriguing contrast in personalities. They really are chalk and cheese. Beats is a gregarious character, which is putting it mildly. At any party, you can virtually guarantee that he will be the life and soul. He is what I call one of life's radiators. Marian is the opposite. When we came in for training each day, we never had to see Beats to know he was there – we could hear him from twenty yards away. Marian could be in the same room and you would still now know he was present.

My sense of humour was totally lost on Marian. At one of our team meetings, when I was talking about an opposing striker, I turned to him and said: 'The first opportunity you get, Marian, I want you to clatter into him and smash him right up in the air.' It was meant as a joke, because Marian, unlike Beats, was noted as a player who did not relish bruising bodily contact. But he did not appreciate that I was taking the mick. He just sat there, straight-faced, and nodded.

One incident which I feel summed him up perfectly was his reaction to having to go into the North Sea when we were at St Andrews in Scotland for pre-season training before the 2003/04 campaign. On what seemed certain to be Wayne Bridges' last day at the club before his transfer to Chelsea, we thought we would do something out of the ordinary to make it one to remember. So after the players had gone through their warm-up on the beach, they were given the choice of either running up and down the sand dunes – which they'd done before and hated – or taking part in a swimming test which involved our two masseurs, Jim Simpson and Chris Lovegrove, going as far out into the sea as they could and the players having to swim around them before returning to the shore.

The sky was black and it was cold, but the players did not appear to have any difficulty in entering into the spirit of things – except for Marian and Fabrice Fernandes, another player who could give the impression he was carrying the weight of the world on his shoulders. As the rest of the players were diving in and heading for Jim and Chris – the 'Chuckle brothers', as we called them because of their wisecracks and practical jokes – Marian and Fabrice were hanging back, moaning to each other. I could hear Marian complaining that he might get a cold or the flu. Knowing Marian as I did, it would not have surprised me in the least if his negative thoughts about the idea had included the fear that he might even get bitten by a shark. He was the quickest player at the club, but the fifteen-yard dash from the beach to the sea must have taken him and Fabrice fifteen minutes.

The annoying aspect of this for the other players was that nobody was allowed to come out of the water until everyone had completed their swim. Thanks to Marian and Fabrice, they were all left trying to tread water. They were freezing.

It is difficult to reconcile this picture of the pair with the wonderful flair and panache they showed on a football field.

Marian is a fantastic striker. I previously tried to sign him for Coventry, and would have been prepared to pay him double the wages we heard he was getting at Southampton. We were not able to enter into any personal negotiations with him, however, because Glenn Hoddle, my first point of contact over the matter, told me he was not willing to let him go. Southampton had paid £800,000 for Marian but to me he was more like a £10 million player. Apart from his pace, he had a great fitness level and was tremendous in the air for someone of five foot nine. Above all, he was far and away the best finisher I had at the club.

All of which made it seem a massive blow for us when Marian, having struggled to regain his fitness after a hernia operation in the 2002 close season, then suffered an ankle injury – in November – which put him out of action for almost a year. The fact that we were able to progress as far as we did without him, though, becomes easier to understand when you consider the strength of character of the player who took over from him, Brett Ormerod – and, of course, the irrepressible Beats.

They are not the most technically gifted strikers in Britain, but the amount of running Ormerod and Beattie did, and their determination, made them a nightmare for any defenders to play against. I cannot think of a pair of strikers who burned out defenders as much as they did. Their rapport stemmed from the fact that they had a great deal in common in their backgrounds and that they have had to work exceptionally hard to establish themselves after early setbacks in their careers.

Both, for example, are Lancastrians, and both were released by Blackburn as teenagers. The road to the Premiership was particularly hard for Brett because he then had to go into non-league football with Accrington Stanley and, after being signed by Blackpool, he suffered a badly broken leg. If any professional footballers can be excused for giving themselves a pat on the back for what they have achieved, it is these two. They have squeezed the absolute maximum out of themselves.

I had first seen Brett in action for Blackpool in a 3-1 win at Northampton, shortly after my departure from Coventry. It was almost as if he was the only man playing – no matter where the ball was, he seemed to be there. He scored two of the goals and he just seemed to have a stimulating effect on his whole team. He was like that at Southampton, too. He could look a right mess when he played – his socks would often be rolled down and he resembled a parks player more than a Premiership one.

'I've seen a better dressed wound than you,' I'd tell him. But everybody at Southampton – the fans, players, coaches, myself – loved him.

None more so than Beats. He was more focused on scoring than Brett. Although they both covered a lot of ground, Brett tended to make more runs into wide areas, thus enabling his partner to remain in the key central goal-getting positions. Given Brett's selfless support of Beats, and the rarity of him getting on the score sheet as a consequence – he only scored five goals in his thirty-one league appearances – I do not think any of the goals which helped propel Southampton to the FA Cup Final were applauded as enthusiastically as his headed opener from Chris Marsden's cross in the 2-1 semi-final win against Watford. That put him in the uncharacteristic position of being our top FA Cup scorer, with three. His claims to the man-of-the-match award, and the favourable media attention that went with it, were endorsed by the fact that he also set up Beats for the second goal.

It was great to see his value to the team being highlighted publicly. I was particularly happy for him, because he'd been very nervous about the match. During a long conversation with him beforehand, it struck me that he was looking upon it as a sort of make or break game for him. I said: 'This is not that much of a big game for you. In terms of changing your career, the most important game you have played was probably the one I saw at Northampton. Don't worry about it – just enjoy it.' At the end of the tie, I was so pleased for him; his performance provided one of the best experiences of my managerial career. This also applied to Beats' achievements in breaking into the England team and ending the season with his best ever goal total of twenty-four.

He did not score any in his first nine league matches, only two of which were won. His first goal came in the 1-0 win over

Aston Villa, with a penalty which he earned himself through charging bravely into a situation which a lot of centre-forwards would have backed out of. From then on, he was up and running, and so were Southampton.

Beats, a great athlete as opposed to a great footballer, was always at his most effective for Southampton when he was playing flat out all the time. Because he thrived so much on responsibility, and nobody else appeared to be able to hold a candle to him as a goalscorer – in the absence of Marian – we were happy to build the team around him. The style of play we adopted to get the best out of him meant that some of our individual technical ability had to be sacrificed, but the end justified the means.

Basically, our attacking play was designed to put him in the position of nearly always being the last man in the move. He is an intelligent lad, and his ability to create space for himself – especially through taking his marker towards the ball and then spinning off – was excellent. He got better and better at that. But he did not have the variation in his play of an Henry or a Van Nistelrooy; he wasn't the type of striker who was comfortable in coming short for the ball to be played to his feet, and setting up other players. We knew that the more times we could get the ball into the box early – especially with crosses – the more goals he would score. I know one can say that about all strikers but, because of his need to avoid having to manipulate the ball, it was especially true with Beats.

In repeatedly getting the ball into the box from wide positions, we were (or tried to be) the working class equivalent of Manchester United, when they had David Beckham and Ryan Giggs. With his ability to create outstanding chances with crosses from deep positions – as opposed to on or near the goal line – Fabrice Fernandes was our Beckham.

Fabrice did so well for us that, during the following 2002/03 season, Liverpool expressed an interest in him. In my opinion, this – and, more specifically, our unwillingness to sell him to them – had an unsettling effect on Fabrice. I do not think it was mere coincidence that he was not quite the same player for us after that.

It was a situation I could have anticipated when we signed Fabrice because I did have some doubts then concerning his temperament and personality. Apart from what I'd read about his problems at Fulham, he struck me as intense when I first met him. I thought: 'Oh, I am not sure about you.' As I was to discover – notably after I left him out of our starting line-up for the FA Cup Final – that was the way he was. He worked hard enough – there were no problems with him on that score – but he did not look the happiest of people at the best of times, and there were occasions when, rightly or wrongly, you would be convinced that he was in a sulk.

To make sure that this did not affect the mood of the other players, I would often make a joke about it. I'd say something like: 'Right, lads, before we start, this is just to let you know that Fabrice is in a bad mood again. You know what these temperamental, artistic French types are like. But we aren't going to allow that to get to us, are we?' They laughed. Fabrice, without the trace of a smile, just tutted, shrugged and got on with it.

They did not dislike him and they certainly respected and admired his ability. It might have seemed as if he had a cloud over him off the field, but on it, when he had the ball at his feet, it was as if he was bathed in warm sunshine.

A lot of people were surprised at his success as a right-side player, on the grounds that he could not use his right foot for a cross – he nearly always had to switch it on to his left. It is often claimed that this can be detrimental to a team; that it disrupts its rhythm and creates problems for the players hoping to get on the end of the cross in their attempts to lose their markers. This is not necessarily the case. It depends on the crossing position and where the opposing defenders are positioned. The point is valid when you are trying to get the ball into the middle from on or near the goal line, but much less so when it is being put in early from deeper positions.

Whenever I played on the left, I found that defenders tended to find it harder to stop me crossing the ball with my right foot than they did when I was on the other flank, especially when I had someone creating an extra couple of yards for me by making an overlap. Paul Telfer helped Fabrice a lot in this way. I also found that, because of the trajectory of the crosses in these circumstances – the way they bent towards the goal like inswinging corners – they were more dangerous.

Despite the work of players like Fabrice, Beats and Brett, we were not a team which found goals easy to come by. Our total of league goals that season amounted to just forty-three, but this was offset by the fact that we only conceded forty-six, one of the best defensive records in the Premiership. Bearing in mind the result we suffered at the hands of Arsenal in May, one curious aspect of all this was that the ten matches in which we managed to score more than one goal included a 3-2 home win over the Gunners in November.

In the 2002/03 season, with Michael Svensson having been signed from the Swedish club Troyes for £2 million to form a new central defensive partnership with Claus Lundekvam, this was an area in which we were exceptionally strong. It would be wrong, however, to give them all the credit for our defensive record. We did a lot of work in training on this side of our game, which involved all the players, not just the keeper and back four, or just Michael and Claus in the middle. However, these two together were special by any standards. Claus was already a really good central defender, but Michael – probably a better defender, but not as skilful as Claus on the ball – made him even better. Michael is an excellent communicator, and that in itself has been a big plus for Claus. He is not the most assertive of people in this way and reacts well to having people alongside him who are.

All manner of explanations have been put forward for Southampton's relegation in 2005. In my view, the loss of Michael through injury for the season was possibly the biggest factor of all.

Our defence was no less impressive in the FA Cup than it was in the Premiership. No more than three goals were conceded in our six ties, and the bonus for us was that our total at the other end was thirteen, four of which came in the third round, with the 4-0 home win over Tottenham. As Tottenham's manager was Glenn Hoddle, a man who seems destined never to be forgiven by Southampton fans for leaving the club to go to White Hart Lane, that success meant more to our followers than any of our other wins in the competition. My own reason for remembering it concerns the physical power of our performance. It was probably the most vivid example of the level of fitness I tried to instil into the team. We had also played Spurs at home three days earlier in the Premiership, beating them 1-0 with a James Beattie goal eight minutes from the end. It was a hard match, but this affected them more than us. Spurs were not a very fit or strong team in my opinion, and because of the amount of work they had to do against us they had nothing left for the second match. The only player who seemed as if he could cause us problems was Robbie Keane. But we ran them off the pitch.

Of the other ties leading to the final – against Millwall, Norwich, Wolves and Watford – the ones that concerned me the most were the clashes with Millwall. Just the fact that Millwall's manager was Mark McGhee was enough to bother me. Mark is among the brightest people I have known in professional football and, because of our long, close friendship, I reckon he can read me better than almost anyone. I think that every team that reaches the final experiences at least one match in which it could easily have been knocked out of the competition, and the tie with Millwall was the one in that category for us.

We were drawn against them at home and Millwall, who took the lead through Steve Claridge early in the first half, would have had another but for a goal line clearance by Francis Benali. In the last few minutes, Kevin Davies was brought on for Fabrice, which was no more than a last, desperate throw of the dice on my part; and Kevin, who had been at Millwall on loan earlier in the season, equalised in stoppage time. We beat them 2-1 in the replay, thanks to two Matt Oakley goals – the winner coming in injury time.

When we beat Watford I was particularly happy for Brett Ormerod and Chris Marsden. They must have viewed the possibility of taking part in an FA Cup Final as an impossible dream during the early part of their careers. I had a special reason for congratulating Chris, who was thirty when Southampton brought him into the Premiership from Birmingham in 1999 and was now team captain.

I get a lot of satisfaction out of creating an atmosphere in which players feel comfortable about querying and making me think about my decisions; provided it is done at the right time and in the right way, I have no problems at all with it. It is good for me – it is good for everybody. One of the things that Chris deemed it necessary to question was my attitude to the FA Cup.

In my first season at Southampton, all that had really mattered to me was that we avoided relegation. We were fifteenth in the table when we lost 2-1 at Rotherham in the FA Cup third round on 16 January, and with a home Premiership match at home to Liverpool three days later, I just told the players: 'Forget about this – just clear your minds for Saturday.' It was disappointing to get knocked out of the Cup; although we did not play well at Rotherham, Agustin Delgado must have had about half a dozen chances. But in the context of our position in the league, I did not feel it was the end of the world.

At least one player felt differently. At about 9 p.m. on the eve of the Liverpool game, while I was relaxing in my room at our hotel, there was a knock on my door. It was Chris.

'I would like to speak to you about your attitude on Wednesday [to the tie against Rotherham],' he explained.

'Attitude?' I replied. 'We were thorough in our preparation for the game, weren't we?'

'Yeah,' he said. 'But after the match, it did not look as if the defeat had hurt you.'

When I explained my preoccupation with the league, he made a point that I could not argue against. He said: 'It is okay for you because you have won cups. I have not won anything. It is the same with many of the other players. We were busting a gut out there but your attitude made it seem as if you were dismissing that.' He was right, so, in one way, Southampton's achievement in getting to the final the following year felt almost like some kind of redemption for me.

As for the team I selected against Arsenal, the decision to omit Fabrice Fernandes from our starting line-up and replace him with a 21-year-old defender – Chris Baird – who had only made his first full appearance in the previous match at Manchester City, was inevitably the one which created by far the most fuss. I think that a lot of people interpreted it as me being negative. I don't believe I was being negative. I was being realistic. Nobody appreciated Fabrice's attacking talents more than I did, but against a team like Arsenal I had to take into account the question of whether he was liable to see enough of the ball to be able to use them. I also had to look at what he could contribute in other departments.

It always irritates me when managers and players say: 'It's great just to take part in an FA Cup Final – whatever the result, we are going to enjoy the occasion.' I doubt whether any of them truly believe this. It still hurts like crazy if you are on the losing team; and because the match attracts such a vast, worldwide audience, I can think of nothing worse than not even being able to make it a decent contest and being hammered. We had less to lose than most other FA Cup finalists. We were already guaranteed the FA Cup winners' slot in the Uefa Cup, thanks to Arsenal getting into the European Champions League. But we wanted to beat Arsenal, and I did not see the point in kidding ourselves that we could do it by taking them on at their own game.

I did not believe any team in the Premiership was fitter than we were, so our game plan was to push the game into extra time and try and gain the edge from there.

It was well known that Arsenal were particularly dangerous on the left. In addition to the attacking bursts of left-back Ashley Cole, this is the side of the field where Robert Pires and Thierry Henry created or scored most of the Gunners' goals. I was more concerned about Pires than I was about Henry because of his ability to take the ball past opponents. Once he gets into his stride, his pace, strength and control make it very difficult to stop him – and that aspect of his game is often what brought Henry his scoring chances. How many times did we see Pires draw the opposing right back towards him, and Henry going into the space he had left? Pires operated in an old fashioned-type inside left position, so had Fabrice been in our FA Cup Final team, we would have needed him to slightly adjust his position to make himself the first Southampton player his fellow Frenchman had to beat and to deny Pires the chance to build up any momentum.

I always had doubts that Fabrice could do this and I think these were confirmed when Arsenal's beat us 6-1 the week before the final. He tried hard enough but tackling is not one of his strong suits and Pires was much too good for him. Every time Pires got the ball, he practically waltzed past him. Fabrice was not even able to put enough pressure on Pires to help his next Southampton opponent to stop him. Pires scored a hat trick that night. Ironically, he also scored the goal – a close-range shot from a rebound just before half-time – that beat us at the Millennium Stadium. However, I still feel that the team we picked, with Fabrice on the bench – alongside Paul Jones, Jo Tessem, Paul Williams and Danny Higginbotham – was the right one.

Initially, we intended to have Paul Telfer in his usual right-back spot, with Chris Baird in front of him. But it did not work properly at Manchester City – it was too much to ask of the inexperienced youngster to play up the field, so the roles of the two players were switched. In helping Chris, and keeping Pires reasonably subdued, Paul was tremendous. Arsenal did deserve their win on the run of play – but we could easily have equalised in stoppage time when James Beattie's header was cleared off the line by Cole. It could be that Fabrice himself might have been able to save us from defeat if I had managed to bring him on when I wanted to do so. But the problem was that he himself did not appear to be enthusiastic about coming on. It seemed to me that the blow of not being in the team was just too much for him.

I had been due to name the team after our morning training session on the eve of the Final, but to save Fabrice the embarrassment of being told he was not in the side, in front of all his colleagues, I got up at 6.30 and spoke to him about it before he went in for breakfast.

Fabrice was so distraught he could hardly speak. I would like to have explained the decision to him more fully, but I knew that, like most players in this position, he was in no mood to listen. I just told him and walked away because, had I stayed with him for a bit longer, I am pretty sure we would have ended up having a row.

During the match, whenever I looked at him in the dugout, it seemed to me that he was not showing any interest whatsoever in the game. He appeared to be looking everywhere but the field. Even when I asked him to go for a warm-up – a signal to most subs that the manager is thinking of bringing them on – I got the impression that he was disinterested. I eventually asked him: 'Look, do you want to go on or not?' He just nodded. He replaced Baird four minutes from the end.

When we all returned to our hotel after the match, to join our families and friends, Lesley and I went up to our room so that we could have five or ten minutes together on our own. There were only three other people in the lift taking us back down to the ground floor – Fabrice and his parents. No one said a word. You could have cut the atmosphere with a knife. When we got out, I whispered to Lesley: 'It's a horrible feeling to be hated.' On decisions like the one I took with Fabrice, you can easily end up hating yourself.

One thing I admired him for is that he did not moan to the media – sadly, an all too common occurrence for players with an axe to grind against their managers. To my knowledge he never has. I think he showed a lot of dignity in that respect.

Fabrice was not the only Southampton player who felt particularly hard done by over the Final. The other was Kevin Davies. He probably had even more to moan about than Fabrice because, despite having been selected as a substitute in the earlier rounds – and his dramatic equaliser against Millwall – he was not included in the 16-man squad.

Having once gone through the same experience at Aberdeen when I was left out of their Scottish Cup Final pool against Rangers, I could understand why Kevin was upset about the decision. Even so, I was disappointed by some of the comments attributed to him in a newspaper interview a few months after his free-transfer to Bolton in the summer. Kevin was quoted as saying: 'I think Strachan knows I am a good player, but there was something personal between him and me. He said it was to do with something other than me as a footballer. I proved in training and reserve games that I could do it, but I did not get a start until the second-last league game of the season [the 6-1 drubbing by Arsenal]. James Beattie had been scoring a lot of goals but the other strikers had done nothing and for me not to start before this was a bit strange. Given the players we had, I thought I would have made the bench.'

I cannot ever remember telling Kevin – or anybody else – that my decisions concerning his non-selection for the Final and his departure from Southampton were based on anything more than his ability as a player. There was nothing remotely 'personal' in any of this from my point of view.

Indeed, in recognition of his part in helping to get us to the Final, I even gave him my medal. Outside the medals presented to the 11 players in the starting line-up, and the five substitutes, we had only three left for the four others who had been involved in the Cup run. In addition to Kevin, these were Jason Dodd and Rory Delap, who were unavailable for the Final because of injury, and Francis Benali. Kevin was the odd one out, in that his only appearances for us in the competition had been as a substitute. But to ensure that he did not feel that way, I gave up the gong I was allotted, to him.

It is likely that Kevin would have been involved against Arsenal had Fabrice not been on the bench. As it was, in order to cover myself for all eventualities, I did not feel we could accommodate two strikers and plumped for Jo Tessem ahead of Kevin mainly because I considered that Jo was more versatile and gave us more options in the styles of play we could use. I also had to take into account that we had already decided to let Kevin go at the end of the season – to make way for the signing of someone more suitable to the type of football I wanted to produce – so it seemed only fair to me that Jo be made to feel part of the set-up.

It was a difficult decision, which partly explains why Kevin and Jo only learned about it about an hour and a half before the kick-off. My first priority had been to name the team – hence the fact that Fabrice and goalkeeper Paul Jones, who could both have reasonably expected to be in it, learned their fate the day before. The question of who the other substitutes would be was a different matter. I needed to give myself as much flexibility as possible. I know that this made it even worse for Kevin, but managers cannot always pay as much heed to the feelings of their players as they would wish. You have do what you feel is in the best interests of your team and club.

I think it is fair to say that Kevin, after rejoining Southampton from Blackburn in August 1999, generally struggled to re-produce the scoring form he had showed in his first spell at the club. He'd had a miserable time at Blackburn, mainly because of injuries, and though he was one of the big earners at Southampton when I joined the club, he gradually slipped from third in our strikers' pecking order – behind Beats and Marian Pahars – to fourth or fifth. Because of serious family health problems, he had to cope with a great deal of pressure off the field as well. Through all this, however, I feel we did our utmost to help him. I gave him all the time off he wanted to look after his mother, who had cancer, and I also tried as hard as I could to improve his situation with us on the football side.

Kevin has done a good job at Bolton. This does not surprise me because he is perfectly suited to their football. He is their only central striker and they knock long balls up to him and try to play from there. One reason why he struggled to get a first-team place at Southampton was that we already had one striker who played up front – Beats – and I believed that Kevin was too similar in some ways to make an effective partner for him. I worked a lot with Kevin to try and help him add more strings to his bow. The main aim was to get him to come deeper and have the ball played to his feet. But after a while, he said: 'Gaffer, I am just not comfortable doing this.'

Finding a striker who could play in this way had become very much a priority for me. Teams had started to make it more difficult for us to give Beats the service he and we wanted by pushing up on us and forcing us to play more passes – more short passes – in order to get through them. When we won the ball deep in our own half, it was now taking us six or seven passes to get into a position where we could bring Beats into the picture, whereas before, it was maybe only three or four. The result was that Beats was having to come towards the ball, away from the positions in which he was most dangerous, and into those in which his limitations in touch and control were bound to become more exposed.

The search for someone who could play in that deeper role ended in August 2003, when Kevin Phillips, once a great goal poacher who had reinvented himself to become a tremendous all-round forward, was bought from Sunderland for £3.25 million. He did well for us; he did bring greater imagination to our play. However, one problem was that after getting three draws and three wins in our opening six Premiership matches, which put us into fourth position, we lost central midfielder Matt Oakley – possibly our best passer of the ball – through injury for the rest of the season.

I also suspect that I might have tried to make too many changes to our approach too quickly – that some of the players were not ready to take the development steps I was expecting of them.

Perhaps the best example is David Prutton, the former England Under-21 midfielder we bought from Nottingham Forest in January 2003. David was signed very much on the basis of his potential. He has the ability to fill any position in midfield, and also full-back. Still just finding his way in football, he will be an excellent player in my view. However, whether working with me at Southampton might have helped him is a moot point. In attempting to get him to stop playing on sheer energy and enthusiasm – to think about the game more – I tried to change his style of play too dramatically. Indeed, when I left, I felt it necessary to apologise to him.

I used to say that Southampton were brilliant at being ordinary and playing from the heart. It could be argued that in striving to make us more polished technically, I might have taken us too far away from this. This perhaps was another example of why I believed I could do with a rest from football.

It was a strange season. Following that encouraging start, we had only one win and as many as five defeats in our next eight Premiership matches to drop to twelfth. Although a run of three successive wins took us back to fourth, we quickly headed back to the middle of the table. Southampton were eleventh when I left – after the 2-0 defeat at Arsenal on 10th February – and eventually finished twelfth.

The amazing aspect of all this was we tended to perform better in matches that we lost than in matches that we won. By that criteria, one defeat which was more disappointing than most was the one against Steau Bucharest at our first Uefa Cup hurdle. Steau were the most powerful of the non-seeded teams in the competition, but by the time they scored the late goal in the second leg which gave them their 2-1 aggregate victory, they could easily have been at least two-down. It was a sore point with Kevin Phillips, who twice failed to find the net when clean through their defence with only the keeper to beat.

Ironically, it was only when I was about to leave that I really saw what I considered to be the best results of my work at the club. Just before the curtain came down on my Southampton career, we were beaten 3-2 at Manchester United, and in my last match on 10th February, we lost 2-0 at Arsenal. Leaving aside the refereeing blunders which caused those results, our performances were without doubt the best produced by any of the teams I have managed in games at Highbury and Old Trafford. After the clash with Arsenal, I said to Garry Pendrey: 'That is exactly how I have wanted this team to perform.'

My lasting memory of that final Southampton game is of the short conversation I had with Arsenal's assistant manager, Pat Rice. 'Why are you going?' he said. 'We can't understand it. You see to have the makings of a really good team there.'

It would have been nice to have had the chance to further emphasise this by remaining at St. Mary's until the end of the season, as had been the plan. But, once the announcement had been made that I would not be signing a new Southampton contract, an earlier parting of the ways was inevitable. I cannot blame Southampton for this – that announcement, in January, was virtually forced on them. It had been known for some time that my existing agreement was due to expire in the summer and that I had not signed a further one. The longer that Rupert and I tried to deflect the media's attention away from the matter, the greater their fixation about it had become. It reached the stage where it was starting to be unsettling for everybody at the club, not least the players. Unfortunately, this was even more the case after Southampton had issued the public statement clarifying my situation – a step which led to the media turning their attention to speculation about who my successor would be and whether there was more to my intended departure than met the eye.

The other factor which prompted Rupert to make his managerial change sooner rather than later was that Glenn

Hoddle – his No. 1 choice as my successor – was not in a job at that time. Of course, Rupert already had Hoddle lined up to replace me when I left, but was forced to change his mind because of the fierce opposition to the move by Southampton fans.

At that point, Rupert suggested that I return for a couple more weeks to give him a bit more breathing space to find a solution to the problem. But as I had already said goodbye to the players and coaching staff – and had conditioned myself to my sabbatical – I felt I had to decline.

Having never had a proper break from football before, I did not know what to expect. But it proved one of the best decisions of my life – not least because of where it ultimately led me.

## CHAPTER THIRTEEN
# HOOP DREAMS

When I was at Coventry and Southampton, the fact that I was based at their training grounds during the week meant I could live in a world of my own. Those places, out of bounds to the public and media, and frequented mainly just by the players and coaching staff, were very much my havens.

It is different at Celtic. I occupy an office just off the foyer at the main stadium, virtually at the hub of everything that goes on at this huge club. The window by my desk actually looks out onto the stadium concourse. Thus, even outside match days, I am constantly reminded of the sheer scale of the Parkhead operation and my responsibility in producing good results on the field. It can be nothing if not scary at the best of times, but especially when things are not going well. It was stressful enough to be in that situation at Coventry and Southampton; at a club like Celtic, where the expectations are so much higher, the pressure is obviously a lot greater.

I doubt whether I would have been able to cope with it at an earlier stage in my managerial career. It is different now. Apart from having being a more knowledgeable manager since I started in the job in 1996, I feel I have become a stronger manager, too. Even so, not being a masochist, I could have done without the tests of this belief that marked my first season at Parkhead.

For some strange reason, disappointing starts have been par for the course for me over my managerial career. But the one I made at Celtic was by far the most traumatic. Throughout all my time in professional football, no one result or performance has shocked me more, and put a darker cloud over my club, than the 5-0 European Cup defeat by Artmedia Bratislava in my first competitive Celtic match in July 2005 – the heaviest European defeat in the club's history and their biggest in any competition for some forty-two years. It is still horrible to have to acknowledge those facts (I was hoping to overlook them in this book, but the editor would not let me).

The picture became even gloomier three days later, with a 4-4 draw at Motherwell, after we had been 1-0 and then 3-1 ahead, in our first Premier League match. This brought the additional unwanted distinction of giving us the worst defensive record over two successive matches for fourteen years. Shortly afterwards, we were beaten 3-1 in our first Old Firm game of the season at Rangers, where we had two men, Alan Thompson and Neil Lennon, sent off. That meant that, in addition to being out of Europe at the Champions League qualifying stage – a massive financial blow as well as a footballing one – we were five points behind Hearts in the Championship race after just four matches.

There might not seem much point in dwelling on all this now. But it is the memories of those bad times – which, of course, also included a 2-1 defeat by First Division Clyde in the Scottish Cup in January and provoked one newspaper to give me the sort of treatment meted out to England managers like Graham Taylor and Sven-Göran Eriksson by publishing a mocked-up picture depicting me as a clown – that made the good times that followed so special for me.

Managers under pressure can be a bit like caged animals; if you prod them, they are bound to snap back at you. This characteristic has always been part of my nature, but because of the enormity of the Celtic job, and the over-the-top tabloid media reaction to my setbacks, it has probably never been stronger than it was during my first couple of months at Parkhead. Despite my experience of the game in Scotland, the ways in which being involved with Celtic or Rangers can affect your life outside of football did take a while to get used to.

My most unpleasant experience came after the 3-1 defeat by Rangers, when I stopped at a garage for some petrol. Lesley was also in the car with her mother, who had come down from Dundee to stay with us for a few days, and as I got out, a lad in a vehicle being filled up by a middle-aged guy at the neighbouring pump to mine wound down his window and started taunting me.

'Three-one, three-one, three-one,' he sang.

It was not having much effect on me but I could sense the discomfort in Lesley and her mother. The lad, who must have been fourteen or fifteen, appeared to sense it as well. No doubt encouraged by getting some kind of reaction, he kept going.

'Three-one, three-one, three one.' He went on and on, and as he did so, the middle-aged guy, whom I took to be his father, started laughing.

Eventually, when I'd finished at the pump and was ready to pay – with 'three-one, three-one, three-one' – still ringing in my ears – I went over to the lad. 'What's all that about, son?' I said.

'It's just a laugh, Strachan,' the guy replied, smirking.

'Well, you might think it is a laugh,' I said, 'but I have my wife and mother-in-law in the car and we are all feeling low enough [about the Rangers result] without you trying to make it worse.'

With that, they went through the 'three-one, three-one, three-one', routine together.

By this time, I knew full well that Lesley and my mother-in-law were upset. What really got to me was that the guy still seemed to think his son's conduct was funny. I turned to the lad again. 'Look, son, I don't blame you for being a moron,' I told him. 'I blame the moron who brought you up to be a moron.'

'What are you talking about?' the middle-aged man said.

'It's not the kid's fault,' I replied. 'Someone had to show him how to conduct himself and as you are his dad, it must have been you.'

The guy erupted. He called me every name under the sun. I was an effing this, an effing that. 'You are a cocky little \*\*\*\*,' he said. The language was something else. Once more, I addressed myself to the lad. 'Hear that, son? Your dad has some new words for you – or have you heard them from him before?'

It was back to 'three-one, three-one, three-one' as we went into the garage shop. The father of the lad was in front of me in the queue when it was my turn to pay, the lady behind the counter, clearly on my side, said to me, 'Sorry about that.'

'It's not your fault that he's a moron,' I told her.

As the guy and his son were driving off, they gave me the finger. Lesley and her mum did not say a word. 'What a world we live in eh?' I said.

One day I even managed to have a clash with someone who was being given a guided tour of Parkhead. As I was heading for a meeting elsewhere in the stadium, this particular person approached me to ask if he could have his photograph taken with me. 'No problem,' I said. It is amazing how insensitive people can be because as he passed the camera to his female companion, and put an arm around my shoulder, he remarked to her: 'You'd better be quick. He will probably get the sack next week.'

I know he meant it as a joke, but he did not pick the best time and place for it. He hit such a raw nerve with me that I actually ejected him from the ground. He thought I was joking as well. He was laughing as I was pushing him through the door. I can still see the stunned look on his face as he stood outside in the rain and the penny dropped that I was serious.

A more uplifting experience for me was the encouragement from a lad I met while travelling back to Scotland after watching a player I was interested in signing in Sweden. We had a short chat about the club and the extraordinary commitment to it by its followers before boarding our flight to Glasgow; and on our arrival, his parting shot to me was: 'When you are the manager of Celtic, you will never walk alone. Just remember that.'

I don't think he realised how much those words meant to me. It was the same with the faith that Dermot Desmond showed in me. Dermot, who as Celtic's major shareholder played the biggest part in bringing me to Parkhead, told me: 'I promise you that the moment I start to feel that you are not the right man for this job, I will immediately tell you. But I really cannot see that happening – in fact, I would bet a million on you still being here at the end of the season.'

Whether even he would have been bold enough to bet on Celtic going on to win the CIS Cup, and then the Championship by twenty points, with six matches to spare – not to mention me being voted 'Manager of the Year' by the Scottish Football Writers' Association – is another matter.

Nobody can have visualised any of this. In the early weeks of the season, Garry Pendrey remarked: 'We are going to have to brace ourselves for more flak. I think we will have to accept that this season is going to be a write-off for us, and just put on the armour and focus on building a team that can achieve success next season.' I honestly could not see any reason to disagree with him. So the way it all turned out for us made this not just the most successful season of my managerial career, but also the most surreal.

That is also the word one could use about my arrival at Parkhead in the first place. For my part, I should imagine that a lot of the people close to me, who knew what I went through at Coventry, and how it affected me, will have been surprised that I should want to take on the pressures of the Parkhead post as badly as I did.

I was flattered to be linked to various other jobs before the Celtic opportunity came along. But, as I have said, I was keen to try and hold out for the doors to the Manchester City job to swing open for me through the takeover bid for the club by Bryan Richardson. Only a small handful of the posts for which I was sounded out during my break from the game had the same appeal for me as that of working with Bryan again, especially at a club with City's potential.

It was important to me to return to football in a job that truly stimulated me. The last thing I wanted, when I felt the time was right to end my sabbatical, or when I needed to do so to maintain my standard of living, was to be forced into a position that was more or less the same as the ones I had filled previously and provided little scope for me to develop further. It was for this reason that a return to Southampton – an idea apparently mooted by many of their supporters – was not an option for me. When my successor, Paul Sturrock, left the club in August 2004, after only thirteen matches in charge, the number of fans campaigning for me to come back prompted a telephone call from Rupert Lowe to ask how I felt about it.

'I am about to issue a statement to the effect that you would not be interested in re-joining us,' he said. 'But I thought I would just check this with you first.' I had the feeling that Rupert

himself would not have been averse to seeing me as Southampton manager again. But, as much as I'd enjoyed my time
there, and liked living in the area, I knew that in order to be at
my best, I needed to move on.

The irony of all this was that Portsmouth also sounded me
out following Harry Redknapp's controversial departure – to
Southampton, of course – in December 2004. I suspect that even
Harry was surprised at the level of ill-feeling towards him, from
both Southampton and Portsmouth supporters, over that switch.
He was subjected to so much hostility that, when it was revealed
publicly that Portsmouth had me in mind as his successor, he
telephoned me to point out that I could lift a lot of the pressure
and stress off him by taking the job.

What a character. Not even Portsmouth's chairman, Milan
Mandaric – whom he had fallen out with – could have worked
harder at trying to sell the club to me than Harry did. 'They pay
well, better than Southampton,' he told me. He also talked in
glowing terms about the Portsmouth team spirit and the Fratton
Park atmosphere. Then, after discussing the negative aspects of
his relationship with Mandaric, he added: 'Take the job.'

'What?' I said.

'You've got to take it. If you don't, it will make me look
worse than ever. I will look a right ****.'

'To be honest, Harry, not making you look a **** is not one
of my priorities,' I joked. I think we both ended up laughing.

Harry has said that he looks upon Fratton Park as his spiritual home. This, of course, was borne out by his return there as
manager in December 2005, possibly the most remarkable twist
of all in his eventful career, along with his achievement in saving
them from relegation.

I sense that some people might have felt that my spiritual
home is Leeds United. The success I had at Elland Road as a
player has led to a number of approaches to become their

manager. United offered me the chance when I was at Coventry and also Southampton. I also had the prospect dangled in front of me by the various consortiums who were interested in buying the club before Ken Bates gained control in January 2005. For example, in Leeds' 2003/04 relegation season, after I had left Southampton and Lesley and I were in Australia, I received calls on my mobile from the representatives of three different potential Leeds takeover groups on the same day. I do feel a special affinity with Leeds. However, for one reason or another, the opportunities to work at Elland Road again have always come at what I have considered to be the wrong time.

During my sabbatical, the job vacancy that unquestionably held the biggest attraction for me, outside Celtic, was the one at Liverpool following Gérard Houllier's departure. It was a big surprise when they made contact to ask if I was interested and even more so when I was told at my interview with Liverpool's chief executive, Rick Parry, that I was on a shortlist of three. I cannot deny that I was disappointed not to get the job. But I knew from the start that I was very much an outsider – Rick confirmed that Rafael Benitez was by far the number one candidate – and I did get a lot of satisfaction just through having been considered for the position.

That was also the case regarding the Scottish Football Association's interest in me as a successor to Bert Vogts as the national team coach. Here again, I was under no illusions. It might have appeared to boil down to a straight SFA choice between Walter Smith and myself, but the reality of the situation was that I was not as strong a contender for it as some might have imagined. Whereas I was said to be the more popular candidate among the Scotland supporters – which only goes to show what a decent international playing record and a lot of television appearances can do for you – Walter was the one the SFA most wanted in the post. I had the feeling that the SFA's approach to me, and my subsequent interview with their chief executive, David Taylor, stemmed mainly from them wanting to at least show that the wishes of the fans were not being brushed aside. This did not bother me, partly because I was not sure myself if I could do the job at that stage of my career, I had mixed feelings about whether I could handle the long periods between matches and not being involved with players on a daily basis. Indeed, it was not just the SFA who thought Walter was the right man for it. Deep down, I thought so, too.

Unlike me, he never played for Scotland. But his CV was much better than mine with regards to management experience. He had already had spells as coach or assistant manager with Scotland's Under-18, Under-21 and senior national teams; and he seemed happier about the terms of the post than I was. David Taylor's head must have been spinning after his chat with me on the subject. Instead of just being the national team coach, which I feared would be too limiting and frustrating for me, I wanted my remit to include all the other representative teams and to have the scope to reconstruct the entire coaching structure.

'We only have the money to change one thing, and that's the national team coach,' he told me. My ambitious vision of the radical part I could play in their setup probably frightened the life out of David.

If anybody can handle a national team manager's job – and, more specifically, the high expectations that go with it – it is Walter. He was Scotland's assistant manager, to Alex Ferguson, when I played for the team in the 1986 World Cup Finals in Mexico. At that time, he had also been appointed Graeme Souness's second in command at Rangers – a move that was to propel the Ibrox club to the greatest spell of success in their history. Rangers, of course, went on to equal Celtic's amazing record of the 1960s under Jock Stein, with nine successive Championship triumphs; and Walter, having stepped into the number one spot after Graeme left to join Liverpool in April 1991, had the distinction of being the manager for seven of them.

It was then Celtic's turn to be the most dominant force in Scottish football – initially under Wim Jansen, who steered them to the title in 1998, and two years later, my predecessor Martin O'Neill. In his five seasons in the job, Martin proved the best Parkhead manager since Stein by bringing Celtic the Championship three times, the Scottish Cup three times, the League Cup twice and steering the club to a Uefa Cup Final. Both as a player and a manager, I have never had to follow an act quite like that. But then this is one reasons why the job was irresistible to me.

After twenty-one years in England, I never expected to find myself working back in Scotland; and not in my wildest dreams did I think that my next club after Southampton would be Celtic. It is well known that the chance arose because of Martin's decision to step out of football to give more support to his wife, Geraldine, who had become seriously ill. As for the background to Dermot Desmond electing to plump for me as Martin's replacement, all I know is that it was partly due to the recommendation of Eddie Jordan, the former Grand Prix Formula One motor racing supremo. Eddie, whom I'd originally met through Bryan Richardson – and who had become involved in Bryan's Manchester City takeover bid – is a close friend of Dermot's as well as a fellow Celtic shareholder.

I first became aware of Dermot's interest when we met by chance, for the first time, at the Cheltenham Festival in March 2005. I am not a horse racing fan, but as I had never been to the event, a friend from my Coventry City days, an associate of the club's directors by the name of Eric Groves, invited Lesley and myself to be his guests in his hospitality box there. The suite next to it was occupied by Dermot, Eddie and various Irish football personalities like Kevin Moran and Liam Brady, and when Lesley and I bumped into Eddie and Liam as we were going for a walk, Eddie asked us to join him for a drink in their box. I had only been in the room for a few minutes when I became conscious of a vaguely familiar distinguished-looking guy with a moustache looking at me. It was Desmond. He came over to introduce himself, and asked what I was doing football wise.

I told him: 'I would like to return to football, but a lot of the jobs aren't that much different from the ones I had at Coventry and Southampton. Maybe that's my true level as a manager, but I would like to try something more exciting.'

There was no way I was angling for Martin's post – it was just a general comment about my situation. However, Dermot said: 'Well, we don't know how long Martin is going to be here. He will never get the sack from Celtic, but maybe he will want to go somewhere else.'

Referring to the Manchester City situation, I then said: 'There is something in the pipeline for me, so I could be going somewhere myself in the few weeks.' But Dermot said: 'If you do, make sure you have a get-out clause in your contract,' That was it. I rejoined Eric and his friends and just tried to forget about the conversation. There had been plenty of drink flowing in that room and I really did not know how seriously I should take Desmond's comments.

Two days later, I received a telephone call from Kevin Moran. He had been listening to my conversation with Desmond and he said: 'I bet you couldn't believe what Desmond was saying to you. But take it from me – he meant every word. He does not tell porky pies and he is not a flanneller.' Then came the call from Desmond to tell me that Martin would be leaving at the end of the season, and to invite me to have further talks about the job.

My biggest concern was how much Dermot's approach to me was backed by the other members of the Celtic hierarchy. At our meeting, my only stipulation about joining Celtic was that the approval of it had to be unanimous. I said: 'I know you are the major shareholder but I am not coming along if it's just you who wants me here.'

I considered it particularly important that Celtic's chief executive, Peter Lawwell, the boardroom figure with whom I needed to have the closest working relationship, was in agreement with my appointment. I actually pulled him aside and said: 'Look, if you don't fancy me, just let me know and I won't come here. You have my promise that if this is the case, I won't drop you in it – I will just make an excuse.' Peter seemed aghast at the suggestion. He stressed that he was just as enthusiastic about me being at Celtic as Dermot and Martin O'Neill were. But I did have a major credibility hurdle to overcome with the Celtic fans. It could be that I still do.

I have lost count of the number of times I have heard it said that I am not a true 'Celtic man'; and I cannot dispute that. I was not born in Glasgow, did not support Celtic as a boy and I would have been the last person that any Celtic follower would have thought of approaching for an autograph when I played for Aberdeen. For much of that period, the two most powerful sides in Scotland were not Celtic and Rangers but Celtic and Aberdeen; and in matches between us, the perception of me as the cocky little ginger-haired guy with the big mouth – combined, I like to think, with my performances – made me the Aberdeen player who got up the Parkhead faithful's noses the most.

The more stick I took, the more belligerent I became. There was something about a match against Celtic which brought out the worst (or should I say best?) in me. All I can say in my defence is that it was partly Fergie's fault for winding us up so much for these games. On one occasion, the Celtic crowd got so uptight about me that one guy came onto the pitch in an attempt to batter me.

It is easy to see why Celtic fans looked upon Martin as a kindred spirit. Most managers find it difficult to keep their emotions in check during matches; most of us show that we care about our teams. But few do so as demonstratively as Martin does. I am reckoned to be one of the most animated of managers, but from what I have seen of Martin's technical area conduct, he has sometimes made me seem as restrained as Sven-Göran Eriksson. In other words, Martin mirrored the passion for Celtic that is felt by the club's hundreds of thousands of followers.

No club provokes a more powerful sense of sense of pride and devotion than Celtic. Because of their well-documented social and religious backround – their standing as the so-called 'people's club' of the west of Scotland – this has hardly taken me by surprise. But it is only when you are involved in the Parkhead setup that you fully appreciate the vast number of people who support the club and what the club means to them. Manchester United are the biggest club in Britain, if not the world, but when I played for United, I never really sensed the sort of overwhelming commitment to them that I have seen from those who attach themselves to Celtic.

My sister is married to a Celtic supporter and, though they live in Aberdeen, they are both Celtic season ticket holders and hardly miss a single match home or away. I used to think they were exaggerating when they talked about the number of miles they had travelled to see games – until I met up with them at Celtic's 2005 pre-season friendly at Fulham. They had made the ten-hour journey from Aberdeen on a Celtic supporters' coach on the morning of the game and headed back to Aberdeen immediately afterwards.

I tease them about it. 'Why don't you two get a life?' I say. But, by Celtic standards, their devotion to the club is by no means unusual – as we saw in May 2006, when some 25,000 made the trip across the border for Roy Keane's testimonial at Manchester United.

I have never had that sort of emotional attachment to any club. But you would have to be made of stone not to be moved by the reaction to Celtic's Championship and League Cup successes. I often liken the feeling a manager gets on such occasions to that of watching your family and friends open the Christmas presents you have bought them. You tend to get more enjoyment out of that than you do from unwrapping your own gifts. In terms of football trophies, it's a great feeling for a manager to make so many people happy – but especially at a club like Celtic.

When Celtic clinched the title at Parkhead, the explosion of noise and excitement from the 60,000 crowd made it one of the most remarkable experiences of my life. It was overwhelming. I just looked at the scenes of celebration and thought: 'You have played a part in creating this.' As I have said, the elation I felt was partly as a result of what we had to go through in order to reach this point.

The fact is that, despite the traditional advantages that Celtic and Rangers have over the other clubs in Scotland through their attendances and commercial standing, this has been a more difficult post than many outsiders might have anticipated. When I took over, Celtic were still a club in shock following the 2-1 defeat at Motherwell that had enabled Rangers to snatch the title from their grasp on the last day of the previous season. The psychological effect of that blow, inflicted by two out-of-the-blue Motherwell goals in the last three minutes of the game, seemed to affect the mood of people at the club for ages.

On top of this, the Celtic squad needed to be rebuilt; and, with the club struggling to cope with their wage bill – apparently the sixth highest in British football – and finances having fallen £20 million into the red, I had to do it on a considerably smaller budget than the one with which Martin had started his Celtic career.

I had to laugh at a comment by Paul Telfer. When I pulled him up after a game for messing about with the ball instead of trying to turn the opposing defence. Paul, signed from Coventry to help us out of a right-back shortage crisis, joked: 'Well, what do you expect from a 32-year-old who only cost £200,000?' There was no answer to that.

I did not have a transfer-market kitty when I started. I could only spend what I brought in on outgoing transfer deals. One example of the financial guidelines on which I had to operate was our inability to hold onto Craig Bellamy, on loan from Newcastle. He did an excellent job for Martin in the 2004/05 season, and his partnership up front with John Hartson – which, of course, I had previously initiated at Coventry – was one I was keen to maintain. Newcastle, though, were not prepared to let us have him on loan again; and because of the £5 million fee they wanted for him, and what we would have had to pay him, buying him would have put me in the position of not being able to afford anybody else.

The transfer fees Celtic paid in my first season amounted to less than half the figure forked out in Martin's first season; and none of the newcomers got more than 45 per cent of the wages given to the highest paid footballers under Martin. One top earner brought in by Martin was on £34,000 a week – a figure that covered the total salaries for our major foreign signings: Artur Boruc, Maciej Zurawski and Shunsuke Nakamura after he left.

The need for Celtic to tighten their purse strings even applied to the signing of Roy Keane. When Roy joined Celtic on a free transfer in December 2005, most people were left wondering how we could afford him and why he should be interested in playing in Scotland. He had been reckoned to be on something like £80,000 a week at Manchester United and it was clear that, though the Premiership clubs who were interested in him could not match that, they would nevertheless be able to take him closer to this figure than we could. When he signed for us, a number of reports indicated that he would be on £40,000 a week at Parkhead and that the deal would be funded partly by Dermot Desmond. But neither was correct.

The salary we agreed with him was considerably less than £40,000 a week, and even then it was dependent on the number of first-team appearances he made. Far from being Celtic's highest earner when he joined, he was no higher than eighth on the list. Dermot was brilliant in this matter. As one of Roy's Irish admirers, he wanted Roy on board as much as anybody – but not at the expense of leaving us short of money for the group of younger players I wanted to sign.

I had known for some time that Roy's United contract was due to expire in the summer of 2006 and that he had expressed the hope that he might be able to end his career with Celtic. Various people around the club – and especially his Irish fans like Eddie Jordan – had alerted me to this almost from the day I started at Parkhead. But it was very much a long shot as far as I was concerned. With more pressing matters to deal with, I just pushed it to the back of my mind. I was amazed when it came off. Coming to Celtic was some decision on Roy's part. One could argue that he already had enough money in the bank following his brilliant twelve-year career at Old Trafford. But he was still only thirty-four and I cannot think of many people of that age in professional football who would be willing to pass up opportunities to give themselves and their families further financial security. Perhaps the most surprising aspect of his decision was that I could not even promise him a regular place in the team. At our meeting to discuss the move, at Dermot's house in London, I told him: 'I still see you as a central midfielder. But the problem is that Neil Lennon and Stilian Petrov are doing too well in that area to be left out or moved elsewhere. If I had select a team for the next match, and the three of you were all fit, I would have to plump for Neil and Stilian.' He was perfectly happy with that, for the simple reason that because of his affection for Celtic during his upbringing in the Irish Republic – an affection shared by countless other people there – he had genuinely set his heart on playing for the club.

This sort of occurrence is very much the exception rather than the rule among most leading modern-day players. As far as non-Scots in other countries are concerned, it has to be accepted that the Scottish Premier League does not have the same appeal – in purely footballing terms – as the top leagues in England and other bigger soccer nations. Not long ago, one agent said to me: 'Generally, it is not easy to get players to come to Scotland. In a number of cases, outside blindfolding and drugging them, the only way you can do it is to pay them fortunes.' OK, he was exaggerating – but I feel that his basic point was valid. So having Roy Keane at Celtic was a considerable boost to the international image of the club. It was just a shame that he had to retire at the end of the season: it was a privilege to work with him.

All clubs have to keep making changes to their playing staffs each season. But in Celtic's case, the twin objectives of easing our financial problems and improving the squad took the form of a major reconstruction job. In the close season alone, between my appointment on 25 May and our first match on 25 July against Artmedia, no fewer than fourteen players left the club and seven were brought in. Of the men who had been in Martin's starting line-up for his last match as manager, the 1-0 win over Dundee United in the Scottish Cup Final, the ones in that position against Artmedia were Balde, Stilian Petrov, Neil Lennon, Chris Sutton, Alan Thompson and John Hartson. For the match in which we clinched the title, against Hearts in March, the list was down to four – Balde, Petrov, Lennon and Hartson. As for that first leg against Artmedia, the argument that the game came too early for us was best illustrated by the upheaval to our defence in the full back slots. The regular incumbents under Martin had been Didier Agathe and Jackie McNamara, Celtic's captain. But with the former unavailable through injury and the latter having left for Wolves – much to my regret – following a contractual dispute which I am convinced would have been settled to the satisfaction of both parties had Jackie and his agent adopted a more patient negotiating stance, we were forced to give debuts to both Paul Telfer and Mo Camara.

The other back four headache concerned Bobo Balde's contractual situation. Bobo had a clause in his agreement stipulating that, at that particular time, he could leave Celtic for any club prepared to match or better his terms with us. He had every right to explore this possibility, but in the build-up to a game as important as the one in Bratislava, his meetings and telephone conversations with other clubs were a distraction that we – not to mention Bobo – could have done without.

For all this, there is little doubt that we should have done better against the Slovakian champions. I had the impression that their coach was as shocked about the scoreline as I was. Celtic did not play well, but up to Artmedia's young striker Juraj Halenar getting the first of his three goals two minutes before half-time, I was thinking that the likeliest outcome would be a 0-0 draw. Even when Altmedia made it 2-0 early in the second half, I really could not see us taking the hammering we did. Hence the fact that, while some managers might have tried to bolster their defence and opted for a damage-limitation approach, I went the other way.

My substitutions after Artmedia's second goal – Shaun Maloney for Maciej Zurawski, who had struggled to make an impact on his Celtic debut, and then Jeremie Alliadiere for Alan

Thompson, who had not been fully match fit – were later described by some pundits as naive. However, because of the importance of away goals in European matches, and my belief that Artmedia would prove as vulnerable at the back as we had been if we could put greater pressure on them, I felt that the gamble was justified. I still do. It could easily have paid off for us – Shaun Maloney missed one excellent chance and Aidan McGeady, who had come on in the first half for the injured Chris Sutton, failed to convert an even better one. The roof then fell on us again, but bearing in mind that we beat Artmedia 4-0 in the return leg at Parkhead, we would still have gone through had one of those opportunities been taken.

Almost every player or manager is bound to find himself at the wrong end of a thrashing at some stage in his career. Depending on the standard of the opposition, some of those experiences are easier to accept than others. When I was at Southampton, I saw no reason to throw myself off a bridge after we had been outclassed by Manchester United and Arsenal. The heaviest defeat I experienced as a Scotland player was when we lost 4-1 to Brazil in the 1982 World Cup Finals in Spain. However, I looked upon it as an honour just to be on the same field as a team of that quality; and whenever I look back on that match now, I find it impossible not to smile.

I think we all knew that it was mission impossible for us even when we were lined up with the Brazilians in the tunnel before taking the field. The temperature was 100 degrees in Seville that night, and most of the Brazilians had their tops off, revealing bodies that seemed to have muscles in places where we did not even have places. I took one look at their six-packs and said to Alex McLeish: 'There is something wrong with these guys. They look deformed.' This prompted Alex to suggest that we should take off our tops as well. 'You keep your one on, big man,' I said. 'With your white spotty chest, you are going to look a bit out of place here.' The sense of impending football doom grew stronger when David Narey gave us the lead. It was a wonderful moment for David, but I think the rest of us were thinking: 'We could be in right trouble here – this is going to fire them up.' We weren't wrong.

I was taken off about twenty minutes from the end, which was disappointing, if only because it effectively ruined my chance of being in a position to swap shirts with one of the Brazilian stars like Zico, Falcao or Socrates. It was just my luck that the only Brazil jersey I could get was that of their centre forward, Serginho who was widely considered to be by far the least impressive member of their team and who was being substituted at the same time as me. When he offered to swap jerseys with me – much to the amusement of some of the other Scotland players – I thought: 'Oh no, anybody but you.' I almost felt like feigning a heart attack, or making an excuse along the lines of: 'I would love your jersey, but unfortunately I am saving mine for my grannie.' The other lads all wanted Zico's shirt. It must have been embarrassing for him because in the last five minutes of the match, he had about six Scottish stalkers.

In the dressing room afterwards, nobody said a word. We were disappointed obviously, but it was mainly down to the fact that the amount of energy expended in trying to get the ball off the Brazilians – in that heat – had left us absolutely shattered. Suddenly, you could hear the sound of studs coming down the tunnel. The dressing room door opened, and it was Scotland's keeper, Alan Rough. Still clearly finding it difficult to get his head around the way that Eder had chipped the ball over him from the edge of the penalty area for the third Brazil goal, he said: 'That chip – anyone here think that he was going to do that?' At that, everybody just burst out laughing. A few minutes later, he was on about it again. 'That's it, you know – all the great players in the world have chipped me.' Such incidents have always appealed to my sense of humour. But I cannot find anything to laugh about over what happened to Celtic against Artmedia. When I die, I reckon the inscription on my headstone should read: 'This is much better than Bratislava.'

As my target on becoming Celtic manager was to win the Championship-Scottish Cup-CIS treble, as Martin did in his first season at Parkhead, the defeat at Clyde was a big disappointment as well. It is important for managers to look at themselves before anybody else when things go wrong, and in this instance, I have to hold my hands up and concede that I did not choose the right team. Having watched Clyde at home in their previous match, and checked the weather forecast for the area for the two or three days before our tie, I fully expected the pitch to be heavy and lumpy. In anticipation of a gruelling, physical slog, I picked the biggest and strongest side I could get.

When we arrived at the Broadwood Stadium, though, I was taken aback to find that the pitch, having been covered overnight to keep the rain and snow off, was like concrete – so hard and slippery in places that had it been a league match, I feel sure the match would have been postponed. In my team talk, I said: 'Right, let's keep getting the ball in behind their back men and turn them.' However, it never really happened. Instead, John Hartson repeatedly came short for the ball to be played to his feet, which allowed Clyde to push up on us and deny us the space to properly feed off him. John, and the players on whom he tended to rely on the most to find him with the ball, the full backs, were still locked into the style of play that had helped us recover from 2-0 down to win 3-2 at Hearts the previous week. It was a massive victory for us – it increased our Championship lead over the Edinburgh club to seven points – and John's ability to take the ball in deep positions and link our play up front was a big factor in it. He caused Hearts' central defenders Stephen

Pressley and Andy Webster a lot of trouble. But then you could pass the ball more on the Tynecastle pitch than on the Clyde surface.

As is often the case when a centre-forward is not stretching the play, John – one of our strongest runners in training – argued that the full backs were not giving him the service necessary for him to do this, whereas they countered that he was not taking up the right positions. The bottom line is that Clyde were spot on with their personnel and tactics – they belted the ball forward and played on the knock-downs – and we weren't. The crucial difference between the two teams was Clyde's sheer hunger to run. For us, it was all a bit of a mess.

If any Celtic player deserved sympathy, it was Du Wei, the centre-half and captain of China's national team. He made his full debut, along with Roy Keane, but like Mo Kamara when he was adjudged to have been partly responsible for two of the goals we conceded on his debut in Bratislava, the experience was a nightmare for him. Wei had been looking tremendous in training and, as he certainly had the height we felt we needed at the heart of our defence, all the coaching staff agreed that he should play. It was not entirely his fault that he did not do well. Usually, if one member of a back four is having a bad afternoon, he can rely on others to help him. Unfortunately for Wei, they were all struggling in this match. They could not even help themselves. Another problem for Wei was the language barrier. He could understand a bit of English but the noise from the crowd at Clyde made it more difficult for him to hear or understand instructions from his team-mates than had been the case in training and reserve team matches. That's why I had to substitute him at half-time. We were 2-0 down and I knew that the tactical changes I had to make to get us back into the game can only have made his communication headaches worse. That was his one and only game for Celtic. I would have liked to have kept him, but his club, whose asking price for him to join us on a permanent transfer was £700,000, were unwilling to give us more time to assess him.

Celtic have always been noted as a team better in attack than defence. Going forward in search of goals, without worrying too much about the opposition being able to create scoring opportunities as a consequence, is an important part of the club's tradition. In most of their matches in Scotland, Celtic are so much on top that the men at the back don't have a great deal of defending to do anyway. The other side of the coin – how this tactic can rebound on Celtic – was seen in the lack of concentration that brought that devastating 2-1 defeat at Motherwell in May 2005. This is one of the reasons for the changes I have tried to make to Celtic's style of play. My goal has been to retain the attacking spirit that Celtic showed under Martin O'Neill, but for the team to show it in a different way.

Under Martin, Celtic were generally more direct and open than they have been under me. When I looked at videos of their previous season's matches, it struck me that the games at Parkhead had the sort of cut-and-thrust element usually associated with cup ties. There were a few times when you would see Celtic charging forward en masse and then, when the move broke down, the opposition only needing one or two passes to make life uncomfortable for them on the break. I can't knock it – generally it worked superbly for Martin. But, notwithstanding the desire for all new managers to put their own stamp on their teams, I thought the time was right to expand or redefine their approach.

To an extent, I took a leaf out of Chelsea's book. They have been labelled a boring team because they retain possession of the ball for long periods and string a lot of passes together. I don't go along with that criticism – they certainly do not bore me. What their football does to the brains of the teams who face them is another matter. When Chelsea are in possession, some opposing sides have to expend so much energy in trying to get the ball from them that by the time they do so, they are too knackered to do anything with it. Chelsea mesmerise teams. Also, their style of play means that they nearly always have plenty of people behind the ball. When the opposition get it, they have to make six or seven passes in order to get into a position where they can threaten the Chelsea goal. Little wonder that Chelsea, through their ability to control the play, can create all manner of attacking options without making themselves vulnerable.

I always remember Fergie extolling the virtues of this style of football when we were at Aberdeen. It is the football I have always wanted to produce as a manager myself. I say to players: 'Every time you receive the ball, your first thought should be: "Can I knock it forward to create a scoring chance?" But if such a pass is not on, there is no point giving the ball away.' It was not possible to truly bring that principle to reality at Coventry and Southampton – the teams I had there did not have the necessary ability. Celtic do, which is another reason why I wanted to come here so badly. Managers are only as good as their players. In any rationalisation of the recovery from my dreadful start, and notably the winning of the Championship on the back of a run in which we had twenty-four wins and only one defeat in twenty-eight games, that maxim has to be the most valid starting point.

Of the newcomers to the club, it is fair to say that Maciej Zurawski and Shunsuke Nakamura made the biggest impacts. Maciej, or 'Magic' to give his nickname, was our top scorer and Shunsuke was the player who created the most chances. It has been reported that Shunsuke was the one who cost us the highest transfer but in fact it was Maciej, at £2 million. Shunsuke's fee, quoted as £2.5 million originally, was not even half that.

When I watched him previously on TV, in his Confederation Cup matches for Japan against teams like Brazil, I actually thought my eyes were deceiving me. I kept asking people: 'Is he really as good as I think he is?' At Celtic, it quickly become clear that he was. His touch and vision are outstanding. I thought that Fabrice Fernandes, who filled a similar right-side midfield role for me at Southampton, was the bee's knees in these respects. But I would say that Shunsuke is ahead of him. I loved watching him, possibly more so than any other Celtic player. The changes to Celtic's style of play made him a crucial figure for us because when we were knocking the ball around, you could rely on him not to miss any opportunities to penetrate the opposing defence. Being able to pass the ball is one thing – to be able to play the pass that is going to give your team a scoring opportunity is another. In goal-assists, I really do not think there is a player in Scotland to touch him. The way that he and Maciej linked up sometimes was a joy to behold.

It was a big plus for me to be able to get such players. I was also fortunate to inherit the likes of Bobo Balde, Neil Lennon, Stilian Petrov, Alan Thompson and John Hartson from Martin. These players had long formed the influential nucleus of Celtic's team and had reached the stage where they just needed other players to take some of the weight off them. In that context, apart from Shunsuke and Maciej, the major bonus for us was the way in which youngsters who had previously been no more than bit-part players thrust themselves into the first-team picture. The most notable of these, of course, were Stephen McManus, who established himself at the heart of our defence alongside Balde, and Shaun Maloney, a striker whose success in a wide left attacking role led to him gaining both the 2006 Scottish Young Player of the year and Player of the Year awards. I would love to be able to claim that I always recognised their ability but the truth is that I knew very little about either when I arrived. Had I immediately been given £20-30 million to buy players for their positions, I would have done it, and Stephen and Shaun would have remained on the fringes. One could argue that, in developing themselves as first-team players so quickly, they might also have been helped by Celtic going out of Europe so early. This gave us extra time to work with them in training. It gave us more coaching time with the entire squad, but for obvious reasons, it was particularly beneficial for Stephen and Shaun and the other comparatively inexperienced lads such as Craig Beattie, Aiden McGeady, Stephen Pearson and Ross Wallace.

Their enthusiasm and energy brought new life to the team. There was no better example than that 3-2 win over Hearts and the increase in our physical dynamicsm in midfield following the substitution of Stephen Pearson for the injured Stilian Petrov. I also remember Stephen McManus's first match of the season in that 4-4 draw at Motherwell. Stephen, a long way down in the first-team centre-back pecking order the previous season, was as hyped up as any player I have ever seen in the first ten minutes of that game. He gave the impression of looking upon it as a trial game that would decide his entire career. We had to shout at him to calm down – had he not done so, he would have blown up in a cloud of smoke or got sent off. Being kept in the team inevitably did wonders for his confidence. One of the great things about him, apart from his willingness to learn and technical ability, was his communication.

Shaun Maloney had been hit by a cruciate ligament injury the previous season, and it says much about the way he viewed his chances of quickly breaking into the team when I arrived, that he asked if he could go somewhere else on loan. I thought that giving him the chance to play first-team football at another club would be the ideal way for me to assess him, but the two Championship clubs I approached on this said they could not take him.

Maloney is not a big lad – at five foot seven inches he is certainly no giant compared with a lot of other strikers – but one of the first things I noticed about him in his training matches was his unwillingness to be put off by any stick dished out to him. On a couple of occasions, when I watched his reaction to people like Bode Balde kicking him, I thought: 'You're really brave, you are.' You could not fail to notice his skill on the ball and work-rate either, which prompted us to look upon him not so much as a striker but a player who could operate in a wide-left attacking role.

This turned out to be unfortunate for Alan Thompson – an excellent player in that position for Martin, and one I have always liked as well. But on the basis of striving to give us more versatility in our team shapes and systems, I was looking for players who could operate more like inside forwards in the wide areas as opposed to the more conventional winger-types; and Shaun, like Shunsuke on the other side, fitted the bill perfectly.

For the likes of Stephen and Shaun, the next challenge – that of maintaining their progress – will be the most difficult part. The same, of course applies to me. In terms of the Celtic team I dream of producing, I have only scratched the surface. I believe I am capable of raising my managerial profile further.

But this being the crazy job that it is, I do not rule out the possibility of having to go parasailing again either.

# INDEX

Aberdeen, 51, 63, 86, 91, 286
Aberdeen FC, 18, 25, 180
  challenges Old Firm stranglehold,
    25, 54–7, 67, 285
  fans, 57, 59–60
  under Ferguson, 24, 52–5, 60,
    62–7, 73–4, 76–7, 79–84, 94,
    104–5, 237, 285, 297
  Strachan joins, 47–9, 85
  Strachan leaves, 74, 84–94
  Strachan's career, 6, 24–5, 36,
    38–9, 50–71, 73–4, 79–84,
    104–5, 109, 119–20, 124–6,
    129, 131, 237, 251, 268, 285
  style of play, 129
  vs Arges Pitesti, 81–2
  vs Celtic, 57–8, 62, 91
  vs Hearts, 92
  vs Ipswich, 131
  vs Liverpool, 67–70, 79
  vs Partick Thistle, 38
  vs Porto, 90–1
  vs Rangers, 51, 54, 60, 62, 79–81,
    268
  vs Real Madrid, 55, 67, 70–1, 80
  youth system, 62
Abramovich, Roman, 192
Accrington Stanley FC, 257
Adams, Tony, 162–3
Adebayor, Emmanuel, 146
Africa, 177
Agathe, Didier, 291
Airdrie FC, 56
Aitken, Roy, 122
Albion Rovers FC, 37
Albiston, Arthur, 116
Allardyce, Sam, 10–11
Allen, Ronald, 225
Alliadiere, Jeremie, 292
alligators, 132

Alloa, FC
Aloisi, John, 202, 215
Anderlecht, 132
Anderson, Viv, 115
Anfield, 10, 68–9
Arbroath FC, 37–8
Archibald, Steve, 51, 55–6, 58, 63,
  77, 109
Arges Pitesti, 81
Arsenal FC, 51, 88, 146, 186, 190,
  215
  vs Aston Villa, 253
  vs Coventry, 162–3, 192, 194
  vs Dundee, 35
  vs Southampton, 167, 241, 252,
    254, 261, 265–6, 268–9,
    271–2, 292
Artmedia Bratislava, 2, 187, 218,
  275, 290–2, 294–5
Aston Villa FC, 148, 150, 186,
  223–4, 238
  signings from Coventry, 152,
    172–6
  vs Arsenal, 253
  vs Coventry, 99, 187, 199, 217
  vs Manchester United, 81
  vs Southampton, 259
Atkinson, Ron, 73, 100–6, 118,
  120, 142
  approach to coaching, 102–6, 114
  and Carlton Palmer signing, 205–6
  character, 101–2, 105
  farewell party, 160
  manages Coventry, 157–62, 165,
    177, 181, 184, 190, 205–6,
    220–1
  manages Manchester United, 65,
    94–5, 104–6, 112–15
  sacked from Manchester United,
    113

Audi (sponsors), 218
Australia, 281

back-pass rule, 129
    change in, 140
Bailey, Gary, 93, 113
Baird, Chris, 264, 266–7
Balde, Bobo, 291, 298, 300
Ball, Alan, 35–6
Bannon, Eamonn, 24
Barcelona, 94, 205, 214
Barnes, Peter, 79
Barnsley FC, 198
Bates, Ken, 123, 281
Bath City FC, 251
Batty, David, 128, 132–6
Bayern Munich, 55, 67, 70, 74
Beattie, Craig, 299
Beattie, James, 239, 246, 252, 255,
    257–9, 261–2, 266, 268–70
Beckenbauer, Franz, 102
Beckham, David, 74, 96, 260
Beglin, Jim, 126
Belgium, 67, 132
Bellamy, Craig, 189, 212–17, 223,
    288
Benali, Francis, 251, 263, 268
Benidorm, 287
Benitez, Rafael, 281
Bennett, Steve, 168
Bergkamp, Dennis, 239
Berne, 121
Berwick Rangers FC, 35
Best, George, 34
bio-kinetics, 28
Birkenhead, 213
Birmingham, 165
Birmingham City FC, 222, 263
Black, Eric, 60, 63, 92, 109
Blackburn Rovers FC, 201, 213,
    257, 269
    and Dion Dublin transfer,
        172–3
    vs Coventry, 191
    vs Leeds, 128–9
Blackpool FC, 252, 257
Blyth, Jim, 166, 219–20, 226
Boateng, George, 152, 166, 199,
    211
    transfer, 173–7
Bolton Wanderers FC, 10, 145, 268,
    270
    vs Coventry, 198, 200–1
    vs Southampton, 11–12, 246

Booth, Tim, 21–2
Boruc, Artur, 288
Bosman ruling, 5
Boston United FC, 180
Bothroyd, Jay, 215
Bournemouth FC, 127–8
Bowyer, Lee, 56
Bradford City FC, 224
Brady, Liam, 284
Brazil, 292–3, 298
Brechin FC, 37
Breen, Gary, 194
Bremner, Billy, 36
Brenna, Mark, 134–5
Bridge, Wayne, 147, 251–2, 255
Bristol, 16
Brown, Craig, 38, 121–2
Brown, Steve, 246
Bruce, Steve, 140
Burley, George, 70
Burrows, David, 159, 194

Cadamarteri, Danny, 13
Caldwell, Alec, 37–42, 44
Caldwell, Carol, 42
Camara, Mo, 291, 295
Canary Islands, 229
Cantona, Eric, 136, 138–40
Cardiff, 252
    Millennium Stadium, 266
    Ninian Park, 16
Carrick, Michael, 208
Celtic FC, 33, 45–7, 50, 54–7, 223
    finances, 288–90
    'Lisbon Lions', 48
    and Old Firm dominance, 54–7,
        285, 287, 290
    Roy Keane joins, 288–90
    Strachan manages, 2, 8, 19, 21,
        32, 142–3, 173, 181–2, 184,
        187, 197, 214, 222, 250,
        274–9, 283–300
    style of play, 296–8
    supporters, 286–7
    vs Aberdeen, 57–8, 62, 91
    vs Bratislava, 2, 187, 218, 275,
        290–2, 294–5
    vs Clyde, 182, 294–5
    vs Dundee, 45, 57–8
    vs Hearts, 291, 294–5, 299
    vs Motherwell, 275, 287, 296,
        299
    vs Rangers, 47, 275–7
Chala, Kleber, 240, 242

Chapman, Lee, 128–9, 137–40
Charlton, Bobby, 107
Charlton Athletic FC, 145, 216
  vs Southampton, 246–7
Chelsea FC, 87, 89, 147, 255
  provoke hostility, 192–3
  style of play, 297
  vs Coventry, 165–6, 188, 192–4,
    198
  vs Leeds, 123
  vs Liverpool, 193
  vs Manchester United, 193
  vs Southampton, 254–5
Cheltenham Festival, 283
Cheshire, 107
Chippo, Youssef, 170–1, 174, 208
Christie, Tony, 24
Claridge, Steve, 263
Clark, John, 50, 54
Clarke, Bobby, 57, 61
Clarke, Ray, 235
Clough, Brian, 67, 182
Clyde FC, 51, 182, 275, 294–5
Cole, Ashley, 265–6
Coles, David, 236
Cologne, 86, 90–2, 96–7
Connolly, Chris, 11–12
Coombe Abbey hotel, 149
Cooper, Davie, 17
Cooper, Neale, 60, 62–3
Cooper, Terry, 146, 235
Cormack, Peter, 27
Countdown, 8
Coventry, 210
Coventry City FC, 33
  Atkinson manages, 157–62, 165,
    177, 181, 184, 190, 205–6,
    220–1
  fans, 218–19, 222–5
  finances, 144, 148, 151–5, 227–8
  Gavin Strachan's career, 198–9
  relegated, 19–20, 99, 154–5, 174,
    211–12, 214, 223
  signings, 149–54, 159, 187
  stadium, 155
  Strachan as assistant, 101–4,
    141–3, 157–8, 161, 205–6
  Strachan manages, 2, 4, 14–15,
    19–21, 32, 38, 61, 74, 87, 136,
    142–5, 148–59, 162–4,
    168–226, 235–6, 250, 256,
    274, 279–80, 283, 288, 297
  Strachan sacked, 1–2, 22, 210,
    226–30

strikers, 201, 213–16
transfers, 171–6
vs Arsenal, 162–3, 192, 194
vs Aston Villa, 99, 187, 199, 217
vs Blackburn, 191
vs Bolton, 198, 200–1
vs Chelsea, 165–6, 188, 192–4,
  198
vs Derby, 99, 187, 192, 194–5,
  203
vs Everton, 13, 157, 174–5, 202,
  204, 217–19, 221, 224
vs Leeds, 142, 191
vs Liverpool, 185, 192
vs Luton, 172–3
vs Manchester United, 198
vs Newcastle, 190–1
vs Nottingham, 224
vs Southampton, 185, 192, 194,
  198
vs Tottenham, 157–8, 181, 187,
  192, 194–7, 216
vs West Bromwich, 165
vs West Ham, 155–6, 163–4, 217
vs Wimbledon, 167, 187
youth system, 38
Cowen, Andrew, 232–3
Crouch, Peter, 148, 202, 238–9
Crystal Palace FC, 172, 180, 184,
  198

Daily Echo, 243
Daish, Liam, 159
Dalglish, Kenny, 31, 61, 68, 200
Dalziel, John, 33
Danson, Paul, 165
Davies, Kevin, 51, 251–2, 263,
  267–70
Day, Mervyn, 128
Delap, Rory, 148, 250, 268
Delgado, Agustin, 239–45, 264
Delgado, Marcos, 242
Denmark, 23
Dens Park, 25, 34–5, 37, 44, 49,
  109
Deportivo La Coruna, 170
Derby County FC, 148, 180, 250
  vs Coventry, 99, 187, 192, 194–5,
    203
Desmond, Dermot, 278, 283–5,
  289–90
Di Matteo, Roberto, 193
Dinamo Tirana, 59
Dodd, Jason, 250–1, 268

Donald, Dick, 53–4, 92
Dorigo, Tony, 128, 136
Dublin, Dion, 161, 181
    Coventry career, 152, 158, 161,
        185, 187, 190–1, 194–5, 198,
        202
    transfer, 172–4, 176
Dugmore, Dr Dorian, 15–16
Duncan, John, 36
Dundee, 37, 41–3
Dundee FC
    dressing-room atmosphere, 46
    financial difficulties, 48
    Strachan's career, 5, 23–4, 26,
        34–7, 40–9, 109, 120
    Strachan leaves, 47–9, 85
    vs Arsenal, 35
    vs Celtic, 45, 57–8
    vs Hearts, 49
Dundee United FC, 23–5, 38, 58,
    80, 182, 290
Dunfermline FC, 41
Dunn, Steve, 166–8
Duxbury, Mike, 66, 116
Dyer, Kieron, 56

Ecuador, 239–40, 242–3
Eder, 293
Edinburgh, Justin, 158
Edinburgh, 26, 33, 35, 37–8, 54,
    226
Edinburgh Thistle FC, 33
Edwards, Martin, 92–3, 96–7
Elgin City FC, 37
Ellis, Doug, 174
England, 34, 86
England football team, 39, 58, 202,
    213, 239, 259
    Under-21s, 271
Eriksson, Sven-Göran, 39, 276,
    286
Errol, 48
Español, 152
Everton FC, 95–6, 116, 157, 239
    vs Coventry, 13, 157, 174–5, 202,
        204, 217–19, 221, 224
    vs Manchester United, 93, 110–12
    vs Southampton, 167–8

Fairclough, Chris, 140
Falcao, 293
Fashanu, John, 115
Fenerbahce, 153
Fenn, Neale, 196

Ferguson, Sir Alex, 36, 46, 69, 150,
    184
    joins Manchester United, 92–4
    manages Aberdeen, 24, 52–5, 60,
        62–7, 73–4, 76–7, 79–84, 94,
        104–5, 237, 285, 297
    manages Manchester United, 61,
        63, 73–4, 76, 79, 81, 83–4,
        94–101, 104, 113, 116–17,
        237, 253
    management style, 75–81
    manages Scotland, 14, 18, 94,
        121, 282
    predicts end of Strachan's career,
        136
    regrets about football, 7
    relationship with Beckham, 74
    relationship with Strachan, 73–99,
        116, 171
    sacked by St Mirren, 53
    temperament, 14, 23, 25
Ferguson, Cathy, 7, 93
Ferguson, Darren, 7
Ferguson, Duncan, 218
Ferguson, Jason, 7, 170–1
Ferguson, Mark, 7
Fernandes, Fabrice, 51, 252, 256,
    260–1, 263–7, 269, 298
Feyenoord, 174
Finland, 120
Firth of Forth, 26, 30
fitness coaches, 31
Florida, 132
football
    financial growth, 3–4
    greed and dishonestly, 4
    importance of money, 145
    macho aspect, 131
    media interest, 6, 209
    nature of game, 110–11, 114–16
    schoolboy, 27–8, 215
    transfer market fears, 209
    wage bills, 154
football agents, 4, 87, 168–71, 209
football club chairmen, 4, 53,
    142–6, 152, 237
football managers, 2–22, 100, 105,
    142, 237
    and back-pass rule, 129
    emotions, 10–13
    European, 5
    and finances, 4–5, 130
    fitness and training, 29, 31–2
    health hazards, 15–16

insecurity, 173
lifestyles, 9, 16
national, 17
remuneration, 154
stress, 2–3, 9, 14, 18
subject to abuse, 20
and transfers, 87
football pitches, 116
football players
 ageing, 28
 bad behaviour, 160–1
 contracts, 75, 172
 foreign, 6, 111, 203, 240–1
 insecurity, 173
 and media, 267
 pampered, 44, 177
 professionalism, 6
 salaries, 5
 Scottish, 34, 86
 strikers, 201, 213
football referees, 164–8
football supporters, 6, 20
Forfar FC, 37
Forrester, Jamie, 129
Fotherby, Bill, 123–4, 126
France, 17
Fry, Barry, 15
Fulham FC, 147, 260, 286

Gallacher, Dermot, 193
Gallacher, Kevin, 201
Gascoigne, Paul, 188
Gayle, Howard, 137
Gellalty, Ian, 48
Gemmell, Tommy, 36, 45–8
Genoa, 90
Germany, 90–2
Gerrard, Steve, 29
Ghana, 175, 177
Gidman, John, 66
Giggs, Ryan, 63, 260
Gillingham FC, 187
Glasgow, 33, 278, 285
Gleneagles Hotel, 66
golf, 27, 78, 127, 132
Gothenburg, 55, 70, 80, 161
Gould, Bobby, 162
Gould, Jonathan, 161
Graham, George, 144
Grasshoppers Zurich, 153
Gray, Andy, 110
Gray, Stuart, 240, 246–7
Green, Tony, 165
Gregory, John, 150

Grimsby Town FC, 225
Groves, Eric, 283–4
Gullit, Ruud, 193

Hadji, Moustapha, 170–1, 203–5, 208, 223
Halenar, Juraj, 291
Halesowen Town FC, 30
Halifax, 140
Hamburg, 70, 91
Hansen, Alan, 3, 68, 94
Hart, Tom, 33
Harte, Ian, 141
Hartlepool FC, 30
Hartshill, 124
Hartson, John, 181
 Celtic career, 223, 288, 291, 294–5, 298
 Coventry career, 152, 212, 214–16
Harvey, Andy, 15, 219
Heart of Midlothian FC, 49, 92, 275
 vs Celtic, 291, 294–5, 299
Hedman, Magnus, 180, 183
Hendrie, Tom, 35
Hennigan, Mick, 73, 123–5
Henry, Thierry, 167, 259, 265
Hewitt, John, 63, 71
Hibernian FC, 27, 33–4, 58–9
Higginbotham, Danny, 266
hockey, 232–3, 237–8
Hoddle, Glenn, 256, 262, 273
Holland, 174, 177
Holt, John, 24
Houllier, Gérard, 9–10, 15, 68, 281
Hover, Graham, 169
Huckerby, Darren, 152, 187–91, 197, 202, 204
Hughes, Lee, 224
Hughes, Mark, 107, 109, 111
Hughes, Paul, 194
Hull City FC, 133
Humperdinck, Engelbert, 225
Hungary, 58

Inter Milan, 45, 150
internet, 6
Inverness, 91
Inverness Caledonian, FC, 37
Ipswich Town FC, 70, 131, 246
Irish Republic, 290
Italy, 90, 120, 216

Jackson, Mike, 49

Jansen, Wim, 283
Japan, 298
Jarni, Robert, 152–3
Jarvie, Drew, 57, 68
Jess, Eoin, 159
Joachim, Julian, 224
Johnstone, Jimmy, 47–8
Jones, Paul, 51, 246, 266, 269
Jones, Vinnie, 127, 132–6
Jordan, Eddie, 283–4, 289
Joyce, Jimmy, 242–3
Juventus, 39

Kamara, Chris, 132–6
Kanu, Nwankwo, 215
Keane, Robbie, 150–2, 203–5, 216,
    262
  joins Inter Milan, 209–10, 212
Keane, Roy, 36, 287
  joins Celtic, 288–90, 295
Keegan, Kevin, 143
Kennedy, Ray, 68
Kennedy, Stuart, 65–7
Killat, Bernt, 90–1
Kilmarnock FC, 55
Kilner, Andy, 10
King, Martin Luther, 200
Kinnear, Joe, 15
Klinsmann, Jürgen, 157
Knox, Archie, 13, 88, 219
Konjic, Mo, 218

La Manga golf complex, 31
Lampard, Frank, 29
Lancaster, Burt, 66
Larsson, Henrik, 214
Latchford, Peter, 58
Lawwel, Peter, 285
Le Tissier, Matthew, 250
League Managers' Association, 15
Leboeuf, Frank, 165, 193
Lee, Sammy, 69
Leeds United FC, 4, 144, 158, 166,
    189, 204
  fans, 128, 138
  finances, 123
  Gavin Strachan joins, 198
  promoted, 127–8
  Strachan coaches reserves, 140–1
  Strachan joins, 21, 98–9, 117–19
  Strachan leaves, 101
  Strachan's career, 47, 66, 73,
      118–41, 157, 177–8, 185, 206,
      251, 280

Strachan's spiritual home, 280–1
style of play, 129–30
vs Blackburn, 128–9
vs Bournemouth, 127–8
vs Chelsea, 123
vs Coventry, 142, 191
vs Leicester, 126–7
vs Liverpool, 140
vs Manchester United, 98
vs Middlesbrough, 134–5, 195
vs Rangers, 139
vs QPR, 139, 164
vs Sheffield United, 137
vs Southampton, 254
youth system, 136
Leicester City FC, 126–7, 136, 191
Leighton, Jim, 18, 60–1, 68
Lennon, Neil, 275, 290–1, 298
Lennox, Bobby, 57
Lens, 96–7
Lincoln City FC, 190
Liverpool FC, 3, 112, 116, 187,
    200, 239
  and David Thompson, 212–13
  Gary McAllister joins, 208–9
  mascot, 193
  Souness joins, 283
  Strachan as possible manager, 281
  vs Aberdeen, 67–70, 79
  vs Chelsea, 193
  vs Coventry, 185, 192
  vs Leeds, 140
  vs Manchester United, 137
  vs Southampton, 9–10, 254, 264
Livingston, FC, 180
Local Hero, 66
London, 41, 93, 244
Lovegrove, Chris, 256
Lowe, Rupert, 11, 142, 146–8, 169,
    230–42, 245, 247–9
  and Strachan's departure from
      Southampton, 272–3
  and Strachan's possible return,
      279–80
Lundekvam, Claus, 252, 261–2
Luton Town FC, 136, 172–3

McAllister, Gary, 127
  Coventry career, 158–9, 181,
      184–7, 191, 194–6, 199, 205
  friendship with Strachan, 136–7,
      177
  Leeds career, 128, 136–7, 177,
      185

transfer to Liverpool, 208–10, 212
McCluskey, George, 58
McCormick, Peter, 166
McDermott, Terry, 68
McGeady, Aidan, 292, 299
McGhee, Mark, 204, 234
  Aberdeen career, 57–8, 60, 68, 82, 87–9, 109
  friendship with Strachan, 63–4, 88–9, 263
  joins Hamburg, 91
  manages Millwall, 263
McGinnity, Mike, 220, 222, 227–8
McGovern, John, 182
McGrath, Paul, 95, 106–8
  and drinking culture, 107, 113–14
McGregor, Jimmy, 106, 108, 115
Mackie, George, 37–41, 219–20
McLean, Doris, 24
McLean, Jim, 23–6, 36, 43, 46
McLeish, Alex, 59–62, 66, 80, 83–5, 292–3
McManus, Stephen, 298–300
McMaster, John, 51, 59, 67–8, 81
McNamara, Jackie, 291
McNeill, Billy, 48–50, 53–4
McVeigh, Paul, 196
Makelele, Claude, 208
Malbranque, Steed, 147
Maloney, Shaun, 292, 298–300
Manchester City FC, 33, 171
  Richardson's takeover bid, 143, 279, 283
  Strachan as possible manager, 143, 279, 284
  vs Southampton, 264, 266
Manchester United FC, 7, 34, 137, 147, 150, 152, 260
  under Atkinson, 65, 94–5, 104–6, 112–15
  and back-pass rule change, 140
  Cantona joins, 138, 140
  drinking culture, 113–14
  under Ferguson, 61, 63, 73–4, 76, 79, 81, 83–4, 94–101, 104, 113, 116–17, 136, 237, 253
  Ferguson joins, 92–4
  gate receipts, 154
  Old Trafford pitch, 116
  Roy Keane and, 287, 289
  ruthlessness, 253–4
  Strachan joins, 86, 88, 91–3
  Strachan leaves, 21, 74, 94–101, 117

Strachan's career, 65–6, 73, 83–4, 93–9, 104–16, 118, 120, 124, 126, 129, 131, 136, 223, 237, 251
  style of play, 129
  supporters, 286
  vs Aston Villa, 81
  vs Chelsea, 193
  vs Coventry, 198
  vs Derby, 99
  vs Everton, 93, 110–12
  vs Leeds, 98
  vs Liverpool, 137
  vs Nottingham, 98
  vs Sheffield Wednesday, 112
  vs Watford, 105
  vs West Bromwich, 112
  vs Wimbledon, 115
  vs Southampton, 252–4, 272, 292
Mandaric, Milan, 280
Maradona, Diego, 102, 124
Marchwood training centre, 234
Mariner, Paul, 70, 131
Marsden, Chris, 251–2, 255, 258, 263–4
*Match of the Day*, 19
Meadowbank Thistle FC, 37–8
Metz, 92, 146
Mexico, 14, 16, 94–5, 282
Middlesborough FC, 134–5, 180, 191, 195–6, 223–4, 246
Milan, 210
Miller, Alex, 187–8, 196–7
Miller, Willie, 60–2, 66, 68, 80, 83, 104
  row with Ferguson, 77–8
  selected for Scotland, 94
Mills, Mick, 70, 131
Millwall FC, 180, 263, 268
Moldovan, Viorel, 153
Molineux, 151
Monaco, 146
Money, Richard, 38
Moran, Kevin, 110, 284
Morocco, 203
Moses, Remi, 116, 131
Motherwell FC, 59, 187, 275, 287, 296, 299
Mourinho, José, 69, 192
Muhren, Arnold, 70
Muirhouse, 26

Nakamura, Shunsuke, 288, 297–8, 300

Narey, David, 24, 293
Ndlovu, Peter, 157–8
Neal, Phil, 152
Newcastle United FC, 63, 126–7,
    171, 188, 223, 288
  Alan Shearer testimonial, 287
  Dyer–Bowyer clash, 56
  vs Coventry, 190–1
  vs Southampton, 254
Nicholas, Charlie, 62
Niemi, Antti, 236, 238
Nilsson, Roland, 203
Nimes, 138
North Sea, 255
Northampton Town, FC, 228,
    257–8
Northern Ireland, 58
Norwich City FC, 189–90, 212–13,
    263
Nottingham, 179
Nottingham Forest FC, 33, 195,
    205, 207, 271
  under Clough, 67
  vs Coventry, 224
  vs Manchester United, 98

Oakley, Matt, 252, 263, 270–1
Ogrizovic, Steve, 61, 181, 183, 187,
    196
Oldham Athletic FC, 132
Olsen, Jesper, 105, 107, 116
O'Neill, Geraldine, 283
O'Neill, Keith, 224
O'Neill, Martin, 283–6, 288, 290–1,
    294, 296, 298, 300
Ormerod, Brett, 252, 257–8, 261,
    263
Overmars, Marc, 190
Owen, Michael, 202

Pahars, Marian, 246, 252, 255–7,
    259, 269
Paisley, Bob, 69–70, 130, 200
Pallister, Gary, 140
Palmer, Carlton, 74, 205–8, 214,
    218–19
parasailing, 1–2, 300
Park, Donald, 38
Parry, Rick, 68, 281
Partick Thistle FC, 37–8, 58
Pearce, Stuart, 98, 111, 143, 220–3
Pearson, Stephen, 299
Pele, 102
Pendrey, Garry, 226

assistant at Celtic, 15, 278
assistant at Coventry, 8, 15, 157,
    159, 168, 196–7, 199
assistant at Southampton, 15,
    233, 241, 254, 272
threat to position at Coventry,
    220–2
Perugia, 216
Petrescu, Dan, 165
Petrov, Stilian, 290–1, 298–9
Phillips, Kevin, 270, 272
Pires, Robert, 265–6
Platt, David, 207
Pletikosa, Stipe, 236
Poland, 58
Poom, Mart, 194
Porto, 90–1, 170
Portsmouth FC, 202, 280
Portugal, 40, 91
Powell, Chris, 194
Pressley, Stephen, 295
Prutton, David, 271
Putney, Trevor, 134–5

Queen of the South FC, 49
Queens Park Rangers FC, 139, 164

Rangers FC, 59, 96, 216, 282
  and Old Firm dominance, 54–7,
    285, 287, 290
  vs Aberdeen, 51, 54, 60, 62
  vs Celtic, 47, 275–7
  vs Leeds, 139
Real Betis, 152–3
Real Madrid, 33, 39, 74, 87, 124,
    153
  vs Aberdeen, 55, 67, 70–1
Redknapp, Harry, 280
Reid, Peter, 110
Rennes, 252
Rennie, David, 103
Revie, Don, 132
Rice, Pat, 272
Rice, Peter, 23
Richards, Dean, 250
Richards, John, 151
Richardson, Bryan, 142–4, 148–56,
    167, 234–7
  and Carlton Palmer, 205–6, 218
  and Dion Dublin, 173–4
  and Gary McAllister, 208–9
  leaves Coventry, 227
  and Manchester City, 143, 279,
    283

negotiations with agents, 169–70
and Strachan's departure from
  Coventry, 220–2, 226
Richardson, Dick, 149
Richardson, Kevin, 159, 181,
  185–6, 191
Richardson, Peter, 149
Ricoh Arena, 155
Ripley, Stuart, 128
Roach, Dennis, 90
Robinson, Geoffrey, 220, 222
Robson, Bobby, 70, 171
Robson, Bryan, 95, 104, 106–8,
  112, 116, 223
  dislocated shoulder, 112–13
  and drinking culture, 107,
    113–14
Rofe, Dennis, 146, 235
Romania, 81
Ronaldo, 210
Rooney, Wayne, 157, 188
Rotherham FC, 264
Rough, Alan, 293
Rougvie, Doug, 57, 63, 89, 131
Rousell, Cedric, 215
Rowett, Gary, 194
Roxburgh, Andy, 38, 65, 121–2
Royle, Joe, 171
rugby, 232, 238
running, 30–1
Rushden & Diamonds FC, 228

Saha, Louis, 147
St Andrews, 80, 255
St Johnstone FC, 37
St Mary's Stadium, 231, 245, 272
St Mirren FC, 35, 53, 58, 85
St Tropez, 39
Scotland, 290, 296
Scotland football team, 58, 65, 69,
  86, 120–1
  fans, 281–2
  Strachan as possible manager,
    281–2
  Under-15s, 33
  Under-16s, 38
  Under-17s, 38
  Under-18s, 282
  Under-21s, 30, 282
  World Cup squad, 14, 16–17, 66,
    84, 94, 292–3
  youth team, 23
Scott, Jocky, 36
Scott, Teddy, 51–2, 124

Scottish Football Association, 38,
  281–2
Selway, Ronnie, 40
Serginho, 293
Seville, 152, 292
Shackleton, Len, 237
Sharp, Graeme, 110
Shaw, Richard, 159, 181, 184
Shearer, Alan, 191, 287
Sheffield United FC, 47, 126–8, 136
  vs Coventry, 198
  vs Leeds, 137
Sheffield Wednesday FC, 112
  under Atkinson, 101, 118, 205
  vs Coventry, 183, 198
  under Wilkinson, 125, 138
Simpson, Jim, 256
Simpson, Neil, 60, 62–3
Siveback, John, 66
Sky TV, 167, 203
Smith, Walter, 13–14, 281–2
Socrates, 293
Soltvedt, Trond-Egil, 199
Souness, Graeme, 68–9, 232, 282–3
Southall, Neville, 110–11
Southampton, 20, 67, 127
Southampton FC
  board meetings, 233–5
  fans, 231, 262
  media interest in, 272–3
  possible return of Strachan,
    279–80
  relegated, 262
  signings, 146–8
  stadium, 155
  Strachan leaves, 7, 68, 110, 272–3
  Strachan manages, 2, 8–9, 21, 32,
    51, 87, 142, 145–8, 167,
    181–2, 186–7, 200, 222,
    230–59, 274, 281, 292, 297–8
  vs Arsenal, 167, 241, 252, 254,
    261, 265–6, 268–9, 271–2, 292
  vs Aston Villa, 259
  vs Bolton, 11–12, 246
  vs Charlton, 246–7
  vs Chelsea, 254–5
  vs Coventry, 185, 192, 194, 198
  vs Everton, 167–8
  vs Leeds, 254
  vs Liverpool, 9–10, 254, 264
  vs Manchester City, 264, 266
  vs Manchester United, 252–4,
    272, 292
  vs Middlesbrough, 246

Southampton FC – *continued*
  vs Millwall, 263, 268
  vs Newcastle, 254
  vs Tottenham, 254, 262
  vs Watford, 258, 263
  vs West Ham, 247–8, 251, 254
Spain, 38, 84, 153, 292
Speed, Gary, 136
sports psychologists, 76
sports science, 238
Stanton, Pat, 27, 54
Stapleton, Frank, 107–10
Stark, Billy, 85
Steau Bucharest, 272
Stein, Jock, 16–18, 24, 45, 50,
  282–3
Sterland, Mel, 66, 126
Steven, Trevor, 95–7, 110
Stevens, Gary, 110
Stewart, George, 37
Stockport County FC, 10, 224
Stoke City FC, 106, 124
Strachan, Catherine, 26
Strachan, Craig, 7, 30, 85, 179, 199
  and move to Southampton, 247–8
Strachan, Gavin, 7, 30, 85–6
  Coventry career, 198–9
  and move to Southampton, 247–8
Strachan, Gemma, 7, 179
Strachan, Gordon
  boyhood and family, 26–7, 30–3
  car swap, 107–8
  character and temperament,
    11–13, 72–3, 75, 78, 83, 95
  collapses, 14–15
  courtship and marriage, 7–9, 39,
    42–3, 50–1
  drinking, 9, 23–4, 43–4, 47–8
  drinks spiked, 160–1
  fitness and training, 29–32
  and Gavin's career, 198–200
  health, 9
  holidays, 1–2, 31, 39, 226
  incident with boys on bus, 176
  lives with friends in Dundee,
    40–2, 44
  living in Aberdeen, 51, 53, 63–4,
    85–6
  living in Manchester, 94, 107
  living in Southampton, 20, 67,
    127
  mental state, 20
  and money, 19, 85–6, 90, 118–19,
    123, 154, 227–8

  off-field conduct, 36
  put up at Coombe Abbey, 149
  wedding anniversary, 39
Strachan, Gordon, football career
  plays for Scotland Under-15s, 33;
    joins Dundee, 34; approached
    by Manchester United, 34;
    Dundee career, 5, 23–4, 26,
    34–7, 40–9, 109, 120; captains
    Dundee, 46; joins Aberdeen,
    47–9, 85; Aberdeen career, 6,
    24–5, 36, 38–9, 50–71, 73–4,
    79–84, 104–5, 109, 119–20,
    124–6, 131, 237, 251, 268,
    285; voted Footballer of the
    Year, 58, 137; plays for
    Scotland, 17–18, 58, 69, 84,
    94–5, 113, 120–1; playing
    abilities, 64–5, 69; called best
    player in Britain, 69;
    relationship with Ferguson,
    73–99, 116, 171; leaves
    Aberdeen, 74, 84–94; voted
    Scotland's best player, 84;
    approached by European clubs,
    89–90; agreement with
    Cologne, 90–2, 96–7; joins
    Manchester United, 86, 88,
    91–3; Manchester United career,
    65–6, 73, 83–4, 93–9, 104–16,
    118, 120, 124, 126, 131, 136,
    223, 237, 251; dislocated
    shoulder, 112–13; leaves
    Manchester United, 21, 74,
    94–101, 117; negotiations with
    Lens, 96–7; joins Leeds, 21,
    98–9, 117–19; Leeds career, 47,
    66, 73, 118–41, 157, 177–8,
    185, 206, 251; eye injury,
    118–19; sciatica, 119–20;
    relationship with Wilkinson,
    120, 122, 126, 129–30; Leeds'
    Player of the Year, 128; and
    Leeds captaincy, 135; top-flight
    career ends, 136, 140–1; leaves
    Leeds, 101; assistant at
    Coventry, 101–4, 141–3,
    157–8, 161, 205–6; manages
    Coventry, 2, 4, 8, 14–15,
    19–21, 32, 61, 74, 87, 99, 136,
    142–5, 148–59, 162–4,
    168–226, 235–6, 250, 256,
    274, 279–80, 283, 288;
    relationship with Whelan,

160–61, 177–80; altercations with officials, 164–8, 193; relationship with Palmer, 205–7, 218–19; and Coventry fans, 218–19, 222–5; sacked from Coventry, 1–2, 22, 143, 210, 226–30; manages Southampton, 2, 8–9, 11, 21, 32, 51, 87, 142, 145–8, 167, 181–2, 186–7, 200, 222, 230–59, 274, 281, 292, 297–8; attends board meeting, 233–5; leaves Southampton, 7, 68, 110, 272–3; break from football, 7–8, 18–19, 68, 110, 143, 148, 248–9, 273, 279, 281; and possible managerial posts, 279–82, 284; joins Celtic, 283–5; manages Celtic, 2, 8, 19, 21, 32, 173, 181–2, 184, 187, 197, 214, 222, 250, 274–9, 283–300; voted Manager of the Year, 278
Strachan, Jim, 26
  meets Bobby Charlton, 107
Strachan, Laura, 26
  support for Celtic, 286
Strachan, Lesley, 6–7, 19, 24, 67, 81, 160
  and Celtic, 276–7, 283–4
  and Gavin's career, 199–200
  holidays, 1–2, 31, 226
  incident with boys on bus, 176
  living in Aberdeen, 53, 63–4, 85–6
  living in Manchester, 94, 107
  living in Southampton, 20, 67
  marriage, 7–9, 39, 51
  and move to Southampton, 247–8
  put up at Coombe Abbey, 149
  and Fernandes, 267
  and Strachan's break, 248–9, 281
  and Strachan's departure from Coventry, 1–2, 219, 225–6, 229
  wedding anniversary, 39
  and Whelan, 179–80
Stratford-on-Avon, 176
Sturridge, Dean, 194–5
Sturrock, Paul, 24–5, 279
*Sunday Post*, 36
Sunderland FC, 191, 195, 196, 270
Sutton, Alan, 119
Sutton, Chris, 201–2, 291–2
Svensson, Anders, 241, 252

Svensson, Michael, 261–2
Sweden, 120, 278
Switzerland, 121

Taylor, David, 282
Taylor, Graham, 275
technical area, 167–8
Telfer, Paul, 179–81
  Celtic career, 32, 288, 291
  Coventry career, 32, 159, 181–3, 188
  Southampton career, 32, 250, 255, 260, 266
Tenerife, 1, 226
tennis, 211
Terry, John, 255
Tessem, Jo, 252, 266, 269
Thijssen, Frans, 70, 131
Thompson, Alan, 275, 291–2, 298, 300
Thompson, David, 212–13
Tingey, Mike, 166–7
Tottenham Hotspur FC, 36, 56, 94, 216, 250
  vs Coventry, 157–8, 181, 187, 192, 194–7, 216
  vs Southampton, 254, 262
Troyes, 261
Turkey, 153
Turnbull, Eddie, 33

Uefa, 92
Upton Park, 247

Van Den Hauwe, Pat, 111–12
van Nistelrooy, Ruud, 253, 259
Venables, Terry, 223
Verona, 90
Vialli, Gianluca, 193
Vogts, Bert, 281

Wadsworth, Mick, 247
Wales, 16–17, 58, 162, 214
Wallace, Gordon, 36
Wallace, Rod, 129
Wallace, Ross, 299
Wark, John, 70, 131
Waterschei, 67
Watford FC, 105, 218, 258, 263
Watson, Andy, 58–60
Wayne, John, 20–1
Webster, Andy, 295
Wei, Du, 295–6
Weir, Peter, 70, 82, 131

Welsh, Irvine, 26
Wenger, Arsène, 69, 101, 253
West Bromwich Albion FC, 112,
    165, 205, 224
West Ham United FC, 221, 223, 241
    vs Coventry, 155–6, 163–4, 217
    vs Southampton, 247–8, 251, 254
Whelan, Noel, 15, 141, 159
    Coventry career, 177–80, 185,
        187, 190, 194, 200, 202, 215
    relationship with Strachan,
        160–61, 177–80
White, Davie, 36, 45
Whiteside, Norman, 95, 106–8,
    110–12, 131
    and drinking culture, 107, 113–14
Whyte, Chris, 140
Wigan Athletic FC, 145
Wigley, Steve, 235
Wilkinson, Howard, 73, 100,
    120–30, 132–3, 136, 142
    and Cantona, 138–9
    media portrayal of, 122
    Strachan's relationship with, 120,
        122, 126, 129–30
Williams, Paul, 159, 181

Coventry career, 184, 194, 196
Southampton career, 181, 250,
    266
Wilson, Mark, 182
Wimbledon FC, 115, 135, 162, 195
    and Hartson transfer, 215–17
    vs Coventry, 167, 187
Winter, Jeff, 166
Wolverhampton Wanderers, 150–1,
    204–5, 224, 263, 291
Woodward, Sir Clive, 238
World Cup
    (1982), 58, 66, 84, 94, 292–3
    (1986), 14, 16–17, 95, 113, 282
    (1990), 120
    (1998), 202–3
    (2002), 239–40, 242
    (2006), 146
Wyllie, Keith, 40–2

yob culture, 20, 83

Zico, 293
Zola, Gianfranco, 193
Zuniga, Ysrael, 215
Zurawski, Maciej, 288, 292, 297–83